Scepticism

A critical reappraisal

NICHOLAS RESCHER

Scepticism

A critical reappraisal

ROWMAN AND LITTLEFIELD
TOTOWA, NEW JERSEY

FIRST PUBLISHED IN 1980
BY BASIL BLACKWELL PUBLISHER
5 ALFRED STREET, OXFORD OX1 4MB

FIRST PUBLISHED IN THE UNITED STATES 1980
BY ROWMAN AND LITTLEFIELD, TOTOWA, NEW JERSEY

Library of Congress Cataloging in Publication Data

Rescher, Nicholas.
  Scepticism, a critical reappraisal.
.
  1. Skepticism. 2. Reasoning. 3. Knowledge,
Theory of. I. Title.
BD201.R47   149′.73   79–22990
ISBN 0–8476–6240–3

PRINTED IN GREAT BRITAIN

For (though also against)
ARNE NAESS

Table of Contents

Preface

Scepticism has been touched on in several of my earlier books. There are chapters on the topic in *Essays in Philosophical Analysis* (Pittsburgh, 1969; see Chap. XV), *The Coherence Theory of Truth* (Oxford, 1973; see Chap. XIII), *Methodological Pragmatism* (Oxford, 1977; see Chap. XII), and *Dialectics* (Albany, 1977; see Chap. VI), and some aspects of scepticism are also discussed in *Cognitive Systematization* (Oxford, 1978). The aim of the present discussion is to consolidate and round off these somewhat sporadic forays.

It may seem plausible to wonder why one should take scepticism so seriously as to devote a whole book to this subject. Surely "common sense" suffices to show that the sceptic's contention that we do not have – and cannot obtain – any *knowledge* regarding the world we live in is just incorrect and altogether untenable. Why, then, make all this fuss about scepticism?

But the matter is not to be settled quite so easily. The perspective in question neglects two important considerations. For one thing, what "everyone knows" to be so (or not so) can turn out to be quite otherwise. The *consensus gentium* is far from being a totally reliable authority. Another point is no less important. Even though the sceptic is undoubtedly wrong on the central issue of the unattainability of knowledge, his arguments nevertheless repay close scrutiny. In endeavoring to secure our knowledge against the sceptic's critique, we can acquire a great deal of useful insight into its nature. For it emerges that our knowledge of matters of objective fact is potentially defeasible and that what we claim as "our knowledge of the world" is and is bound to remain presumably incomplete, potentially incorrect, and possibly inconsistent as well. The explanation and analysis of these circumstances is the object of the present critique of scepticism. The book will accordingly endeavor to sift the wheat from the chaff in the sceptic's argumentation.

In outline, the programmatic route of the present work proceeds as follows. Chapters I–IV define more sharply the lines of sceptical argumentation that provide the basis for the purported infeasibility of obtaining factual knowledge. Chapters V–VIII indicate how this sceptical doctrine rests on an improper and incorrect view of the nature of knowledge. Chapters IX–XI show how the more realistic conception of knowledge that ensues can meet various further sceptical denials of knowledge. Chapters XII–XIII argue against the sceptic's insistence that we could actually "live with" the unattainability of knowledge, maintaining that such agnosticism is untenable both from the angle of theory and from that of practice. Finally, the closing Chapter XIV maintains that although the sceptics' conclusions are wrong, many of his supporting arguments are largely correct and convey useful and important lessons whose bearing the sceptic himself misinterprets.

Accordingly, the present examination of scepticism is rather positive than negative in tendency, combining a destructive critique of the central doctrines of traditional scepticism with a constructive assessment of many of its subsidiary positions.

The first draft of the book was prepared in Oxford during an academic visit in the summer of 1977. These materials provided the substance for a series of lectures on scepticism delivered at the University of Pittsburgh during the Winter Term of 1978 and presented again – in somewhat modified form – in the School of Literae Humaniores of Oxford University during the Trinity Term of 1978. I am most grateful to Corpus Christi College for affording me an academic home in Oxford on these as on various other occasions.

I owe thanks to Jay Garfield and Jean Roberts for reading a draft version of the book and helping me to improve its presentation. And I am grateful to Virginia Chestek for the patience and competence with which she steered the typescript through its many revisions.

PITTSBURGH
October 1978

Introduction

SYNOPSIS

(1) A survey of some varieties of scepticism. The presently relevant sort deals with specifically *factual* knowledge. The opponent of scepticism is a *cognitivist*, but by no means necessarily a *dogmatist*. (2) The tenacity of scepticism as one of these perennial issues where every solution evokes its objection and every answer its questioning doubts. (3) Scepticism is in one sense irrefutable – one cannot dislodge the sceptic himself from his position by rational counterargumentation. The best one can do is to build up a case capable of dissuading the uncommitted "rational man" from ever espousing scepticism in the first place.

1. THE SCEPTICAL POSITION AND ITS OPPONENTS

Scepticism has various forms. There are as many sorts of scepticism as there are types of knowledge or purported knowledge. And there are many of them, as for example:

(1) Factual knowledge relating to descriptive information regarding the contents of the natural universe and their modes of operation (specifically including man and his works).

(2) Formal knowledge relating to the structure of the relationships of concepts and the operation of symbolic systems (pure mathematics, formal logic, formal linguistics).

(3) Normative knowledge relating to such evaluative issues as rightness, goodness, beauty, desirability, etc.

(4) Theological knowledge relating to the existence and

nature of the deity, His relations to the world and to man, cosmic creation, teleology in nature, angelic and demonic spirits, etc.

There is thus not only the all-out, global sceptic who takes *all* knowledge to fall within the scope of his theory, but also a wide variety of specialized or thematic local scepticisms. The religious sceptic questions or denies the veracity of theological doctrines. The ethical sceptic questions or denies the tenability of moral rules. The mathematical sceptic questions the validity of mathematical principles. Our concern here, however, is exclusively with *cognitive* scepticism of a *factual* orientation – a scepticism that questions or denies the prospect of man's capacity to attain knowledge or rationally warranted conviction regarding factual matters. The scepticism with which we are concerned questions, doubts, or denies man's capacity to obtain factual information about "the real world," a scepticism oriented specifically towards what Hume characterized as "matters of fact and existence." Unlike its other counterparts – religious, ethical, etc. – this historic form of scepticism is agnostic specifically with regard to man's capacity to attain knowledge about his environing world.

The cognitive sceptic does not hold that what we think we know about the world is *false*. He simply maintains that our knowledge-claims in this domain are *unwarranted* – that we inevitably lack due justification for making them. He regards the evidential basis we normally invoke in support of such claims to factual knowledge as inevitably being probatively insufficient. The sceptic exploits the fact that the unending why/because cycle of question and answer can also be traversed with respect to a claim and its grounding:

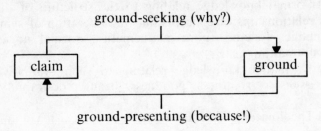

ground-seeking (why?)

claim   ground

ground-presenting (because!)

Gleefully noting the endless regress inherent in such a cycle, the sceptic insists that we can never know anything because knowledge must be altogether certain – secure against every question – whereas the list of potential questions is always endless. His thesis is that whatever we accept as known always rests on an ultimately defective title in point of rational warrant.

Sceptics have seldom been minded to contest factual claims which are strictly subjective in that they are couched wholly in the language of impressions and appearances ("I take myself to be seeing an apple over there").[1] It is the issue of the validity of claims regarding the *objective* circumstances of "the real world" that they wish primarily to put on the agenda. The bone of contention is the veracity of our commonplace processes of knowledge-acquisition such as the sense, memory, and inductive inquiry in science and in everyday life.

The objective of the book is accordingly to examine critically the main arguments in support of such factually oriented cognitive scepticism. It will endeavor to show that the sceptic is wrong and to argue that we are indeed in a position to stake rationally warranted claims to objective knowledge about the world.

What is one to call the sceptic's opponent – the person who maintains that empirical knowledge is accessible – that we can stake appropriate claims? The sceptic prefers to characterize his opponents as *dogmatists*. But the use of this perjorative term distorts the issue. A dogmatist is not simply someone who claims to *know* something, but one who closes his mind on the issue – who refuses to entertain objections and heed difficulties. Accordingly, we have adopted the term *cognitivist* to designate the sceptic's opponent. The cognitivist crosses the threshold into dogmatism only if he maintains that once we claim knowledge we "close the book" on the matter and take the stance that under no circumstances or conditions would we ever retract such a claim. The position to be developed here does not take this dogmatic stance. It propounds a fallibilist theory of factual knowledge which

---

[1] Indeed for the ancient sceptic appearances (*phenomena*) were the guide of life, the working substitute for the orthodox philosopher's real truth (*alētheia*).

recognizes that in principle a perfectly valid claim to knowledge may have to be withdrawn in the light of "unforeseen developments."

Recent discussions of scepticism have tended to focus exclusively on the issue of the availability of *knowledge*, but historically sceptics have concerned themselves no less with acceptance or belief. Their question has not just been "Do we ever actually *know*?" but has moved towards the more radical position of one who asks "Do we ever really have adequately supportive grounds for what we accept?" – "are our beliefs ever really justified?" To focus our epistemology upon the theory of knowledge (*epistēmē*) exclusively is to do less than justice to this inherently complex and diversified enterprise.[2]

It thus emerges that sceptical positions can differ not only in point of *scope* (ranging from the totalitarian agnosticism of the doctrine that nothing whatsoever can be known to the doctrine that nothing can be known in some particular delimited domain), but also, and no less importantly, sceptical positions can differ in point of *degree* – ranging from the narrower insistence on the unattainability of *knowledge* as such, to a more audacious and enlarged insistence on the further unattainability of "reasonable belief" or plausibility or probability or such-like weaker epistemic categories. For in rejecting all prospects of realizing *knowledge*, a sceptic can yet mitigate the impact of his position with words to some such effect as: "Accept claims about the world by all means – you may well be quite justified in doing so. Only call this "reasonable belief" or "justified opinion" or "warranted assertability" (or, as the Greeks had it, *to pithanon* or *to eulogon*), but don't claim it to be actual *knowledge* (*epistēmē*)."

The particular type of scepticism which will primarily concern us here, however, is that which maintains the unachievability of *knowledge* in the domain of empirical fact – even though it might be prepared to concede the prospect of something weaker, such as reasonable acceptance or plausi-

---

[2] Compare the remarks along these lines in William W. Rozeboom, "Why I Know So Much More Than You Do" *American Philosophical Quarterly*, vol. 4 (1967), pp. 281–290, and O. A. Johnson, *The Problem of Knowledge* (The Hague, 1974), p. 127.

ble belief. For our purpose here is antisceptical and positive: the task of our discussion is to work towards the legitimation of claims to knowledge. And clearly, if one is able to validate such claims, one is *a fortiori* in a position to validate its weaker cognates such as "reasonable belief."

Accordingly, the present discussion will endeavor to argue that it is proper, appropriate, and legitimate to accept as the warranting basis for our knowledge claims the usual standards of everyday-life experience and its systematization in natural science. This strategy, if successful, will defeat not only the sceptical agnostic who denies knowledge but also the radical sceptic who denies the realizability of any sort of rationally warranted belief.[3]

While there are many sorts of sceptics and a wide variety of sceptical positions, the present discussion will thus not endeavor to argue against all of them. The following three theses are primarily at issue:

1. That man is inherently so circumstanced that it is impossible in the epistemic nature of things for him to obtain *knowledge* of matters of fact.
2. That this is so because *knowledge* by its very nature requires a certainty (precision, finality, and other such marks of absoluteness) to which we cannot ever attain.
3. That this circumstance is something we can live with because it does not lead to stultifying consequences for thought and action.

The sceptical position defined by these theses provides the prime target of the present deliberations.

2. THE TENACITY OF SCEPTICISM

After receiving short shrift from the philosophical community during the interval from David Hume to the present century, scepticism regained the focus of attention after World War

---

[3] The designation of *radical scepticism* for this position stems from Gilbert Harman, *Thought* (Princeton, 1973).

II, when it found a series of important opponents.[4] The occasion for these critical discussions of scepticism was provided by G. E. Moore. His support of our ordinary knowledge-claims – while not directed against the sceptics but against the idealists – put an antisceptical position prominently upon the agenda. Subsequently, the natural dialectic through which any philosophical doctrine generates its own opposition once more roused up defenders of scepticism. (We have here one of those not infrequent episodes in the history of philosophy where attacks upon a "dead horse" brought it to life again.) A host of champions have entered the lists on its behalf, and there is no exaggeration in ranking it among the main topics of contention in current epistemological controversy. This revival has re-established scepticism as one of the great perennial issues in philosophy.[5]

It is incumbent upon any convinced cognitivist to account for the tenacity of scepticism. Despite rejection, obloquy, and rebuttal over the centuries, scepticism has managed time and again to rise, Phoenix-like, from the ashes. Surely nothing can explain this fact apart from the recognition that scepticism embodies a grain of truth – and perhaps many of them. This at any rate is the stance of the present discussion, which will maintain that, while scepticism is, in the end, incorrect and untenable, nevertheless there is much to be said for many sceptical theses and arguments, and a consideration of the sceptic's views can contribute greatly to a proper understanding of the nature of knowledge. In his tireless (and sometimes tiresome) probing for the basis of the valid-

[4] Especially Ludwig Wittgenstein, *On Certainty* (Oxford, 1969); J. L. Austin, "Other Minds" in *Philosophical Papers* (Oxford, 1961), pp. 44–84; and A. J. Ayer, *The Problem of Knowledge* (Harmondsworth, 1956).

[5] For an excellent overview of the history of scepticism see Richard H. Popkin's article, "Scepticism," in *The Encyclopedia of Philosophy*, vol. 7 (1967), pp. 449–461. Some useful publications in this area subsequent to the references given there are: Charlotte L. Stough, *Greek Scepticism* (Berkeley and Los Angeles, 1969); A. A. Long, *Hellenistic Philosophy* (New York, 1974); Richard H. Popkin, *The History of Scepticism from Erasmus to Descartes* (Assen, 1960); Craig B. Brush, *Montaigne and Bayle: Variations on the Theme of Skepticism* (International Archives of the History of Ideas: The Hague, 1966). A good anthology of very recent controversies about scepticism is G. S. Pappas and M. Swain, *Essays on Knowledge and Justification* (Ithaca and London, 1978), which contains a bibliography. And cf. also another relevant anthology: R. M. Chisholm and R. J. Swartz (eds.), *Empirical Knowledge: Readings from Contemporary Sources* (Englewood Cliffs, 1973).

ity of our beliefs, the sceptic manages to put his hand on something deep and correct regarding the nature of knowledge.

3. THE IRREFUTABILITY OF SCEPTICISM

Scepticism is, in a way, irrefutable, at any rate in the sense that the standard and straightforward sorts of refutatory argumentation cannot successfully be deployed against it. Discursive argumentation standardly proceeds from premises and it is clear that scepticism cannot be refuted by counter-argumentation proceeding along such standard lines. For, insofar as such argumentation is seemingly successful, it is open to the sceptic simply to reject the premises at issue. (However plausible they seem, the sceptic is thick-skinned enough to be as soon hung for a sheep as a lamb.) Factual claims can never be supported by purely formal considerations: any adequately supportive evidence that we could introduce to substantiate the thesis that our factual claims are warranted would itself have to be of the factual sort. Thus it would itself fall at once under the sceptic's ax. Moreover, it is unlikely that the premises from which this refutatory reasoning would proceed would be more plausible than those which support the initial knowledge claims themselves, and it seems anomalous to justify something disputed by what is no less controversial. As Hume wrote:

> This sceptical doubt, both with respect to reason and the senses, is a malady, which can never be radically cur'd . . . . 'Tis impossible upon any system to defend either our understanding or senses; and we but expose them farther when we endeavor to justify them in that manner.[6]

But even if the factual sceptic cannot be refuted by an appeal to unproblematic grounds, he can perhaps be rebutted with reference to the *consequences* of his position.

[6] David Hume, *A Treatise of Human Nature*, Book I, Pt. IV, Sect. II.

Might one not manage to invalidate scepticism by showing that it leads to untenable results?

Untenable for *whom*? As one proceeds in the elaboration of these refuting consequences, it is always open to the sceptic to defeat these efforts by simply accepting these "unacceptable" consequences. (The sheep and the lamb again.) The sceptic can coolly say: "Those so-called 'bad consequences' aren't really so unacceptable. Indeed we must accept them – given the correctness of scepticism. That's just realism – a matter of accepting things as they are." Confronted by such a strategy, we have no further recourse. There is no way of refuting the committed sceptic who is determined to follow the implications of his doctrine "to the bitter end."

It is thus critically important to distinguish between rather different sorts of "refutations of scepticism," namely:

(1) arguments whose probative force is such as to dislodge the rational sceptic from his position,

and

(2) arguments whose probative force would impede "the reasonable man" from ever becoming a sceptic in the first place.

This difference is decisive. There is no real prospect of achieving a successful refutation of scepticism in sense (1). Whatever supporting considerations we bring in would be met by the dedicated sceptic with "I don't accept that" – a stance entirely in unison with his position. Seeing that the sceptic can simply stand pat in his refusal to accept any counterarguments, he holds a position from which he cannot be dislodged by reasoning. It is thus quite impossible to achieve the first sort of refutation. But *ultra posse nemo obligatur* – what is in principle unachievable cannot reasonably be asked for.

And so the sort of refutation at issue with (2) comes to the fore. This is quite a different matter. For here we do indeed have a basis for resting the Archimedean lever of orthodox rationality – viz., the rational commitments of argumentation and proof to which "the reasonable man" stands committed. Accordingly, while it would be absurd to try to *refute* the sceptic – to tackle him head-on and try to dislodge him on his own grounds – one can indeed *rebut* the sceptic's position before the judgment of a *neutral arbiter* – one who has not yet forsaken orthodox rationality in espousing the sceptical way.

To be sure, such counterargumentation is not a "knockdown, drag-out" refutation to the sceptic, but only an argument that would prevent someone not already *precommitted* to scepticism – and specifically a (hypothetically) "rational man" who is, at this stage, neutral as between scepticism and cognitivism – from espousing this doctrine in the first place. This – to repeat – is as much as one can reasonably ask for. Given that the utterly committed sceptic cannot – as a matter of theoretical general principle – be dislodged by *any* line of argumentation, it is clear that the only sort of "refutation" of scepticism that is worth developing is one which proceeds along the lines of this second alternative.

Our over-all strategy of argumentation is thus to address the question: "Why should one who is not *already* a precommitted sceptic abstain from espousing scepticism?" And here the answer is this, that scepticism incurs grave sanctions on both the cognitive and the practical side, exacting a price that is simply not worth paying. The antisceptical argument to be developed in the ensuing pages will accordingly endeavor to show that the adoption of scepticism would exact a price unacceptable to the rational man who does not already share the sceptic's predilections.

The central task of the present book is thus to present a rebuttal of scepticism. Yet this nutshell statement fails to do justice to a rather complex venture. For the validity – and utility – of many of the sceptic's views and arguments will, in the end, be fully recognized and admitted. The position here defended is that the sceptic *misconstrues* the bearing of his own doctrines, in that these do not demonstrate the unattainability of knowledge, but rather indicate certain mundanely realistic limitations upon the sort of knowledge we actually can and do obtain.

I

The "No Criterion" Argument: "The Wheel"

SYNOPSIS

(1) A presentation of the Wheel Argument (*diallelus*) to the effect that one cannot validate a standard of truth unless one *already* has a standard of truth in hand. (2) This argument can be met by (i) differentiating between ground-level *factual* truth and various sorts of higher-level, *fact-abstractive* truth, thereupon (ii) noting that the issue of the validation of a standard of factual knowledge regarding the occurrences of nature can proceed on higher-level grounds of cognitive methodology, and (iii) that the appropriateness of these grounds to their appointed task can – without vicious circularity – be established by further abstract considerations. (3) In fact, this distinction between our ground-level factual knowledge and our higher-level metaknowledge is also crucial for the articulation of scepticism itself as a viable philosophical doctrine.

1 *DIALLELUS:* THE WHEEL ARGUMENT

An important negative line of reasoning regarding man's prospects of attaining knowledge about the world has been known from the days of the sceptics of antiquity under the title of the "*diallelus*" (*ho diallēlos tropos*) – or "the wheel" – which presents a particular sort of vicious-circle argumentation (*circulus vitiosus in probandi*). Montaigne presented this Wheel Argument, as we may term it, as follows:

To adjudicate [between the true and the false] among the appearances of things we need to have a distinguishing method (*un instrument judicatoire*); to validate this method we need to have a justifying argument; but to validate this justifying argument we need the very method at issue. And there we are, going round on the wheel.[1]

The classical formulation of the argument comes from Sextus Empiricus:

[I]n order to decide the dispute which has arisen about the criterion we must possess an accepted criterion by which we shall be able to judge the dispute; and in order to possess an accepted criterion, the dispute about the criterion must first be decided. And when the argument thus reduces itself to a form of circular reasoning (*diallēlus*), the discovery of the criterion becomes impracticable, since we do not allow them to adopt a criterion by assumption, while if they offer to judge the criterion by a criterion we force them to a regress *ad infinitum*. And furthermore, since demonstration requires a demonstrated criterion, while the criterion requires an approved demonstration, they are forced into circular reasoning.[2]

It is difficult to exaggerate the significance of this extremely simple line of reasoning, which presents the sceptic's "No Criterion" Argument to the effect that an adequate standard of knowledge can never be secured.

The ancient sceptics – who originated this argument –

[1] "Pour juger des apparances que nous recevons des subjects, il nous faudroit un instrument judicatoire; pour vérifier cet instrument, il nous fault de la démonstration; pour vérifier la démonstration, un instrument: nous voilà au rouet." *Essaies*, Bk II, ch. 12 (" An Apologie of Raymond Sebond"); p. 544 of the Modern Library edition of *The Essays of Montaigne* (New York, 1933). Francis Bacon, with the characteristic shrewdness of a lawyer, even managed to turn the *diallelus* into a dialectical weapon against his methodological opponents: "no judgement can be rightly formed either of my method, or of the discoveries to which it leads, by means of ... the reasoning which is now in use, since one cannot postulate due jurisdiction for a tribunal which is itself on trial." (*Novum Organon*, Bk I, sect. 33).

[2] *Outlines of Pyrrhonism*, Bk. II, sect. 20 (tr. R. G. Bury); compare Bk. I, sects. 114–117. See also the article on Pyrrho in Bayle's *Dictionary*.

sought to use it to enmesh in absurdity their Stoic opponents, who advocated a certain criterion of truth. The sceptics argued (in effect):

> *Quis custodiet ipsos custodes?* How are you going to validate your criterion itself. Surely not on its own ground, in terms of itself? That's just begging the question. In terms of another? But that just starts an infinite regress – like the ancient myth about supporting the earth on the back of an elephant, and this on the back of an alligator, and so on. The choice before you is an unattractive one – that between a vicious circle or a vitiating regress. Either way, you have no adequate means to support the truth-criterion which lies at the foundation of your cognitive enterprise.

This ancient Wheel Argument formulates with exemplary clarity a key plank in the sceptic's platform: How can one hope to validate a standard for claims to truth unless one *already* has in hand a standard of truth by whose means the validating grounds can themselves be evaluated? The crucial point here was formulated with pointed clarity by the French philosopher Theodore Jouffroy (1796–1841):

> We consider scepticism invincible, because we regard it as the last word of reason on itself. . . . That we believe is simply a fact. But are we justified in believing what we do believe? . . . That is a problem which the mind cannot help raising. . . . But from the fact that reason raises this doubt about itself, does it follow that reason can settle it? The *vicious circle* is too glaringly manifest. If reason can so doubt itself as to feel the need of a control, clearly it cannot trust itself to exercise this control.[3]

We arrive once again at the ancient sceptical problem of how reason can legitimately sit in judgment on itself and validate its own deliverances. Or, to look at the issue from a somewhat different angle, how can one possibly provide a system-

---

[3] Preface to the *Oeuvres de Thomas Reid*, Vol. I, p. clxxv, reprinted in T. Jouffroy's *Mélanges philosophiques* (4th ed.; Paris, 1866), p. 219. Quoted in P. Coffey, *Epistemology or the Theory of Knowledge* (London, 1917), Vol. I, p. 141.

atic noncircular validation for the system of our beliefs as a whole?

2. MEETING THE WHEEL ARGUMENT

Plausible though this argumentation seems, it can be met – and overcome – by sufficiently careful countermoves.

The most crucial of these lies in effecting a division of labor. It should be recognized – and indeed stressed – that a dualism of criteria must be adopted. First, there is the question of validating our specifically *factual* truth-claims regarding nature and its *modus operandi*. These have their own verificatory method (or "criterion") – in effect, the *scientific* method. (Other species of truths – e.g., the formal truths of mathematics, logic, theoretical grammar – may be put aside for the purposes of our present discussion.) Secondly, there comes the question of validating this *method* itself. This is a matter of elaborate theoretical (or "philosophical") argumentation – argumentation which is fact-abstractive in its orientation, and accordingly subject to rather different standards (since factual issues are no longer, or no longer *wholly* involved).

This division of labor accomplishes an important advance. It effectively splits the problem into two distinct parts: (1) the establishment of *factual* truth-claims with reference to certain probative methods of inquiry and substantiation, and (2) the validation of this method by strictly theoretical *fact-abstractive* argumentation. This division rids us of the objection that we are appraising our criterion of facticity by means of itself and are simply setting this standard up as a judge in its own case.

Viewed from this vantage-point, what the "No Criterion" argument effectively establishes is that there is no one unilateral, all-inclusive criterion of truth-validation. For the best way to meet the argument is to recognize that there are a variety of types of truth, each with a characteristic criteriology of its own. The argument renders the important service of manifesting the need to shift from epistemic monism to epistemic pluralism.

But once rid of the circularity, the prospect of a vicious regress remains. We now face the question: What validates the standards of methodological validation in their turn?

The short answer here is that they are ultimately validated not in advance, but only *ex post facto*, through the results of their applications: by their fruits shall ye know them. But this short answer expands into a longer one. We shall have occasion in the course of the ensuing pages to lay out many of the justifying considerations that lurk within in this all too telegraphic summary of the situation.

3. SCEPTICISM MUST ALSO DISTINGUISH TYPES OF KNOWLEDGE

Ironically enough, it turns out that the aforementioned distinction between factual and theoretical knowledge is no less crucial for the sceptic himself than for his cognitivist opponent.

The sceptic regarding factual knowledge about the world is not to be caught in the old trap: "In maintaining that we can know nothing are you not in effect claiming to know something? Is the thesis you maintain not refuted by your very act of maintaining it?" The acute sceptic has a convenient escape-route here. For he can argue as follows:

An important distinction must be heeded: that between concrete factual knowledge of a substantive sort (ground-level knowledge) and theoretical knowledge about knowledge (metaknowledge). In maintaining the infeasibility of the former, I am nowise committed to rejecting the attainability of the latter. The rejection of a factual knowledge claim like "Fire burns paper" is not to be placed on a plane with the case of an epistemological claim to metaknowledge like "Equally good arguments can generally be made for contrary claims."

The distinction between different sorts of knowledge (and in particular between ground-level knowledge and higher-level metaknowledge) is thus also available – and equally crucial – for the consistent development of scepticism as a philosophical *position* or *doctrine*.[4] For the all-out sceptic courts self-refutation in claiming to know that nothing whatsoever can be known.[5] But there is nothing anomalous about a sceptic's claiming to know (by way of higher-level metaknowledge) that no knowledge is obtainable within such and such a particular ground-level domain – or indeed with respect to the domain of factual knowledge as a whole.

[4] Some ancient sceptics took bull by horns and abandoned all doctrine. Scepticism, they held, simply is matter of *attitude* –a disinclination to accept any theses. Even our own arguments, they said, advance not *reasons* but *motivating considerations* wholly outside the rational domain. The stance of rationality is simply abandoned. The unpalatability of this position is relatively clear, but will emerge even more clearly from the ensuing discussion.

[5] Extreme sceptics are sometimes willing to run this risk of self-destruction. Sextus Empiricus wrote: "And just as purgative medicines expel themselves together with the substances already present in the body, so these [sceptical] arguments are capable of cancelling themselves along with the other arguments which are said to be probative. Nor is this preposterous, since in fact the dictum 'Nothing is true' not only refutes every other saying but also nullifies itself as well." (*Outlines of Pyrrhonism*, Bk. II, sect. 188.) This intellectual equivalent of a nuclear warfare that annihilates oneself along with the enemy offers what is clearly a very unattractive position.

II

Some Facts of Cognitive Life

SYNOPSIS

(1) A survey of some fundamental conditions upon knowledge as the concept actually functions in its standard role in our conceptual scheme. (2) The absoluteness of knowledge: its inherent claim to certainty and accuracy. (3) However, all objective factual statements are such that their claim-content transcends the evidence we can ever actually have in hand for them. An "evidential gap" is inevitable here. (4) How these considerations set the stage for the sceptic's argumentation.

1. CONDITIONS OF KNOWLEDGE

Any profitable discussion of knowledge does well to begin by recognizing some basic linguistic facts about how the verb "to know" and its cognates actually function in the usual range of relevant discourse. For if one neglects these facts one is well en route to "changing the subject" to talk about something different from that very conception which must remain at the center of our concern. It would clearly be self-defeating to turn away from *knowledge* as we in fact conceive and discuss it and deal with some sort of so-called "knowledge" different from that whose elucidation is the very reason for being of such a theory. If a philosophical analysis is to elucidate a conception that is in actual use, it has no choice but to address itself to that usage and conform to its actual characteristics.

The first essential step is to recognize that "to know" has both a propositional and a procedural sense: there is the intellectual matter of "knowing that something or other is the case" (*that*-knowledge) and the practical matter of knowing how to perform some action and to go about realizing some end (*how-to*-knowledge). This distinction is crucial because only the former, intellectual and propositional mode of knowledge has generally been the focus of attention in traditional philosophical epistemology, rather than the latter, practical and performatory mode. We shall accordingly focus here upon specifically propositional knowledge – that sort of knowledge which is at issue in locutions to the effect that someone knows something-or-other to be the case ("*x* knows that *p*").

Knowledge has three particularly crucial involvements or implications: truth, acceptance, and justification.

One cannot be said to know something if this is not true.[1] Let "*Kxp*" abbreviate "*x* knows that *p*." It then transpires that the thesis

$$Kxp \rightarrow p \qquad \text{(with '}\rightarrow\text{' for "entails")}$$

represents a sound principle of the "logic" of knowledge. This relation between "*x* knows that *p*" and "*p* is true" is a necessary link that obtains *ex vi terminorum*. The truth of *p* is a presupposition of its knowability: if *p* were not true, we would (*ex hypothesi*) have no alternative (as a matter of the "logic" of the conceptual situation) to withdraw the claim that somebody *knows p*.

Some writers see the linkage between knowledge and truth as a merely contingent one.[2] But such a view inflicts violence upon the concept of knowledge as it actually operates in our discourse. The locution "*x* knows that *p*, but it is not true that *p*" is senseless. One would have to say "*x* *thinks* he knows that *p*, but . . ." When even *the mere possibility* of the falsity of something that one accepts comes to light, the

---

[1] We are not concerned here with "the language as she is spoke," but with the *careful* usage of *conscientious* speakers – with what used to be called "correct" usage in the old, normative days of grammatical theory.

[2] For example, D. M. Armstrong, *Belief, Truth and Knowledge* (Cambridge, 1973), p. 189.

knowledge claim must be withdrawn; it cannot be asserted flatly, but must be qualified in some such qualified way as "While I don't actually *know* that *p*, I am virtually certain that it is so."

Knowledge entails acceptance (endorsement, subscription, credence, belief, etc.). To accept a contention is to espouse and endorse it, to give it credence, to view it as an established fact, to take it to be available as a true premiss in one's thinking and as a suitable basis for one's actions.[3] And a person cannot be said to *know* that something is the case if he is not prepared to "accept" it in this sort of way. And accordingly, the claim "*x* knows that *p*" is only tenable when *x* holds *p* to be the case. It is senseless to say "*x* knows that *p*," but he does not really believe it or "*x* knows that *p*, but does not accept it."[4]

This fact endows our attributions of knowledge with a certain overtness and explicitly *occurrent* dimension. We cannot say that somebody *knows* something when he simply has various good reasons that militate for its being so, but lacks appropriate grasp of the fact itself. Accordingly, we must reject the idea that the logical consequences of a known fact are *eo ipso* themselves known. The implication-thesis

$$(Kxp \ \& \ [p \rightarrow q]) \rightarrow Kxq$$

is *not* a valid principle of the conceptual "logic" of knowledge. For this thesis legislates the implausible circumstance of *logical* omniscience: the ability to make any and all correct deductions from what is known, so that the totality of the logical consequences of that which is known is itself thereby also known. This thesis would have the bizarre-seeming consequence, among others, that someone who knows the axioms of a system – let *p* be their conjunction – *ipso facto* knows *all* of the theorems, even though there are infinitely many of them.

Note that if this just-considered principle were in fact to

---

[3] Acceptance is not quite the same as belief. For belief is episodic and psychological, whereas acceptance is non-transitory and epistemological; moreover acceptance is a matter of choice while belief is involuntary.

[4] Indeed we cannot even say the more guarded "*x* thinks he knows that *p*, but does not accept it." On the other hand, knowledge-avoiding locutions like "*x* says that *p*, but he really knows better" are unproblematic.

obtain, it would be a most powerful weapon in the sceptic's arsenal. For it would yield

$$[(p \to q) \& \sim Kxq] \to \sim Kxp.$$

And so, knowledge of a fact could be defeated by a lack of knowledge of any one of its myriad consequences. Absence of knowledge regarding any one of the theorems would preclude *knowledge* of the axioms. And so, failure to know something one could not possibly know – some yet unestablished, indeed undreamt-of theorem – would block such knowledge.

On the other hand, we must presuppose in our knowers that minimal competency at issue with the capacity to make those inferences that are altogether trivial and unmistakably obvious. They must be credited with minimal rationality. Accordingly, we would have it (*inter alia*) that if both Kxp and $Kx(p \to q)$ then Kxq:

$$(Kxp \& Kx[p \to q]) \to Kxq.$$

Once it is clear that x knows p and that he knows $p \to q$, we cannot refrain from crediting him with knowledge of q. When the handwriting is on the wall *that* clearly, the rational knower must be presumed able to read it. And it follows from this that when $p \to q$ is an "obvious" implication – one which, so it may safely be supposed, "*everybody* knows" – then Kxp would indeed provide a suitable inferential basis for Kxq.

Again, certain other "perfectly obvious" deductions from what is known must be assumed to be at the disposal of every (rational) knower. For example, the conjunction principle

$$(Kxp \& Kxq) \to Kx(p \& q)$$

seems altogether plausible. For once again, it seems only natural to suppose that any rational knower could put two and two together in this way.

Knowledge entails justification (warrant, grounding, evidence, or the like). One can maintain that someone knows something only if one is prepared to maintain that he has an adequate rational basis for accepting it. It is senseless to say things like "*x* knows that *p*, but has no adequate basis for its acceptance," or again "*x* knows that *p*, but has no sufficient grounding for it." To say that "*x* knows that *p*" is to say (*inter alia*) that *x* has *conclusive* warrant for claiming *p*, and, moreover, that *x* accepts *p* on the basis of the conclusive warrant he has for it (rather than on some other, evidentially insufficient basis). It is senseless to say things like "*x* knows that *p*, but there is some room for doubt" or "*x* knows that *p*, but his grounds in the matter leave something to be desired."[5]

In sum, the contention that "*x* knows that *p*" will entail each of the following:

1. *p* is true (that is, simply *p*)
2. *x* accepts *p*
3. there is conclusive warrant for accepting *p*
4. *x* has conclusive warrant for *p*
5. *x accepts p* on the basis of the conclusive warrant he has for it.

All these involvements reflect necessary conditions for the truth of knowledge claims. (Note that we are not dealing with a definitional analysis of knowledge, but only with the enumeration of some of its conceptually necessary consequences. The issue of their conjoint sufficiency is here left open and unconsidered.)

It is also important to recognize that that which is known must be compatible with whatever else is actually known. No part of knowledge can constitute decisive counterevidence against some other part. The whole "body of (genuine)

---

[5] It is worth distinguishing between objective grounding ("there are good grounds for accepting that *p*"), which reflects an altogether impersonal aspect of the epistemic situation, and subjective grounding ("*x* has good grounds for accepting that *p*"). For the person whose knowledge is incomplete may well have good grounds for accepting something whose grounding in itself (taken as a whole) is objectively insufficient. Thus someone can have good grounds for *p* when (unbeknownst to him) decisive grounds for not-*p* in fact exist. However, with the conclusive grounding at issue in knowledge the distinction between the objective and the subjective disappears. One can only have *conclusive* grounds when whatever grounds that one has are in themselves conclusive.

knowledge" must be selfconsistent. Accordingly we shall have

$$(Kxp \ \& \ Kxq) \rightarrow \text{compat}(p, q)$$

and consequently:

$$(Kxp \ \& \ Kxq) \rightarrow \ \sim (p \rightarrow \ \sim q).^6$$

Given this circumstance, logic alone suffices to assure the implication:

$$(Kxp \ \& \ [p \rightarrow q]) \rightarrow \ \sim Kx \sim q.$$

Accordingly, one decisive way of defeating a claim to knowledge is by establishing that its denial follows from something one knows.[7] But of course not knowing something to be false (i.e. $\sim Kx \sim q$) is very different from – and much weaker than – knowing this item to be true (Kxq). And so – as was just noted in the preceding dismissal of "logical omniscience" – the just-indicated principle must *not* be strengthened to the objectionable

$$(Kxp \ \& \ [p \rightarrow q]) \rightarrow Kxq$$

which has already been rejected above.

A further, particularly interesting facet of knowledge-discourse relates to *the automatic self-assumption of particularized knowledge attributions*. It makes no sense to say "You know that *p*, but I don't" or "*x* knows that *p*, but not I." In *conceding* an item of knowledge, one automatically *claims* it for oneself as well. To be sure, this holds only for that-knowledge, and not how-to-knowledge (even how to do something "purely intellectual" – like "answering a certain question correctly"). It makes perfectly good sense to say that someone else knows how to do something one cannot do oneself. Again, abstract (i.e., unidentified) knowledge attributions will not be self-assumptive. One can quite approp-

---

[6] Actually, it is immaterial for these principles whether or not the same knower is at issue in the two cases. Not only must *a person's* knowledge be consistent, but the whole body of what is known (by someone or other) as well.

[7] This tactic is, of course, of no use to a sceptic.

riately say "*x* knows everything (or 'something interesting') about automobile engines, though I certainly do not." But particularized and identified knowledge-that claims are different in this regard. One cannot say "*x* knows that automobile engines use gasoline as fuel, but I myself do not know this." (To be sure, we do not have the omniscience thesis:

$$Kxp \rightarrow Ksp \qquad \text{(with } s = \text{I myself)}$$

One's being entitled to claim *Ksp* follows from one's being entitled to claim *Kxp*, but the content of the former claim does not follow from the content of the latter.)

Moreover, the ground-rules of language-use being what they are, *mere assertion is in itself inherently knowledge-claiming.* One cannot say "*p* but I don't know that *p*." To be sure, one can introduce various qualifications like "I accept *p* although I don't actually know it to be true," But to affirm a thesis flatly (without qualification) is *eo ipso* to claim knowledge of it. (Again, what is at issue is certainly *not* captured by the – clearly unacceptable – thesis: $p \rightarrow Ksp$.)

All these conditions represent straightforward facts about how the concept at issue in our knowledge talk actually functions. Any philosophical theory of knowledge must – to the peril of its own adequacy – accept and come to grips with them.

2. THE ABSOLUTENESS OF KNOWLEDGE

As we have seen "*x* knows that *p*" entails "*x* accepts *p*." And here "*x* accepts *p*" must be construed as "*x* accepts *p* as certain."

For knowledge must be certain, and certain in both the subjective and the objective senses of this idea. One cannot say someone knows something of which *he* is not absolutely sure. It is senseless to say "*x* knows that *p*, but has some small reservations about it" or "*x* knows that *p*, but he is not quite certain of it." Moreover, to say that someone knows something is to claim that *it* is certain in an impersonal and objective sense of the term. The crucial issue is not what is accepted, but what is *worthy* of acceptance. ("I am certain that *p*" is an interesting claim about a person's autobiography: his psychological attitude. "It is certain that p" is a claim about the objective epistemic situation.) It is senseless to say things like: "x knows that p, but it is not certain that p" or "x knows that p, but p's being so is not a sure thing" or "x knows that p, but it is merely probable that p," or "x knows that p, but there is some chance that p is not so." (To be sure, an element of an "internal" uncertainty may yet remain – I may not know a person's exact age, but only that it is between 25 and 30 years. But then this fact itself – of the age's lying in the interval $25 - 30$ – is something that must be certain.)

Moreover, knowledge is absolutistic in other ways as well. It does not admit of any qualification or abridgement. One cannot say things like: "x knows that p, but p is only approximately true," or "x knows that p, but that's not quite the way it is." Knowledge must be exact: it can only be maintained in the context of accuracy and precision. To be sure, this again holds only from the claim-externalized standpoint. The thesis at issue (here schematized as p) may itself well be imprecise or approximate or inexact. Thus one may know merely that "His name is *something like* 'Smith'" or "His age is *around* 30 years" or the like. One can say of the man who knows the decimal value of π to be 3.14???.... that "He knows that π is approximately 3.1 but does not know its value any more precisely." Again, one can say of the man who knows the book is in the room that he knows the book is in the room (i.e., someplace in the room) even though he does not know exactly where in the room it is to be found. Our knowledge can be more or less precise without compromise to its status as knowledge. But here we must again recognize the difference between the proximate and the remote placement of the qualification. One can "know that the value of π is approximately 3.1" but one cannot "know approximately that the value of π is 3.1." Any talk of approximate or imprecise knowledge must keep the qualifier removed from the knowledge as such and attached merely to what is known. Knowledge itself must be uncontaminated with imperfection: it must be *indefectable* to use J. H. Newman's splendid term.[8]

[8] See Chap. 7 of his classic *A Grammar of Assent* (London, 1870).

Its commitment to such conditions of absolutistic import (certainty, precision, etc.) is a crucial aspect of the nature of knowledge. And, as we shall soon see, this aspect of the matter plays an altogether central role in sceptical argumentation. It is easy to see why – every element of absolutism is an Achilles' heel that endows knowledge-claims with some point of vulnerability.

3. THE DATA-TRANSCENDENCE OF OBJECTIVE FACTUAL STATEMENTS: THE EVIDENTIAL GAP

Let us now turn the discussion in another direction, shifting our attention from the conception of knowledge itself to a consideration of the conditions under which we must operate in the endeavor to obtain knowledge about the world.

It is necessary to distinguish from the very outset between objective factual claims – those which make descriptively objective assertions about "the external world" – and those claims which are merely subjectively phenomenological and appearance-oriented. The former deal – or purport to deal – with how things *actually* stand; the latter merely deal with phenomenal matters, with how things appear to people or with what people think about them. (The relevant range of locutions here includes such expressions as "it seems to me," "it strikes me as," "I take it to be," "it reminds me of," etc.) These considerations are of paramount importance for any discussion of factual scepticism, because such a sceptic, as we have seen, has no interest in contesting subjective claims cast in the guarded language of person-relative appearances: it is the range of objective claims that is his target.

This distinction between objective and subjective (or phenomenal) judgments brings us to the very far-reaching point that the assertoric content of objective factual claims is *always* so extensive as to render these claims inherently data-transcending. This state of things is evident with regard to all *general* factual statements – and so specifically for all laws ("All elms are deciduous," "Lions have tails"). Here the data-in-hand always relate to a limited group of particular cases, whereas the claim at issue is generic and unlimited.

And there is also the Humean point that data relate to past-cum-present cases whereas the claim covers future as well.

Furthermore, data-transcendence also holds for *particular* statements of objective fact. There are three main categories of these:

(1) thing-kind classifiers ("This is an apple" or "That is a lump of coal").
(2) property-ascriptions ("This is sour" or "That lump of coal is black").
(3) relatedness-ascriptions ("This is heavier than that" or "This is to the right of that").

And all such statements carry a significant burden of generality nomic lawfulness. To be an apple (or a lump of coal) is to behave in certain characteristic ways across a potential infinitude of cases. The same holds for having a sour taste or being black in color. And to be heavier than (or to the right of) something is also to behave in a certain lawful way. The aspect of nomic generality invades all particular characterizations of *objective* fact. And it inevitably outruns the necessarily finite reach of our data-in-hand.

Moreover, it is clear that, as we ordinarily think about things, *any* thing has more properties than it will ever manifest in experience. This desk, for example, has a limitless manifold of phenomenological properties of the form "manifesting such-and-such an appearance from such-and-such a point of view." It is perfectly clear that most of these will never be actualized in experience. Furthermore, the things of this world are bound to have *dispositional* properties, and these are of the form "when such-and-such circumstances are realized, the thing will exhibit such-and-such a manifest property." Since such a range of circumstances may admit of infinite variation (in position, temperature, illumination, etc.), and since the concomitant manifest properties may vary in a one-one manner with these circumstances, the finitude of experience precludes all prospects of the *exhaustive* manifestation of the properties of any thing. Accordingly, the content of all such objective statements acquires a data-transcending import. The concepts at issue (viz., "experience" and "manifestation") are such that we can only ever *experience* those features of a thing which it actually *manifests.*[9]

Not only do things have more properties than they do or will actually manifest, they have more than they *possibly can* so manifest. This is so because the dispositional properties of things always involve what might be characterized as *mutually preemptive* conditions of realization. This cube of sugar, for example, has the dispositional property of reacting in such-and-such a way if subjected to a temperature of 10,000° C and of reacting in such-and-such a way if emplaced for 100 hours in a large, turbulent body of water. But if either of these conditions is realized, we destroy the lump of sugar as a lump of sugar, and thus block the prospect of *its* ever bringing the other property to manifestation. The perfectly possible realization of certain dispositions may fail to be *compossible.* The claim "this is a glass (i.e. an ordinary drinking glass)" asserts (*inter alia*) that it will break into bits if thrown against a wall and that it will melt into a shining blob if subjected to very high temperatures. Obviously it would be impossible to test *both* of these components of the implication-content of the claim at issue. And this circumstance is quite general. All objective claims have an assertion content whose test-conditions are mutually preemptive in this way. This mutual preemptiveness of the dispositional properties of a thing means that these cannot ever be manifested *in toto* – and not just in practice, but in principle.

The experienced portion of a thing is like the part of the iceberg that shows above water. All things necessarily have hidden depths, and the existence of this latent (hidden, occult) sector is a crucial feature of our concept of a thing. Neither in fact not in thought can we ever simply put it away.

To say of the apple that its only features are those it actually manifests is to run afoul of our very conception of an apple. To deny – or even merely to refuse to be com-

---

[9] This aspect of objective statements led C. I. Lewis to characterize them as "non-terminating" judgments, in contrast to those judgments whose meaning can be completely given in the observations to which they give rise, and which, accordingly, can be exhaustively verified. See C. I. Lewis, *An Analysis of Knowledge and Valuation* (La Salle, 1946).

mitted to the claim – that it *would* have such-and-such features *if* these and these things were done (e.g. that it would have such and such a taste if eaten) is to be driven to withdrawing the claim that it is an apple. A real apple must, for example, have a certain sort of appearance from the (yet uninspected) other side, and a certain sort of (yet uninspected) subcutaneous make-up. And if anything goes wrong in these respects, my claim that it was *an apple* I saw (rather than, say, a clever sort of apple-substitute, or something done with mirrors and flashes of colored light) must be retracted.

The claim to see *an apple*, in short, cannot achieve a *total* (logically airtight) security on the basis of evidence-in-hand. Its content is bound to extend beyond the evidence actually – and even potentially – in hand, and does so in such a way that the claim becomes vulnerable and defeasible in the face of further evidence. If, on the other hand, one "goes for safety" – and alters the claim to "It *seems to me* that I see an apple" or "I *take myself* to be seeing an apple" – this resultant claim in the language of appearance is effectively immune from defeat. Security is now assured. But such assertions purchase this security at the price of content. Direct experience of phenomenal subjectivity is objectively vacuous. As C. S. Peirce put it,

> Direct experience . . . affirms nothing – it just *is*. There are delusions, hallucinations, dreams. But there is no mistake that such things really do appear, and direct experience means simply the appearance. It involves no error, because it testifies to nothing but its own appearance. . . .[10]

No volume of claims in the language of subjectivity and appearance – however extensively they may reach in terms of how things "appear" to me and what I "take myself" to be seeing, smelling, etc. – can ever issue in any theoretically guaranteeable result regarding what *is actually the case* in the world. While they themselves are safe enough, appearance-theses – like theses about one's thoughts, beliefs, perceptions,

---

[10] C. S. Peirce, *Collected Papers*, vol. I, sect. 1.145.

etc. – will inevitably fall short on the side of objective *content*.

Accordingly, objective factual claims are in general such that there is a wide gap between the *content* of a claim and the *evidence* we can possibly have at our disposal to warrant this claim. The milkman leaves a suitable-looking bottle of white liquid on the doorstep. One does not hesitate to call it "milk." A small cylinder of hard, white, earthen material is lying next to the blackboard. One does not hesitate to call it "chalk." The *content* of such claims clearly ranges far wider than our meager evidence and extends to chemical composition, sources of origin, behavior under pressure, etc., etc. And this story is a standard one. For the fact is that all of our statements regarding matters of objective fact (i.e., "That *is* an apple" as opposed to "I am under the impression that there is an apple over there") are such that the *content* of the claim – its overall set of commitments and implications – moves far beyond the (relatively meager) evidence for it that is actually at our disposal. All such objective factual claims have ramifications over whose obtaining we in fact have no rational control in the absence of *ad hoc* verificatory checks – checks we cannot every carry out *in toto* and with respect to which we can obtain only a few specific samples drawn from an infinite range.

All objective factual discourse – be it general or particular – involves claims that are data-transcending in that their contentual commitments go beyond the observational and phenomenal evidence we do (or can) actually have at any particular juncture. If one understands an "hypothesis" in the more or less usual way as a claim that moves beyond the evidence at hand, then our objective factual claims will inevitably fall into this category. A real thing is always conceptualized as having experience-transcending features. All objective claims about such things involve an element of *experience-transcending imputation* – of commitment to claims that go beyond the experientially acquirable information, but yet claims whose rejection would mean that we would have to withdraw the thing-characterization at issue.

Accordingly, the data that are really at our disposal to serve as grounds for an objective factual claim will never actually *entail* that claim (in the logician's sense of this term). The falsity of an objective factual claim is always *logically* compatible with the evidence at our disposal.

The "evidential gap" between the assertoric content of objective claims and the experientially accessible supportive data we can ever obtain for them is thus a fact of epistemic life with which any adequate theory of knowledge must come to terms.[11]

4. CONCLUSION

It is clear that these deliberations set the stage for the sceptic's manoeuvers. For they suggest that our claims to objective knowledge involve an absolutism that cannot in fact be realized, given the inevitability of the evidential gap that is operative here. Just this consideration has been the mainstay of scepticism since classical antiquity. For (so sceptics have always argued) if – or rather since – it is indeed the case that all our actual experience is confined to appearances, we have no appropriate choice but to refrain from making any knowledge claims regarding objective reality, seeing that experience-transcending commitments are always involved in this domain.[12]

[11] This stress on *objectivity* is a key facet of the sceptic's position; his concern is only with claims to real existence – so that purely phenomenal claims as to how things *appear* to someone, for example (as contradistinguished from how they stand in reality), have historically fallen outside the sceptic's negativistic purview. (Compare Charlotte L. Stough, *Greek Scepticism* [Berkeley and Los Angeles, 1969], pp. 92ff.)

[12] But to be *adoxastos* – to live without acceptance of any contention as truly characteristic of reality – is not to operate with a mental blank: appearances, impressions, etc., are by no means ruled out. The classical sceptics did not gainsay the fact that things *appear* to us in a certain light, but only insisted that we could never warrantedly endorse these appearances as affording authentic reflections of objective reality itself. As Sextus Empiricus put it:

[W]e do not employ them [i.e., the strictures of scepticism] universally about all matters, but about those which are non-evident and are objects of dogmatic inquiry; and while we assert that which appears to us, we make no positive declarations about the real nature of external objects. (*Outlines of Pyrrhonism*, Bk. I., sect. 208 [tr. R. G. Bury; slightly modified].)

III

The "No Certainty" Argument

SYNOPSIS

(1) The "No Certainty" Argument: When the absolutistic demand for certainty in knowledge is combined with a recognition of the evidential gap, it appears that knowledge of matters of objective fact is in principle unattainable. A sceptical conclusion thus certainly seems to follow from these deliberations. (2) Absoluteness can be thought to enter into a knowledge-claim either with the *asserted content* of the claim or with its *evidential status*. It is in fact the latter of these constructions that is appropriate, and this leaves room for some qualification as regards the absoluteness of these claims. (3) To claim knowledge is *not* to assert a somehow transcendental certainty, but only certainty in the effective sense that any *real* prospect of falsity can be ruled out. (4) Realistic vs. unrealistic conceptions of certainty. Knowledge claims merely maintain effective (or *practical*) and not transcendental (or *categorical*) certainty. The certainty of knowledge is the certainty of life. (5) The untenability of the locution "I know that *p* but might possibly be mistaken" obtains on pragmatic (rather than absolutistic) grounds.

1. THE SCEPTIC'S "NO CERTAINTY" ARGUMENT

When the two main lines of thought of the preceding chapter are put together, a straightforwardly sceptical conclusion appears to result. For it was maintained there that knowledge-claims do not admit of abridgement by any element of doubt or qualification, but must be unqualifiedly certain and inherently absolutistic. On the other hand, philosophers since Plato's day [1] have stressed the unattainability of absolutes in our knowledge of this world, and – as we have seen – all claims regarding matters of objective fact are subject to an evidential gap between the evidence-in-hand and the substantive contention at issue, a gap which seemingly foredooms any prospect of attaining certainty. [2] To all intents and purposes this circumstance squarely violates the absolutism of claims to knowledge.

A straightforward and plausible argument is at work here. If a contention is to be *absolutely* secure relative to the grounds by which it is supported, then its content must not go beyond the content of those contentions that serve as grounds for the claim. [3] But since – thanks to the "evidential gap" – the actual content of all objective factual statements is always ground-transcending, it would seem that they cannot be absolutely secure – and accordingly that we cannot here actually come to *know* anything. What we have called "the facts of cognitive life" are to all appearances such that the definitive conditions for knowledge cannot be met in the factual domain. This, at any rate, is the sceptic's contention.

The sceptic bolsters this claim by inserting into the evidential gap the sharp wedge of a knowledge-defeating possi-

---

[1] His clear awareness of this made it possible for the Platonic Academy to endorse scepticism throughout the middle phase of its development in classical antiquity.

[2] Thus one acute thinker has written:

> [W]hat are my grounds for thinking that I, in my own particular case, shall die. I am as certain of it in my innermost mind, as I am that I now live; but what is the distinct evidence on which I allow myself to be certain? how would I tell it in a court of justice? how should I fare under a cross-examination upon the grounds of my certitude? Demonstration of course I cannot have of a future event. . . . (J. H. Newman, *A Grammar of Assent*, Chap. 8, Pt. 2, Sect. 1.)

[3] The argument here is as follows. Let $G_1, G_2 \ldots, G_n$ be the grounds for the thesis P. And let G be the conjunction of these grounds: $G = G_1 \& G_2 \& \ldots \& G_n$. Then if P is to be absolutely certain relative to G, we must have $G \rightarrow P$ (where $\rightarrow$ represents some relatively strong mode of entailment). Now if $G \rightarrow P$ (but not conversely) then there will be some nontrivial thesis Q such that $(G \& Q) \leftrightarrow P$. Since P must thus be equivalent to the *conjunction* of G with some nontrivial addendum, it is clear that P cannot go beyond the assertoric content of G.

bility – the supposition that life is but a dream, or the hypothesis of the Cartesian arch-deceiver and its latter-day successor, the wicked powerful scientist. The unattainability of any knowledge in matters of objective fact is supported by the sceptic on the basis of the impossibility in principle of ruling out such certainty-defeating possibilities. Do we, for example, know for sure that the person who jumps off the Empire State Building will crash downwards? Why should he not float gently skywards? This would, no doubt, surprise us, but surprises do happen; in such matters of generalization "we may be in no better position than the chicken which unexpectedly has its neck wrung."[4] After all, the sceptic insists:

> None of us, for example, has explored every corner of the universe to make sure that there nowhere exists a malicious but powerful individual who controls the movements of the sun by means of wires which are too fine to be detected by any of our microscopes. None of us can be sure that there is no such Controller who, in order to play a joke with the human race, will prevent the sun from rising tomorrow. Equally, none of us can be sure that there is nowhere a powerful individual who can, if he wishes, regulate the movement of human bodies by means of ropes which are too thin to be detected by any of our present instruments. None of us therefore can be sure that when a man jumps out of the Empire State Building he will not be drawn skyward by the Controller of Motion.[5]

And even without appeal to Cartesian demonology, how can we ever hold that our knowledge-claims are grounded with absolute certainty? Surely, "we shall never be certain that our clearest truths may not be, in Nietzsche's phrase, merely 'the most useful form of error' that we have known."[6]

---

[4] Bertrand Russell, *Problems of Philosophy* (Oxford, 1912), p. 35.

[5] Paul Edwards, "Russell's Doubts About Induction," *Mind*, vol. 58 (1949), pp. 141-163 (see p. 144). (Note that Edwards does not speak *in propria persona* here.)

[6] Will Durant, *The Mansions of Philosophy* (New York: Garden City Publishing Co., 1928), p. 30. This line of thinking goes back to William of Okham's contention

C. I. Lewis has given powerful statement to the line of thought at issue here. Discussing the statement "A piece of white paper is now before me," Lewis says the following:

This judgment will be false if the presentation is illusory; it will be false if what I see is not really paper; false if it is not really white but only looks white. This objective judgment also is one capable of corroboration. . . . [A]ny test of the judgment would pretty surely involve some way of acting – *making* the test, as by continuing to look, or turning my eyes, or grasping to tear, etc. – and would be determined by finding or failing to find some expected result in experience. But in this example, if the result of any single test is as expected, it constitutes a partial verification of the judgment only; never one which is absolutely decisive and theoretically complete. This is so because, while the judgment, so far as it is significant, contains nothing which could not be tested, still it has a significance which outruns what any single test, or any limited set of tests, could exhaust. No matter how fully I may have investigated this objective fact, there will remain some theoretical possibility of mistake; there will be further consequences which must be thus and so if the judgment is true, and not all of these will have been determined. The possibility that such further tests, if made, might have a negative result, cannot be altogether precluded; and this possibility marks the judgment as, at the time in question, not fully verified and less than absolutely certain. To quibble about such possible doubts will not, in most cases, be common sense. But we are not trying to weigh the degree of theoretical dubiety which common-sense practicality should take account of, but to arrive at an accurate analysis of knowledge. This character of being further testable and less than theoretically certain characterizes every judgment of objective fact at all times; every judg-

---

that God can produce in us by immediate action all that He habitually produces through the medium of created things, and that, moreover, He can make us perceive as real an object that does not really exist. See Etienne Gilson, *The Unity of Philosophical Experience* (New York, 1937).

ment that such and such a real thing exists or has a certain objectively factual property, or that a certain objective event actually occurs, or that any objective state of affairs actually is the case.[7]

To all appearances, these considerations as to the impossibility of "full verification" give the entire game to the sceptic at the very outset. For the nature of "knowing" is such that if someone knows something to be so, then he is entitled to be absolutely certain that it is so. But – so the sceptic has it – no one is ever in a position to be absolutely certain of anything, at any rate, not in the factual domain.

We are thus caught in the inexorable grip of the sceptic's "No Certainty" Argument: [8]

1. All knowledge-claims are committed to a demand for absolute certainty
2. Objective factual claims are always evidence-transcending: they are never in a position to meet absolutistic demands.

∴ Our objective factual claims can never amount to actual *knowledge.*[9]

---

[7] C. I. Lewis, *An Analysis of Knowledge and Valuation* (La Salle, Ill.: Open Court Publishing Co., 1946), p. 180.

[8] It must be realized that the "certainty" at issue in these discussions is *not* the subjective psychological state of a *feeling* of certainty at issue in locutions like "*I feel* certain that *p.*" Rather it is a matter of the objective epistemic circumstances, and the relevant locutions are of the impersonal character of "*It is* certain that *p.*" This is crucial to the sceptic's case, "And once we have noticed this distinction, we are forced to allow what we are certain of very much less than we should have said otherwise." (H. A. Pritchard, *Knowledge and Perception* [Oxford, 1930], p. 97.)

[9] As Keith Lehrer has put it:

[I]t should also be clear why it is that ordinary men commonly, though incorrectly, believe that they know for certain that some contingent statements are true. They believe that there is no chance whatever that they are wrong in thinking some contingent statements are true and thus feel sure they know for certain that those statements are true. One reason they feel sure is that they have not reflected upon the ubiquity of . . . change in all human thought. Once these matters are brought into focus, we may reasonably conclude that no man knows for certain that any contingent statement is true. ("Scepticism and Conceptual Change" in R. M. Chisholm and R. J. Swartz [eds.], *Empirical Knowledge* (Englewood Cliffs, 1973), pp. 47–58 [see p. 53].)

In a similar vein, L. S. Carrier has recently argued, in effect, that since belief concerning material objects can in theory turn out to be mistaken, no one ever knows that

The task of these present deliberations is to examine whether – and how – this sort of sceptical argumentation can be defeated.

2. HOW ABSOLUTES ENTER IN

The absolutistic aspect of our knowledge demands closer scrutiny. To begin with, there is no denying that various sorts of classification are clearly absolutistic: they represent decisive yes/no, on/off dichotomies that exclude the admission of intermediate degrees. A line is either straight or it isn't; an animal is either a dog or it isn't; a statement is either certain or it isn't. Accordingly it might be argued that knowledge is unrealizable because what is known must be absolutely certain, and absolute certainty, like absolute flatness, is simply unattainable.[10] Nevertheless, the matter is never quite that simple. In all such cases, some manner of approach or approximation is possible. A cross-bred animal that has a vast preponderance of dog features can be "almost a dog;" a line that has only a few minuscule wiggles can be nearly straight. Nevertheless, it seems inevitable that if something is not absolutely certain then, surely, it just isn't certain at all – period. And so, it could plausibly be contended that certainty is even more emphatically absolutistic than these other absolutistic conceptions.

But even if one grants this categorical absoluteness of certainty, this does not in fact block any and every prospect of qualification and preclude any sort of "epistemic shading." The crux here is the question of just exactly where this shading enters in. Here the question of grounding is decisive, but when it comes to this issue of the *grounds* for a certainty-claim we must distinguish between such a formula as

$$(1) \left\{ \begin{array}{l} \text{effectively} \\ \text{virtually} \\ \text{practically} \end{array} \right\} \text{conclusive evidence that } X \text{ is} \left\{ \begin{array}{l} \text{flat} \\ \text{canine} \\ \text{certain} \end{array} \right\}$$

---

he knows such a belief to be true. See his "Scepticism Made Certain," *The Journal of Philosophy*, vol. 71 (1974), pp. 140–150.

[10] For this line of argument see Peter Unger, *Ignorance* (Oxford, 1975).

in contradistinction to,

$$(2) \text{ conclusive evidence that } X \text{ is } \left\{ \begin{array}{l} \text{effectively} \\ \text{virtually} \\ \text{practically} \end{array} \right\} \left\{ \begin{array}{l} \text{flat} \\ \text{canine} \\ \text{certain} \end{array} \right\}$$

Very different things are at issue with this remote vs. proximate placement of the shading-qualifier. For while the absolutistic conceptions at issue do indeed so operate as to preclude any *proximate* qualification of the second type, this does not rule out a *remote* qualification of the first type.[11] A "reasonable-sufficiency" qualification within the claim itself is inappropriate. But the idea of a remote, "arm's length" qualification or shading is possible – and does not fly in the face of the fact that absolutistic nature of the item at issue precludes all prospect of a *proximate* qualification.

As the preceding chapter argued, every claim of objective fact is evidence-transcending in that its *asserted content* (or assertive commitment) outstrips the evidence we can actually have in hand for it. And our knowledge claims are themselves no exception here: for them too, *asserted* content transcends *supportive* warrant. Thus when one says "I know that *p*" it is part of the very *content* of one's assertion that *p* is (absolutely) certain. There can be no proximately operative abridgement or abatement of this *internal* absoluteness of the claim's very content. But the content-*external* absoluteness of the claim on the side of its justificatory warrant can – without impropriety – be subjected to that remotely indicated absolutism-shading abatement which is virtually inevitable with any objective factual claim. Here the content-oriented absoluteness of knowledge claims is not incompatible with warrant-oriented qualifications.

To be sure, someone might object as follows:

If "It is certain that *p*" is true, then this must also be so with "It is certain that it is certain that *p*." The warrant-

---

[11] Much of the sceptical reasoning in Peter Unger's interesting book, *Ignorance: A Case for Scepticism* (Oxford, 1975) turns on the argument that "certain," like "flat" is not a matter of degree, and thus precludes what we here call proximate qualification. But once a due distinction between proximate and remote qualification is drawn this particular path to scepticism becomes blocked.

ing ground of certainty can be nothing less than conclusive. It is problematic – perhaps even senseless – to say
"*x* has good (but not conclusive) reasons for thinking
that it is certain that *p*."

There is no reason to dissent from any of this. Certainty is
unquestionably self-redundant; i.e., certain entails certainly
certain. But the idea of a "sufficient ground" for certainty
must be interpreted properly. It is not *logical* conclusiveness
but *realistic* conclusiveness that is at issue. The only cogent
reasons for certainty are indeed conclusive reasons, but their
conclusiveness is not a matter of *logical* conclusiveness – it is
the operative conclusiveness of the relevant probative ground-
rules. The standard gap between asserted content (truth
conditions) and supportive warrant (use conditions) is as
operative with certainty-claims as with any others.

3. TRANSCENDENTAL *vs.* MUNDANE CERTAINTY

One must distinguish between *mundane* or *practical* (or "effective") certainty on the one hand and *transcendental* or *categorical* (or "rigid") certainty on the other. The former is certainty "beyond any *reasonable* doubt," the latter certainty
"beyond any *possible* doubt at all – be it reasonable or
otherwise." And the certainty we claim for our knowledge is
of the former, and not necessarily of the latter kind. It is the
certainty of ordinary life, the certainty of contentions like
"There are rocks in the world," "Houses can be built of
bricks," "All men have bodies," etc., the sorts of claims that
are the staple of our common sense conception of the world
we live in.

The supportive grounding of knowledge claims must be
conclusive, but, as J. L. Austin very properly asks:

Why on earth should one think that such verification
can't ever be conclusive? If, for instance, you tell me
there's a telephone in the next room, and (feeling mis-
trustful) I decide to verify this . . . I can take it to pieces

a bit and find out, or actually use it for ringing somebody up – and perhaps get them to ring me up too, just
to make sure.[12]

The conclusiveness at issue is an *attainable* conclusiveness –
one that suffices, and suffices not just for *everyday* or *practical* purposes, but for *all sensible purposes*. (And what is at
issue here may well differ in context – the requisite checks to
establish that a telephone is present may be one thing in an
office and another on the magician's stage.)

Consider the example of a dialectical situation of a
knowledge-claim subject to sequential challenges:

A. This is a pen.
B. Are you quite certain?
A. Of course.
B. Do you actually *know* it?
A. Yes, quite so.
B. But how can you be sure it's not something done
   with mirrors?
A. I brought it in myself two hours ago and it's in my
   pocket, and I've used it. So I think the mirror possi-
   bility can safely be eliminated.
B. But are you sure no one has put a clever pen-substi-
   tute in its place?
A. No one has been here until you came, and I've been
   working with it.
B. But what if a wicked Cartesian demon has been de-
   ceiving you in all this?
A. ?!??!

It is clear that when the challenger has been pushed to his
final move here he has "overstepped the bounds" of reasonable doubt, and has left the sphere of *plausible* challenges
based upon *real* prospects of error, pursuing the will-of-the-
wisps of purely theoretical and altogether hyperbolic worri-
ments. (We need not be in a position positively to rule out
uncannily real dreams, deceitful demons, powerful evil sci-

---

[12] John L. Austin, *Sense and Sensibilia* (Oxford, 1962), pp. 118–19).

entists operating from other galaxies, etc.[13]) And the reader can readily construct other such dialogical exercises, all yielding the same lesson: that in such interrogative situations, the series of challenges is soon forced to move off *ad absurdum*. One reaches the level of obstacles it is in principle impossible to remove and whose removal cannot for that very reason reasonably be demanded.

The key point is that our epistemological procedures such as explanation, substantiation, justification are all essentially social acts performed in the context of a communal interchange of ideas and information that is subject to communally established ground-rules. A fundamental communicative purpose underlies all these probative activities. The end of the road of the process of justification is clearly reached when anything further that could be brought in would be less plausible than what is already at hand. Even as one must not explain by the yet more obscure (*non est explanandum obscurum per obscurius*), so we must not defend by the yet more dubious. In the preceding dialogue, a stage is reached when the existence of the pen in question is (*ex hypothesi*) something that is as sure under the epistemic circumstances at issue as one could ever be of the further supporting considerations that could be adduced on its behalf. And when this stage is reached, there is no point in going on.[14]

The absolutism of certainty is, we are sometimes told, a kind of *ne plus ultra*. Once something is certain, nothing could possibly be more so: all certainties lie in an even – and maximally elevated – plain. Thus Peter Unger writes:

> Is it reasonable for us now actually to believe that many people are *certain* that there are automobiles? If it is, then it is reasonable for us to believe as well that for

---

[13] Compare the discussion of burden-of-proof considerations in Chapter IX below. The conditional "If a wicked Cartesian demon is deceiving me, then I don't actually know" is perfectly true. But this does *not* mean that its antecedent condition must be specifically rebutted to establish due rational warrant for a knowledge claim. (Compare also p. 258 of the Appendix.)

[14] "What I mean is this: that my not having been on the moon is as sure a thing for me as any grounds I could give for it." (Ludwig Wittgenstein, *On Certainty* [Oxford, 1961], Sect. 111; cf. also Sect. 516.)

each of them it is not possible for there to be anything of which he might be more certain than he is now of there being automobiles. In particular, we must then believe of these people that it is impossible for any of them ever to be more certain of his own existence than all of them now are of the existence of automobiles. While these people *might* all actually be as certain of the automobiles as this, just as each of them presumably feels himself to be, I think it somewhat rash for us actually to believe that they *are* all so certain.[15]

But this view that certainty is the end of the line, period, involves an oversimplification. The certainty of my own existence is one thing, that of the existence of mountains on the far side of the moon another. In the context of our knowledge claims certainty is never certainty *simpliciter* but certainty *sui generis*, relativized to the particular sort of thing at issue. To say that a claim is certain is to say that it is *as certain as something of its kind could possibly be*. To be sure, certainty is not a matter of degree – one certain thing is not more or less certain than another. But this uncontested fact of noncomparability does not mean that there cannot be different contexts for certainty – that the certainties of Assyriology cannot differ in character from those of biochemistry.

To be sure, a sceptical objection may well be offered:

If we sometimes fall into error even when doing the best we can, how can we tell that we have not done so in the present case? And if we cannot *guarantee* truth, then how can we speak of *knowledge*?

The answer is simple. If we have done all that can reasonably be asked of us, the best that can realistically be done, then there can be no need for any *further* assurance. The objection suggests that we must be in a position to do better than the best we can. And of course we cannot – and so this must not be asked of us. *Ultra posse nemo obligatur.*

A wholly justified claim to certainty and knowledge is

[15] *Ignorance* (Oxford, 1975), p. 68.

compatible with a nagging element of *theoretical* doubt. "I am surely right to claim this item as known, but might it not, after all, prove to be false in the end" may be a neurotic thing to say, but it is not an outright contradiction. We can have an impeccable "right to be sure" of a claim, but this generally stops well short of guaranteeing its truth in a *logically* airtight manner.

The "certainty" of knowledge claims can seemingly be understood in two very different perspectives:

1. as an unattainable ideal, a condition at which a knowledge claim aims but which in the very nature of things it cannot attain – to its own decisive detriment.

2. as an assurance, a promise, a guarantee that everything needful has been done for the ascertainment of the knowledge claim, and this must be construed in socially oriented terms as a real-life resource of the operative dynamics of communication.

Various philosophers – and most sceptics – insist on the former interpretation, an insistence which is as unnecessary as it is unrealistic.[16] For it is clearly the second, mundane or realistic interpretation that is operative in the conception of knowledge we actually use within the setting of real life.

[16] Compare Norman Malcolm's right-minded complaint:

> Lewis and Carnap ... make the mistake of identifying ... absolute certainty with "theoretical certainty." Lewis, for example, uses the expressions "absolutely certain" and "theoretically certain" interchangeably. ... In what circumstances, supposing that such circumstances could exist, would it be "theoretically certain" that a given statement is true? The answer is clear from the context of their arguments. It would be "theoretically certain" that a given statement is true only if an *infinite* number of "tests" or "acts or verification" had been performed. It is, of course, a *contradiction* to say that an infinite number of "tests" or acts of any sort have been performed by anyone. It is not that it is merely impossible in practice for anyone to perform an infinite number of acts. It is impossible *in theory*. Therefore these philosophers *misuse* the expression "theoretically certain." What they call "theoretical certainty" cannot be attained even in theory. But this misusage of an expression is in itself of slight importance. What is very important is that they identify what they mean by "theoretically certain" with what is ordinarily meant by "absolutely certain." If this identification were correct then the ordinary meaning of "absolutely certain" would be contradictory. ("The Verification Argument" in Max Black (ed.), *Philosophical Analysis* [Englewood Cliffs, 1950], pp. 278–279.

4. THE CERTAINTY OF KNOWLEDGE *vs.* THE CERTAINTY OF LIFE

It is not possible to overemphasize the important fact that the certainty of knowledge is the certainty of life – realistic certainty and not that of some transcendentally inaccessible world.[17] It is the certainty that precludes any *realistic* possibility of error: any possibility of error that is "worth bothering about," the closing of every loophole that one can reasonably ask for.[18] This is, and must be so because knowledge claims are asserted and denied here, in this world – and not in some transcendentally inaccessible one, so that the norms and ground-rules governing their use must be appropriately applicable (at least in principle) *hic et nunc*. Accordingly, there is no contradiction in terms involved in saying that the absolutistic aspect of a knowledge claim is compatible with an element of (claim-externalized) qualification.

The evidential gap is real and undeniable. And since it exists, it is always possible to insert an hypothesis into it to sever what we ourselves think to be the case from "the real truth of the matter." But there are hypotheses and hypotheses – sensible ones as well as those which cannot but strike us as strained and bizarre. An hypothesis capable of undoing "There are rocks in the world" (to take an ordinary-life example) or that in the present cosmic era $s = \frac{1}{2}gt^2$ (to take a scientific one) would illustrate the latter, farfetched variety. That either thesis is false is "unthinkable" – any hypothesis capable of undoing the thesis at issue is too peculiar and "unrealistic" to afford a *real* possibility of error. Admittedly *there*

[17] The "problem of knowledge" that figures in much of the epistemological literature is thus a creation of those philosophers who endow our knowledge claims with a hyperbolic absoluteness never envisaged in or countenanced by our ordinary usage of knowledge-terminology. Having initially created difficulties by distorting our usage, philosophers are then at great pains to try to revalidate it. This whole project gives an aura of unrealism to much of epistemological discussion. For an interesting discussion of relevant issues see Oliver A. Johnson, *The Problem of Knowledge* (The Hague, 1974).

[18] On this issue see J. L. Austin on "Other Minds" (1946), reprinted in his *Philosophical Papers* (Oxford, 1961), pp. 44–84. To be sure, the operation of the distinction between realistic and hyperbolic possibilities of error will to some extent depend upon "the state of 'knowledge' of the day." But this simply carries us back to the truism that what people reasonably accept as known is state-of-'knowledge' dependent and that the plausibly purported knowledge of one era may turn out to be the error of another.

are such (far-fetched) hypotheses and such (implausible) possibilities. But their very far-fetchedness and implausibility mean that the possibilities of error they pose are not realistic. The upsets at issue are simply too drastic – the whole demonology of deceitful deities, powerful mad scientists, etc. brings our entire view of the world crashing down about our ears. Such possibilities cannot be ruled out from the domain of the *imaginable*, but we can and do exclude them from the arena of the practical politics of the cognitive situation.

As we have seen, the "epistemic gap" between available evidence and asserted content means that the falsity of our objective factual claims is always *logically* compatible with the evidence at our disposal. But this undoubted fact remains epistemically irrelevant. For the *logical* compatibility in view is simply irrelevant to the *real or effective* compatibility that is properly at issue here.

The certainty of knowledge is the certainty of life – realistic certainty. This is still absolute certainty: absoluteness is undoubtedly present within our knowledge claims. And this "absolute certainty" must be distinguished from "practical certainty." We cannot espouse the idea that a knowledge claim can be validated on the basis of being "practically certain." For as these expressions are used, *practical* certainty falls short of *real* certainty: "it is certain" and "it is practically certain" reflect two very different sorts of situations, given the operative ground-rules of our language.[19] The point is that although a genuine and undoubted certainty is at issue, this idea is subject to realistic ("practical" if you will) standards of application. An "absolute certainty" can be subject to realistic standards without thereby becom-

[19] Compare the following astute analysis:

Some philosophers have thought that, when it is said in ordinary discourse that it is absolutely certain that so-and-so, what this means is that it is *practically* certain that so-and-so. This is clearly a mistake. The ordinary usage of "practically certain" is quite different from the ordinary usage of "absolutely certain." "It is practically certain" normally means "It is almost certain." To say that it is practically certain that so-and-so implies that it is *not* absolutely certain. "It is practically certain that *p* is true" implies that it is reasonable to have a slight doubt that *p* is true and implies that the evidence that *p* is true is not absolutely conclusive. "It is absolutely certain that *p* is true" implies, on the contrary, that the evidence that *p* is true is absolutely conclusive and implies that in the light of the evidence it would be unreasonable to have the slightest doubt that *p* is true. (Norman Malcolm, "The Verification Argument," in Max Black (ed.), *Philosophical Analysis* [Englewood Cliffs, 1950], p. 278.)

ing less than what it is, and metamorphosing into "qualified certainty." *Effective* (or adequately conclusive) warrant for "*certain* truth" is something different from *certain* warrant for "*effective* truth."

But the following objection remains:

> Consider the two theses: (1) The evidence at hand makes it reasonable to accept that *p* is certain. (2) The evidence at hand makes it certain that *p* is certain. Their contrast brings out a peculiar feature of certainty. Ordinarily there is a valid contrast here, a genuine gap between evidence which makes it reasonable to accept that *q* and the evidence that *q* is certain. But this distinction is abolished when *q* itself takes the form "It is certain that *p*." The only sort of epistemic circumstances in which the acceptance of *such* a claim is valid is one in which it is rendered certain. In the case of a claim to certainty, the standard contrast between "reasonable sufficiency" and "the guarantee of certainty" is abolished.

One reply to this objection would be to press the question of just *why* it should be that in the case of certainty the usual ground-rules are abrogated and the contrast between (1) and (2) abolished. (This sort of thing is, after all, easier said than done.) But a rather different tack is actually preferable. The argumentation at issue rests on equating two items in the case of certainty claims:

$$\text{reasonable sufficiency} = \text{full guarantee of certainty.}$$

But this equation can clearly be read in two directions. It can be read as the sceptic would have it – as saying "Certainty cannot be guaranteed, *ergo* even reasonable sufficiency cannot be attained." But it can just as well be read in the other direction, as saying: "Reasonable sufficiency can indeed be attained, *ergo* all the certainty it makes sense to ask for can be guaranteed." It is exactly this second, *realistic* reading of the equation at issue upon which our present argumentation has in fact insisted.

To be sure, the certainty at issue here involves more than putting the matter beyond *reasonable doubt*. For there is no question that, as these expressions actually operate in our language, "is certain" is something quite different from "is beyond reasonable doubt." But this must not be misconstrued to mean (as the sceptic would sometimes seem to have it) that the claims at issue must be secured beyond *unreasonable* doubts as well. To claim knowledge we must do "everything that can properly be asked" to ensure not just the *plausibility* but the *certainty* of the claim at issue.

The issue here revolves about what one can *reasonably* call into question, not what one can conceivably call into question with respect to a knowledge claim. What is at issue (particularly as we have factual rather than formal knowledge in view) is the second of these – the idea of a *real* prospect of error. Here a knowledge-claim embodies the contention that we have *virtually conclusive evidence for the thing's being certain in the sense that any REAL prospect of* error can be ruled out.

In this context it is useful to consider the line of reasoning which Norman Malcolm has identified – and criticized – as the "Verification Argument," an argument which runs roughly as follows:

(1) any objective claim p has infinitely many consequences

(2) to be absolutely certain of p, we must verify that all its consequences obtain (i.e., the failure of any of these consequences would block the road to the attainment of absolute certainty)

(3) we are never in a position to verify all of the infinitely many consequences of any objective claim

∴ We are never in a position to claim absolute certainty for any objective claim p.[20]

As Malcolm himself stresses, the argument goes wrong because its second premiss is false. The absolute certainty of

[20] See Norman Malcolm, "The Verification Argument" in R. M. Chisholm and R. J. Swartz (eds.), *Empirical Knowledge* (Englewood Cliffs, 1976), pp. 155 ff.

our knowledge claims is not and cannot be the sort of thing which one is in principle precluded from realizing (as per premiss 3). (*Ultra posse nemo obligatur*. The certainty of knowledge is the certainty of life!)

There is no question that the person who claims to know something also becomes committed thereby to its implications (its logical consequences and its presuppositions).But the commitment in question is strictly implicit. As we have seen, one does not arrive at *Kxq* from the premisses *Kxp* and *p* → *q*. People are not "logically omniscient" and able to make failproof deductions from what they know. It is thus inappropriate to demand as a prerequisite or presupposition of a knowledge claim that one be in a position to pre-establish the falsity of any potential falsifier. A claim to knowledge can be made reasonably and defensibly even by one who realizes that it involves commitments and ramifications that may not stand up in the final analysis to the challenges of a difficult and often recalcitrant world. No assurances that extend beyond the limits of the possible can be given – or sensibly asked for.

It is thus tempting to speak of a contrast between "the hyperbolic certainty of the philosopher" and "the mundane certainty of the plain man" in the setting of the actual transaction of our cognitive business.[21] Philosophers have often felt driven to a conception of knowledge so rigid as to yield the result that there is little if anything left that one ever be said to know. Indeed, sceptical thinkers of this inclination launch upon an explication of the "nature of knowledge" which sets the standards of its attainment so high that it becomes in principle impossible for anything to meet such hyperbolic demands. Against this tendency it is proper to insist that while what is known must indeed be true – and certainly true – it is nevertheless in order to insist that the conceptions at issue can and should be so construed that there are realistic and realizable circumstances in which our claims to *certainty* and to *knowledge* are perfectly legitimate

[21] Compare Harry G. Frankfurt, "Philosophical Certainty," *The Philosophical Review*, vol. 71 (1962), pp. 303–327. However, the philosopher (unlike the natural scientist) is simply not free to switch over to "technical terms." His task is to elucidate the concepts we actually work with and in replacing them by technical reconstructions he merely changes the subject.

and altogether justified. A doctrine which admits the defeasibility of quite appropriate claims to knowledge need involve no contradictions in terms.

5. PRAGMATIC INCONSISTENCY

This line of consideration brings to light the effective basis of the untenability of "I know that *P*, but it is not certain that *P*" or "I know that *P*, but it could possibly be the case that not-*P*." The crux is not that these are *logically inconsistent* but that they are *pragmatically self-defeating* – i.e., self-defeating in the context of the relevant communicative aims and objectives. For it is clear that the former part of these statements extends an assurance which the qualifications of the second part effectively abrogate. The knowledge-claim asserts that the grounding-in-hand is sufficient to preclude any real possibility of error, whereas the but-addendum says that there are still such possibilities worth worrying about. And so the statement as a whole is inconsistent: it takes away with one hand what it gives with the other.[22]

The assertion "I *know* that *p*" does indeed have all of those absolutistic facets we have considered (certainty, unqualifiedness, etc.). All are ineliminably parts of the substance of the claim as asserted in its meaning-content. But with this particular factual claim, as with any other, warranted assertability does not require the establishment of full rational control over the whole gamut of its entailments and implications. *Ex hypothesi*, one can appropriately assert "I know that *p*" only when one has adequate rational warrant for this assertion. But this warrant may well stop at being *adequately conclusive* – rather than *comprehensively exhaustive* –grounding for the claim. (Here too the evidential gap occurs.) For example, we need not in the usual course of things exert ourselves in an endeavor to rule out the imaginative sceptic's recourse to the whole demonology of uncannily real dreams,

[22] On this issue one should consult J. L. Austin's analysis of "I know" as a *performative* utterance which extends a guarantee in that the man who makes this claim stakes his reputation and binds himself to others. See "Other Minds" (op. cit.).

deceitful demons, powerful evil scientists, etc. The general principles and presumptions of the domain suffice to put all this aside. To claim knowledge in specific cases, all we need do is eliminate those case-specific considerations which would countervail against the claim at issue.

This difference between *real* and *merely conjectural* possibilities of error is crucial for rational warrant for claims or concessions to knowledge. A real possibility must be case-specific and not abstractly generic and somehow based on general principles alone. And this, it must be insisted, is *not* incompatible with the existence of a "purely theoretical" (let alone "purely logical") prospect of error. There is thus no real anomaly in holding on the one hand that knowledge "must be certain" (in the *effective* sense of this term) and on the other that a valid knowledge claim "might possibly be wrong" (with "might" construed in the light of a merely theoretical or "purely logical" mode of possibility).

Some philosophers have endeavored to evade scepticism by emptying knowledge claims of any and all pretentions to certainty. For example, in his interesting book, *Knowledge*, Keith Lehrer writes:

> Thus, our theory of knowledge is a theory of knowledge without certainty. We agree with the sceptic that if a man claims to know for certain, he does not know whereof he speaks. However, when we claim to know, we make no claim to certainty. We conjecture that to speak in this way is a departure from the most customary use of the word "know." Commonly, when men say they know, they mean they know for certain. . . .[23]

But this approach of extruding certainty from knowledge – and so of going over to a construction of knowledge at variance with that of our standard usage – avoids scepticism at too high a price. What more, after all, can the sceptic ask than to be granted that his position is correct with respect to the standard, most customary use of the word "know"? To win this battle is to win the war. Our own position, by contrast, emphatically preserves the certainty-involvement of all

[23] Keith Lehrer, *Knowledge* (Oxford, 1973), p. 239.

our knowledge claims. It simply insists that the certainty of knowledge is the certainty of real life – the sort of certainty that is not timeless and untarnishable but can be abrogated by the difficult circumstances of an uncooperative world.

Accordingly, the "No Certainty" Argument becomes invalidated: It is *not* true that knowledge claims are committed to a demand for absolute certainty in any hyperbolically inaccessible way. They are indeed committed to a demand for certainty, but *this* "certainty" must be construed realistically – in the effective, mundane, and practical sense of the term. The *certainty* at issue in our knowledge-claims is not inherently unattainable; it is simply that the grounding in hand must be strong enough to indicate that further substantiation is superfluous in the sense of yielding every reasonable assurance that the thing at issue is as certain as something of its sort need appropriately be. To repeat: it suffices to ask for an *adequate* grounding for these claims; logically *exhaustive* grounding is not a reasonable requirement, for the simple reason – so eloquently stressed by the sceptic himself – that it is in principle incapable of being satisfied.

IV
The "No Absolutes" Argument

SYNOPSIS

(1) The "No Absolutes" Argument maintains scepticism on the basis of the unavailability of exactness, total correctness, incorrigibility, and the like. (2) This line of argumentation commits the sceptic's customary mistake of failing to discriminate between the effective (mundane) and the categorical (transcendental) construction of such absolutes. (3) The sceptic's argument commits his favorite fallacy of illicitly inflating the consequences of our knowledge-claims. (4) Moreover, the argument is self-defeating. To the extent that it shows *in principle* the unattainability of certain absolutes, it *thereby* demonstrates the absurdity of including them among the requirements for knowledge.

1. THE "NO ABSOLUTES" ARGUMENT

Knowledge must meet a variety of absolutistic conditions (as we have seen in Chapter II). It must be exact, altogether correct, incorrigible, etc. To say something like "I know that such-and-such is the case, but this is not quite exactly right" is to perpetrate a solecism. And so the sceptic argues with seeming plausibility that the inherent absolutes of knowledge-claims are not attainable in this imperfect and mundane dispensation, construing this argumentation to establish the unattainability of knowledge. He articulates this position by means of a "No Absolutes" Argument which runs roughly as follows:

1. Knowledge-claims must, for correctness, meet various absolutistic requirements: they must be absolutely correct, exact, incorrigible, etc.
2. In the context of our inquiry in factual matters, all such absolutes are unattainable.

∴ Knowledge in factual matters is unattainable.

This argumentation is simply a replay in the context of other, remaining cognitive absolutes – exactness, correctness, incorrigibility, etc. – of the "No Certainty" Argument examined in the preceding chapter.

2. CIRCUMVENTING THE "NO ABSOLUTES" ARGUMENT

The strategy by which this "No Absolutes" argument can be met runs parallel to that of our reply to the "No Certainty" Argument. There we insisted on drawing a clear line between hyperbolic or transcendental certainty on the one hand, and effective or mundane certainty on the other. In the present case too we must distinguish between the hyperbolic or transcendental construction of such concepts as exactness, correctness, etc., and their mundane or effective interpretation. In the interests of *realism*, the exactness (correctness, etc.) of our knowledge claims must be regarded not as a matter of theoretical idealization, but as one of the practical politics of the epistemological situation. The operative construction here is "as exact (correct, etc.) as one can reasonably and appropriately expect in case of the particular sort at issue." The lesson to be derived from the sceptic's argument is simply that the absolutes in question must be interpreted *realistically*, and viewed in a mundane rather than transcendental light.

3. ILLICIT CONSEQUENCE-INFLATION

A standard fallacy of sceptical argumentation is represented by the sceptic's penchant for inflating the consequences of a knowledge claim by a process of illicit exaggeration. It is, for example, an inherent aspect of the conceptual "logic" of knowledge that a known thesis must be true:

(1) If *Kxp*, then *p*.

Given this fact, the sceptic argues:

> If *x* is to be justified in claiming to know *p*, then *p* must be true. Accordingly, if the truth of a thesis is not decisively and conclusively established (indeed, rendered *logically* certain in the circumstances), then a claim to knowledge cannot appropriately be made.

This is quite incorrect. To know *p* it is nowise required that *p* be *necessarily* the case. To be justified in claiming that one knows that *p*, one must – in virtue of (1) – be *justified* in claiming *p* itself as true. But this critical consideration of *p*'s truth need not be demonstrated with *logical* stringency. Antecedent-justification requires consequent-justification, but no more; it requires no demonstration that the consequent is somehow necessary.

Again, we have it that the conceptual "logic" of knowledge is such that:

(2) If *Kxp*, then there is no conclusive evidence against *p*
 – i.e. $\sim(\exists q)\,(q\ \&\ [q \rightarrow\ \sim p])$.

The sceptic now argues as follows:

> If *x* is to be justified in claiming *Kxp*, then there cannot be any conclusive evidence against *p*. In consequence, if it is not decisively and totally established (indeed, rendered *logically* certain in the circumstances) that there is no conclusive evidence against *p*, then an appropriate claim to knowledge cannot appropriately be made.

This too is quite incorrect. To be justified in claiming that one knows that *p*, one must – in virtue of (2) – be *justified* in claiming that there is no conclusive counterevidence against *p*. But again, this is not something that needs to be demonstrated with logical stringency. Here, as elsewhere, *justification* is one thing, and logically conclusive *demonstration* another.

Ever anxious to show that knowledge is unattainable, the sceptic likes to expound theses of the form

$$Kxp \rightarrow C$$

where *C* is some problematic or unacceptable condition. For whenever this is so, then the contraposed inference

$$\sim C \rightarrow \sim Kxp$$

lies conveniently to hand to defeat knowledge claims. Accordingly, whenever the "logic" of the situation regarding knowledge affords us with a thesis of the form $Kxp \rightarrow A$, the sceptic inclines to the device of an illicit "inflating of the consequences" by substituting for *A* some substantially stronger contention *A'*, with the result of rendering $Kxp \rightarrow A'$ more serviceable to his purposes. For the stronger the consequences of a claim to knowledge, the easier its defeat.

For example, given the plausible contention

$$Kxp \rightarrow (Kx[p \rightarrow q] \rightarrow Kxq)$$

the sceptic proposes to replace this by

$$Kxp \rightarrow ([p \rightarrow q] \rightarrow Kxq)$$

whose (improperly) strengthened consequence underwrites "logical omniscience." (See pp. 18–19 above.) Or again, given that *Kxp* entails that *p* must be compatible with all the *realistic* possibilities of the cognitive situation, the sceptic likes to insist that it must be compatible with all possibilities, whatever, no matter how far fetched and "merely hypothetical."

The sceptic's penchant towards a certain form of modal fallacy is closely allied to this inflating of the consequences. Whenever a thesis of the "logic" of knowledge takes the form $Kxp \rightarrow A$ so that

$$\square \, (Kxp \rightarrow A)$$

is an acceptable contention, the sceptic inclines to read this as

$$Kxp \rightarrow \Box A$$

For this classic confusion of the necessity of consequence (*necessitas consequentiae*) with the necessity of the consequent (*necessitas consequentis*) is very much to his purpose. Since contraposition here yields

$$\Diamond.\sim A \rightarrow \sim Kxp$$

there arises once more the just-discussed prospect of deafeating knowledge claims by the manipulation of *mere* possibilities. Here too there is an illicit inflation or escalation in what must necessarily be so for a knowledge claim to be appropriate.

The crucial point is that in the probative exploitation of an implication-thesis the antecedent and consequent must be kept in a state of parity as regards epistemic status. One cannot ask more of the consequent than of the antecedent. It is through a violation of this basic principle of parity-preservation in the treatment of such consequences that the sceptic's consequence-inflating procedure manifests its illegitimacy.

4. THE SELF-DEFEAT OF SCEPTICAL ARGUMENTATION

Mesmerized by the absolutistic aspect of knowledge, one sceptical writer has written:

> I propose that the subject of "knowledge" is no longer of serious philosophical concern for the simple reason that this concept is far too primitive for the needs of technical epistemology. No harm will be done, I suppose, by retaining a special name for true beliefs at the theoretical limit of absolute conviction and perfect infallibility so long as we appreciate that this ideal is never instantiated. . . .[1]

[1] William W. Rozeboom, "Why I Know So Much More than You Do," *American Philosophical Quarterly*, vol. 4 (1967), pp. 281–290; see p. 289.

Such abandonment appears as the logical outcome of a construction of knowledge that renders it inherently unattainable. In fact, however, our standard conception of knowledge just is *not* of this hyperbolic nature. Not the constructions of our language, but the reconstructions of the philosophers have rendered the absolutes of our knowledge claims beyond the reach of the attainable.

In this context, the position of the "common sense" school is on the right track in its opposition to scepticism. As G. E. Moore wrote: "There is no reason why I should not confidently assert that I do really *know* some external facts. . . . I am, in fact, as certain of this as of anything; and as *reasonably* certain of it." [2] The father of this line of thought is Thomas Reid, the great Scottish common-sense philosopher, who held that if a philosophical doctrine (specifically Humean *empiricism*) has the consequence that we do not know any of those plain facts we commonly take ourselves to know, then this doctrine is *ipso facto* false. [3] The sceptic's ingenious demonstrations of the inaccessibility of knowledge are in fact no more than a *reductio ad absurdum* argument against the conception of knowledge on which his demonstration is based.

The sceptic insists that absolute exactness (correctness, precision, certainty, etc.) are as a matter of principle not to be had in factual matters. (See Premiss 2 of the "No Absolutes" Argument.) This line of thought invites a reply along the following lines:

Let it be even as you say, that these absolutes are unattainable in factual contexts as a matter of principle.

[2] *Philosophical Studies* (London, 1922), p. 113. See also Moore's "A Defense of Common Sense," in *Contemporary British Philosophy*, 2nd Series, ed. J. H. Muirhead (London, 1925), pp. 193–223.

[3] *The Philosophical Works of Thomas Reid*, ed. by Sir William Hamilton; see esp. p. 234. The German philosopher Leonard Nelson took much the same line with respect to mathematical scepticism: Such scepticism, he wrote, calls on us to

sacrifice the clearest and most lucid knowledge that we possess – indeed the *only* knowledge that is clear and lucid *per se*. I prefer to strike the opposite course. If a philosophy, no matter how attractive or plausible or ingenious it may be, brings one into conflict with mathematics, I conclude that not mathematics but my philosophy is on the wrong track. (*Socratic Method and Critical Philosophy* [New Haven, 1949], p. 184.)

This very fact of itself shows the impropriety, indeed the absurdity of such absolutistic demands. It makes no sense to ask for what cannot *in principle* be had: one must not require the impossible.

Philosophical sceptics generally set up some abstract standard of absolutistic incorrigibility and then proceed to show that no knowledge-claims in a given area (sense, memory, scientific theory, etc.) can possibly meet the conditions of this standard.[4] From this fact, the impossibility of such a category of "knowledge" is accordingly inferred. But this inference is altogether misguided. For surely what actually follows is simply the inappropriateness or incorrectness of the standard at issue. If the vaunted standard is such that knowledge-claims cannot possibly meet it, the appropriate moral is not "too bad for knowledge claims," but rather "too bad for the standard." For it is senseless to impose conditions which cannot in the very nature of things be met. Obligation does not exceed the limits of the possible: the old Roman legal precept applies – *ultra posse nemo obligatur*. Once all that is reasonably possible – i.e., all that can *appropriately* be expected – has been done to assure some knowledge claim, it is unreasonable, nay *irrational*, to ask for more.

A certain irony emerges here. To the extent that the sceptic "proves" his case by a clever deployment of considerations regarding the theoretical general principles of the matter, he *thereby* destroys it. When he shows that in the nature of things "knowledge" (as he construes it) cannot be had, then this very fact renders this conception of "knowledge" irrelevant to *knowledge* as we deal with it in real-life situations.

The sceptic's "No Absolutes" Argument wields a double-edged sword that inflicts the more serious damage upon itself, and thus carries the heavy burden of self-defeat. For insofar as it succeeds in demonstrating the inaccessibility *in*

---

[4] For example, the argumentation of William W. Rozeboom's interesting article "Why I Know So Much More Than You Do" (*op. cit.*), leads him to the conclusion that "my conception of 'knowledge' – and presumably yours as well – is so impossibly idealized that no real-life belief episode ever satisfies it" (p. 289).

principle of the absoluteness requisite for knowledge it also –
by this very fact – brings out the inappropriateness of the
hyperbolically absolutistic conception of knowledge on
which it is based.

V

The "No Entitlement" Argument

SYNOPSIS

(1) A statement of the "No Entitlement" Argument: The evidence for a claim of objective fact can never wholly exhaust the contentual ramifications of this claim, and – so it is maintained – we are therefore never fully entitled to make the claim. (2) The grounds for entitlement lie not in the abstract "logic" of the situation, but in the warranting conventions governing the employment of language as an instrument of communication – in their *use-conditions* rather than their *truth-conditions*. (3) And these norms and standards of language use do in fact afford the entitlement the sceptic claims to be lacking. The *ultra posse* principle: it makes no sense to ask for guarantees that cannot in the very nature of the cognitive situation be provided. (5) A probabilism that limits us to assertions of probability and denies us the entitlement ever to make categorical claims itself infringes on the ground-rules governing the proper use of language. (6) The entitlement for regarding *our* truth as *the* truth ultimately resides in the operation of Darwinian principles with respect to the methods by which we proceed in the validation of truth-claims.

1. THE "NO ENTITLEMENT" ARGUMENT

The quarrel between the sceptic and the cognitivist has *knowledge* as its main bone of contention, and to "know" something in the sense at issue in traditional controversies is (*inter alia*) to accept it on a rationally adequate basis – one that renders the contention at issue *worthy* of acceptance by "the reasonable man," and suffices to *entitle* someone to stake a claim to knowledge.

The sceptic's position is basically that *nothing* in the sphere of factual claims about the world is worthy of acceptance as true – that the available rational credentials are here invariably inadequate to underwrite unqualified acceptance. As concerns factual issues, the epistemic circumstances of the human condition are inevitably such that "the rational man" would have to suspend credence – to live, as the ancient sceptics put it, *adoxastos* ("unbelieving"), that is, without belief at any rate as far as concerns the domain of contingent matters of fact.[1]

The sceptic maintains the indefensibility of acceptance in general and in particular acceptance based on the standard probative ground-rules that govern the usual conduct of our cognitive affairs. It is on *this* basis that the arguments of the sceptic must be met. And we shall endeavor to meet them (as the argument unfolds) by an account of how the practical know-how of the norms and practices of knowledge-invoking discourse serve to provide a basis of justification. Our discussion takes a pragmatic turn in seeking to validate theoretical knowledge through praxis-oriented considerations.

Knowledge must, of course, preclude all possibility of error. In authentic *knowledge* there can be no slip between the cup and the lip – between what is claimed and one's grasp thereon. To have knowledge one must be able to rule out all possibility of mistake and establish his "right to be sure" – his *full* entitlement to make the claim at issue on the basis of the grounds at his disposal.[2] And so, to claim knowledge is, in effect, to claim infallibility with respect to the specific case in hand. But is the requisite entitlement for such a claim ever in

---

[1] For the ancient sceptics, this epistemological doctrine was the way station en-route to an ethical conclusion, viz., that happiness (*eudaimonia*) lay in that tranquility of mind and freedom from disturbance (*ataraxia*) which only a total suspension of belief could bring about.

[2] A. J. Ayer, *The Problem of Knowledge* (Harmondsworth, 1956), p. 35.

fact available? Given the evidence-transcendence of all claims of objective fact, are we *ever* actually so circumstanced as to have a "right to be sure"? How can one claim even localized infallibility as long as there remains the prospect of slips between the cup and the lip?

These considerations set the stage for the sceptic's "No Entitlement" Argument, which might be formulated as follows:

1. A claim to knowledge will not be warranted when the person who issues it is not in the possession of grounds which *fully* entitle him to make the claim at issue, beyond any possibility of mistake.
2. In matters of objective fact we never are in possession of grounds that fully and completely govern the entire content-area of the claim. The possibility of mistake can never be altogether excluded, so that the full entitlement at issue in the preceding premiss is not available.

∴ Knowledge is not available in matters of objective fact.

How can this argument be countered?

2. MEETING THE "NO ENTITLEMENT" ARGUMENT: THE CRUCIAL ROLE OF THE WARRANTING CONVENTIONS OF LANGUAGE-USE CONDITIONS *vs.* TRUTH CONDITIONS

The issue of entitlement must ultimately be traced back to fundamental rules governing the proprieties of language use. Clearly, the question of whether or not we are entitled to apply particular elements of our language in a certain way hinges on the established conventions that govern such usage. Our knowledge-claims are expressed in everyday language and are consequently subject to the constitutive ground-rules that govern its use.

A language is subject to built-in conventions of various different sorts. Meaning rules and inference rules are familiar from logical and semantical discussions. The *warranting con-*

ventions or *use-conditions* that underly our standard practice in verbal communication are perhaps less familiar. (They are certainly relatively more variegated and less easy to codify.)

The meaning rules of a language govern the truth-conditions of its statements, and specify what range of the *objective* circumstances (actual or possible) must obtain if these statements are to be made *correctly*. By contrast, the warranting conventions fix the governing norms of assertability of its statements, and specify the *epistemic* circumstances (actual or possible) in which these statements can be made *appropriately* (or defensibly). The truth-conditions for a statement determine its assertive content – the consequences that can be derived from it (the set of all *ontological* circumstances in which what it says is true). And the use-conditions determine its evidential conditions – the warrant that is required for it (the set of all *epistemic* circumstances in which its assertion is warranted). Truth-conditions address themselves to the content-oriented issue of *what is being claimed* when a statement is affirmed. The pivotal question takes the form: "Under what circumstances (actual or possible) is it *true* that *P*?" The use-conditions, on the other hand, deal with the warrant-oriented issue of *when is there entitlement* to affirm a statement. The pivotal question takes the form: "Under what circumstances (actual or possible) is it *legitimately assertable* that *P*?" Given the very *modus operandi* of language, these two issues of declarative content and warranting criteria cannot be equated with one another.[3] The involvements of the former may ramify *ad indefinitum*; the latter must be sufficiently simple and straightforward to put a language at the disposal of children of average capability. The unraveling of meaning-contents may exercise the talents of genius; the determination of usability and warrant must deploy only issues of comparatively stark simplicity.

As we have seen, the "evidential gap" at issue with objective factual claims means that the *content* of every such claim – knowledge-claims included – involves such a variety of implications and ramifications that it would be in principle

---

[3] But which determines the "meaning" of a statement – its truth-conditions or its use-conditions? This question is misguided in its either-or form. The term is sufficiently diffuse to encompass both issues.

impossible to check them all. Such omniverification is *impossible* – and thus becomes an irrational demand. However, the warranting conditions that govern our use of this conception are – and in the very nature of the case *must* be – a great deal more undemanding, straightforward, and manageable. It is crucial to the very viability of language that the truth-conditions at issue with contentual commitments involve more than the conditions of appropriate usage can manage to assure. The fact that the *content* of an objective claim always far *outruns* our *evidence* for it means that the use-conditions of assertion-entitlement – the evidential warranting conventions – will encompass only a modest sector of the range envisaged by the truth-conditions correlative with content-determination.[4] The data-in-hand transcendence of *all* factual discourse makes it inevitable that the reach of truth-conditions should extend beyond the verificational resources at issue in the use-conditions.

We must accordingly resist any temptation to equate truth-conditions with warranting conventions or use-conditions, an identification which would be fatal to the capacity of language to accomplish its proper work. These norms of assertability specify the circumstances under which certain claims are in order – including what sorts of further circumstances abrogate such entitlements.[5] They encompass – *inter alia* – the ground-rules of plausibility and presumption that indicate the standard bases on which claims stand "in the absence of counter-indications," and that inventory the types of moves that defeat such claims. It is thus important to avoid confusing this evidential issue of use-conditions with the semantical issue of truth-conditions or assertive content.

[4] The ideas at issue have entered into recent philosophy at many points. Thus conditions of use and assertability are presumably at issue where Wittgenstein speaks of "criteria." (Cf. Rogers Albritton, "Wittgenstein's Use of the Term 'Criterion'," *The Journal of Philosophy*, vol. 56 (1959), pp. 845–857.) Rudolf Carnap distinguishes between truth-criteria (= truth conditions) and confirmation-criteria (= assertability conditions). (See his "Truth and Confirmation" in H. Feigl and W. Sellars (eds.), *Readings in Philosophical Analysis* [New York, 1949], p. 120.) Roderick Chisholm urges that "*conditions of truth*" must be distinguished from "*criteria of of evidence.*" (*Theory of Knowledge*, 2nd ed. [Englewood Cliffs, 1977], p. 98.) Cognate ideas are at work in Michael Dummett, *Frege: Philosophy of Language* (Oxford, 1973). For various relevant issues see also Chap. I, "The Criteriology of Truth" of the author's *The Coherence Theory of Truth* (Oxford, 1973).

[5] See Ludwig Wittgenstein, *On Certainty*, §18.

These warranting conventions are intrinsic components of the language – a part of what every child learns about the use of his native tongue "at mother's knee." For a crucial part of learning what a word *means* is to learn how it is *used* – i.e., to get a working grasp of the types of conditions and circumstances under which its use in certain ways is *appropriate*. And here it is necessary to realize that this involves an "inductive" component – an implicit view of "the way in which things work in the world." [6] The language of our objectively descriptive discourse is in its very nature a vehicle for evidence-transcending imputations. [7]

To be sure, it would be misleading to speak of use-conditions in terms of assertability-*rules* so as to invoke the idea of "rules" in this connection. For the "rules" at issue are not, strictly speaking, *rules* at all; they are not formulated and codified; doubtless they are not even codifiable, any more than are the "rules" for hitting a forehand in tennis. What is at issue is a matter of the characterizing conditions of a practice, of how-to-do-it guidelines, of tricks of the trade or skills, of what is learned largely through observation, imitation and practice rather than through mastery of and adherence to explicitly specifiable rules.

These considerations lend a special importance to the fact that the warranting conventions or use-conditions of our claims (knowledge-claims included) can – and indeed in the case of all objective claims *must* – fall short of their truth-conditions. To meet the former is not (ever) to meet the latter as well – at any rate within the domain of objective fact.

Many writers fail to recognize this crucial circumstance, and such a failure leads straightaway to scepticism. Consider, for example, the following passage:

[I]t may seem very stringent to require of a belief, before it can qualify as knowledge, that the reasons we offer in its support entail its truth. Such a requirement may well preclude us from claiming to know many propositions which are in fact true and for which we can offer sup-

---

[6] Cf. Chapter VI of the author's *The Primary of Practice* (Oxford, 1973), pp. 107–123.

[7] Compare the author's *Conceptual Idealism* (Oxford, 1973), pp. 86ff.

porting reasons of substance but it does this on the grounds, which I believe to be unexceptionable, that we have no way of identifying the propositions in question. For the very ones we might choose as true could be propositions which are in fact false. As long as truth is a necessary condition of knowledge and as long as the only way of establishing the truth of any proposition is through the reasons we can give in its behalf, we are forced to accept the consequence that, for a proposition to count as knowledge, its truth must be entailed by the reasons which support it. Unfortunately, as we have already discovered, we seem unable to find any propositions which fulfil this very strict requirement.[8]

The entire argument here rests on the idea that the rationally warranting supporting grounds of a claim must *logically entail* its truth, that its warranting conditions must exhaust its truth conditions. And this claim – which is simply false – paves a sure road to cognitive disaster.

There will, of course, generally be *some* fairly intimate relationship between the truth-conditions of *p* and its use-conditions – the authorizing conditions for the warranted assertion of *p*. But these two sets of conditions do not – and in the nature of things relating to discourse and communication cannot – be made to coincide. To identify them would make demands that render warranted assertability of objective factual claims always and inevitably impossible, and do so *a priori*, on the basis of the general principles of the matter.

Effective or practical warrant stops short of categorical transcendental certainty. But just how far short? We have said above that a thesis is *effectively* certain when "it is as certain as, in the nature of the case, a thesis of its type could *reasonably* be rendered." But just what does this call for – what determines the reasonableness at issue?

In the case of knowledge-claims, in particular, such warranting conditions will have to specify, in effect, "how far is far enough" when it comes to closing the "evidential gap" in putting forward a (now duly warranted) assertion. Here too it must be recognized that a "reasonable level of expecta-

[8] O. A. Johnson, *The Problem of Knowledge* (The Hague, 1974), pp. 74–75.

tion" regarding the evidential warrant in knowledge-talk will be part and parcel of what is built into the very *modus operandi* of our language.

In elucidating this issue, it is useful to consider Peter Unger's discussion of absolute terms:

> English is a language with absolute terms. Among these terms, "flat" and "certain" are *basic* ones. Due to these terms' characteristic features, and because the world is not so simple as it might be, we do not speak truly, at least as a rule, when we say of a real object, "That has a top which is flat," or when we say of a real person, "He is certain that it is raining." . . . If a condition of something's being *flat* is, as I shall argue, that nothing could ever possibly be even the least bit flatter, we would be in a strong position to advance the thesis, in the most ordinary meaning of the words, that *at most hardly any* physical objects are *flat*. . . . Now, in the case of any or almost any physical object, you can find another which is flatter. Of course, the flattest object you might ever find *may* itself *not* be flat, or the few tied for flattest *may* themselves actually *not* be flat. At the same time, it or they may be flat. If it is or they are, then it is still true that hardly any are flat, and so, that at most hardly any are flat. If it is not or they are not, it will also be true that *at most* hardly any physical objects are flat. In either case, then, it will be true that at most hardly any physical objects are flat. Similarly, if a condition of someone's being *certain* of something is, as I shall similarly argue, that no one could ever possibly be any more certain of anything than he is of that, we would be in a strong position to advance the thesis that, in the case of every human being, there is at most hardly anything of which he is certain.[9]

Unger now has little difficulty in supporting his key premiss that "It is never all right for anyone to be absolutely certain that anything is so."[10]

[9] Peter Unger, *Ignorance: A Case for Scepticism* (Oxford, 1975), p. 49. The whole of Chap. II ("A Language with Absolute Terms") is relevant.
[10] *Op cit.*, p. 95.

The untenability of this approach in the case of certainty can be seen by examining Unger's own comparison-case of flatness. It is bizarre to think that we find ourselves in the absurd situation that (for example) "flat" is a descriptive term in our language which is without any application virtually in principle – given "the nature of things." Rather, the lesson emerges that the application of the term is no unthinking and mechanical process. What is flat in the context of a dining table is one thing, something in the context of a landscape or a farmer's field, and quite another thing in the case of a precision instrument. There is in the background the "theoretical ideal of perfect flatness" and we have to learn how much deviation (micrometers, millimeters, meters) is allowable in a particular context of application.[11] Learning the standard that governs the applications of a term as part of learning its "meaning."

Exactly the same holds for certainty. It is one thing in the context of pure mathematics, another in that of theoretical physics; one thing for the courtroom, another for egyptology. The standards of attainable deviation from the (in principle unattainable) theoretical ideal of perfect certainty have to be mastered step by step with our mastery of the language itself and the conditions of its use. This is simply part of the background of talents and abilities that constitute linguistic competency. It would thus be a serious mistake to think that such an absolute term is "strictly speaking" such that it can only be applied correctly in the theoretically ideal (and thus unrealizable) case.

3. THE CENTRALITY OF LANGUAGE AND THE POSSIBILITY OF
   ERROR

Knowledge-claims – as we have seen – are crucially predicated upon a "right to be sure." But what is the foundation of this right, the *basis* of the warrant or entitlement at issue? The answer is simple: it inheres in the very *conventions of language-use* themselves. For – as we have stressed – a "lan-

---

[11] It won't do to conjure with "absolute." Analogous considerations hold for absolutely flat landscape *vs.* absolutely flat table.

guage" involves not merely rules of formation (syntactical rules), and rules of meaning and of truth (semantical rules), and rules of inference (logical rules), but also – and most importantly – conventions of application-propriety or assertion-entitlement (evidential ground-rules).[12]

The crucial entitlement-denying premiss of the sceptics' "No Entitlement" Argument thus founders on the fact that we *are* entitled to make knowledge claims by the basic conventions of language-use that govern our discourse about "knowledge." For discourse about knowledge to be a viable and meaningful enterprise there must be norms that govern it, and – given the communicative jobs at issue – there are indeed such that *something* (some realistically realizable conditions and circumstances) does actually count as satisfying them.

It is useful to approach the issue of our entitlement to make knowledge claims from the angle of the traditional distinction between theoretical knowledge-that and practical how-to-knowledge. In our present context how-to-knowledge appears in a basic role. To be sure, the how-to-knowledge at issue here is of a very particular kind, namely knowledge of how to put "knowledge"-terminology to work. It is thus necessary in this context to acknowledge the aptness of the pragmatists' perspective that what a conception *is* lies in what the conception *does*.

The critical issue is that of how to operate with knowledge-talk (or, if you prefer, *how to apply* the conception of knowledge). The validity of our use of "I know that . . ." claims or "He knows that . . ." concessions must be taken to inhere in the ground-rules of use governing such expressions. And here we must be realistic about how our knowledge-terminology actually operates, recognizing that such realism blocks the sceptic's stratagem of arguing on the basis of general principles that one is never warranted in making claims of the form "I know that *p*."[13]

---

[12] Note that these largely take the form of principles of presumption to the effect that such-and-such can be maintained in the absence of indications to the contrary.

[13] Roderick Chisholm describes his own epistemological position as holding

That there are principles of evidence, other than the principles of induction and deduction, which tell us, for example, under what conditions the state we have called "thinking that one perceives" will *confer evidence*, or *confer reasonable-*

It is not a workable policy to *equate* the use-conditions with the truth-conditions. After all, it is not a workable policy to adopt the rule

(i) I shall affirm (assert) *p* only if *p* is true.

in contradistinction to

(ii) I shall affirm (assert) *p* only if I have adequate reason for holding *p* to be so.

There is no way in which I can possibly implement rule (i) except via (ii). And I am not idiosyncratic in this regard, but reflect the situation in which people-in-general find themselves. And so in knowledge-contexts as elsewhere the conditions of truth and those of warranted assertability must be kept apart.

In this connection Arne Naess makes an astute observation. When people are pressed hard with regard to a claim to truth or knowledge they tend, he says, to shift from the issue of the factuality of the claim to that of their warrant for making it: "to shift towards the question of being *justified in asssserting or saying* 'Now it is true' or 'Now it is known.' That is, there is a tendency to estimate what might be, from a social point of view, sufficient to *claim* this or that. Nobody will *blame* anybody for saying 'It is true [and known to be so] that there are mountains on the other side of the moon'."[14] And these considerations are crucial to the cognitivist's case (though Naess himself takes them to substantiate scepticism). For the key fact is that we can stake defensible claims to having knowledge – claims whose appropriateness is validated by the social contract of language use, and that will stand up as having been made appropriately even in the event that "things go wrong" and that matters ultimately so turn out that they are *incorrect*.

---

ness, upon propositions about external things. . . . (*Theory of Knowledge*, 1st ed., p. 62.)

Our present position achieves the same ends by simpler means. Rather than resorting to a new mechanism of *principles of evidence* we see the mission at issue accomplished simply by the very ground-rules of language (assertability conditions) themselves.

[14] *Scepticism* (London, 1968), p. 80.

A. J. Ayer has trenchantly enunciated the key point at issue here:

> If someone wants to know what day of the week it is and, when I tell him it is Monday, asks me whether this is certain, then an answer like "Yes, quite certain; I have just seen it in the newspaper, and anyhow I remember that yesterday was a Sunday" is a correct answer. To answer, "Well, I seem to remember that yesterday was a Sunday, and I believe that this is to-day's newspaper, and I seem to see 'Monday' written on it; but I may be wrong about the newspaper, and anyhow both memory and perception are fallible. Therefore I cannot be certain that it is Monday but I think it very probable" – to give an answer of this sort would be tiresome, and not only tiresome but misleading. It would be misleading because, in the ordinary way, we say that something is not certain, but at best highly probable, only in cases where we have some special reason for doubting, some reason which applies particularly to the case in question. Thus, in the example that I have just given, I might be justified in saying that I did not know that it was Monday if my memory were frequently at fault in matters of this kind, or I had glanced at the newspaper only carelessly, or the newspaper could not be relied on to print the right date. But if my reason for saying that it is not certain is merely the general reason that all empirical beliefs are fallible, then it is not consonant with ordinary usage to say that it is only probable. It is correct to say that it is certain. It is correct for me to say that I know.[15]

Claims to certainty and knowledge under the circumstances are *normal* in the root sense of conforming to the norms of our language-use. And these, as Ayer rightly sees, do not render claims to certainty subject to defeat or demotion into claims of probability by appeal to general principles (like "Man is fallible"), but only by case-specific counterindications.

[15] A. J. Ayer, "Basic Propositions" in *Philosophical Analysis*, ed. by Max Black (Englewood Cliffs, 1950), pp. 59–60.

But cannot a knowledge-claim that is "made appropriately under the circumstances" ever turn out to be false? Of course it can! "They believed that they knew that p – and quite justifiedly so – but it turned out that they were wrong about this" is a perfectly viable locution that presents an all-too-common facet of the human predicament. And to say this is *not* to deny the pragmatic inconsistency of "They knew that p but turned out to be wrong about it.") Knowledge as such is indefeasible, and so (*ex hypothesi*) are *correct* claims to it. But *warranted* claims to knowledge are *not* indefeasible. Thus if I accept something on the basis of appropriately sufficient or adequate (albeit not *conclusive*) evidence – say the on-the-spot report of a radio news broadcast that the President is in Chicago – then I can warrantedly claim to know he is in Chicago, even though I will have to retract this claim if (say) it eventuated that his motorcade turned back at the city limit.[16] The point is that while the inference

$$x \text{ knows } p$$
$$\therefore p$$

is unproblematically valid, the inference

$$x \text{ has adequate rational warrant for claiming } x \text{ knows } p$$
$$\therefore p$$

is not. While the truth of a thesis is indeed a prerequisite for *actual* knowledge of it, this is not – and, given the *modus operandi* of communication cannot be – the case with respect to the *adequate warrant* for a knowledge claim.

Consider a related issue. Philosophers sometimes talk as though knowledge claims could only be warranted by *maximal* warrant – as though x only has adequate warrant for the claim to know that p if it is altogether impossible for x to have any better warrant for anything than he then has for p.[17] They enjoin us to acceptance of the inference:

---

[16] Compare Norman Malcolm, "Knowledge and Belief" in *Knowledge and Belief* (Englewood Cliffs, 1963), pp. 60–61.

[17] Compare Bertrand Russell's contention that a proposition is certain in the "epistemological" sense only "when it has the highest degree of credibility." And he at once goes on to add that "Perhaps no proposition is certain in this sense; i.e.,

$$\frac{x \text{ has adequate rational warrant for claiming } Kxp}{\therefore \ x \text{ has maximal rational warrant for claiming } p}$$

But there is no reason to think that this inference holds. To exploit $Kxp \rightarrow p$ as basis for laying down the inference in question is yet another instance of that "inflation of the consequences" of which we have complained above. (See sect. 3 of Chapter IV.) Indeed, given the stringent sense of "maximal warrant" taken to be at issue here, we simply have another instance of that hyperbolic exaggeration which sceptical philosophers incline to attribute to knowledge claims. There is no reason to think that all the things we warrantedly claim to know lie on one and the same epistemological plane – that of maximal warrant. This just is not the way in which the concept operative in our knowledge-discourse actually works. I know that Peking is in China but could no doubt augment my evidential basis for making this claim by visiting the place. To be sure, having *adequate rational warrant* for Kxp entails having *adequate rational warrant* for p. (Kxp, after all, entails p.) Adequacy or sufficiency there must be, for parity must be preserved in the move from premiss to conclusion. But to insist on maximality is to carry things too far and to perpetrate the sort of illicit escalation against which our earlier discussion has already admonished. (See pp. 53–54 above.)

The key point is that knowledge-talk is part of the ordinary, run-of-the-mill use of language for communicative purposes. There are relatively well defined – workable, learnable, and implementable – conventions for making such claims, and for accepting and rejecting them. Our knowledge-attributions are subject to certain understandings or conventions governing the capacity of evidence to count as conclusive – rules of presumption and burden of disproof whose force is not logical but a part of our inductively secured view of the ways of the world. The relevant conventions about conclusiveness are not absolute – they are (as we have said) rules of presumption, and these presumptions are defeasible, exactly

---

however certain it may be in relation to a given person's knowledge, further knowledge might increase its degree of credibility." (*Human Knowledge* [New York, 1948], p. 396.)

as with the legal presumption that a person missing for seven years is dead. Yet they are not to be defeated by considerations of general principles or outlandish hypotheses, but only by definite, case-specific considerations (which can come into operation only when themselves established in a manner incompatible with dogmatic scepticism). Language is a purposive instrumentality, evolved in the course of the dealings of mundane beings for mundane purposes of communication. Its assertions – those about knowledge preeminently included – are subject to the social and communally established standards of linguistic propriety and normality: here, as always, the use of our linguistic resources is governed by the apposite ground-rules.

Some sceptics are perfectly prepared to accept these consequences and take the hard line of flatly rejecting our linguistic usages as simply improper and incorrect in this context of knowledge-claims. For example, we are told that:

> Whenever you or I assert, as we often do, ... "He knows that ...," etc., we are uttering falsehoods which would come closer to the truth if revised as ... "He almost knows that ...," or the like. The paradigm-case rejoinder, that what we *mean* by "know" is defined by these ordinary-life, applications, no more shows that this usage is literally correct than the everyday paradigmatic ascription of "spherical" to roundish objects of irregular curvature demonstrates that a thing's surface does not really have to be a constant distance from its center in order for it to be literally a sphere. On matters philosophical as well as scientific, ordinary language teems with simplistic presuppositions and coarse-grained, uncritical categories which do slovenly justice to reality. ...[18]

But this dismissal of the realities of our communicative praxis has little to recommend it. There is no shirking the fact that one key task of the philosopher is to clarify the conceptions we actually employ – the conceptions that set the stage of philosophical deliberations. He has no real use

---

[18] William W. Rozeboom, "Why I Know So Much More Than You Do," *American Philosophical Quarterly*, vol. 4 (1967), pp. 281–290 (see p. 289).

for technical constructs, such as the "work" of the physicist in contrast to the *work* of everyday life. These technical devices have a real job to do in science. But this is not so in philosophy. Where is the discipline in which the philosopher's technical variant of "knowledge" performs a useful job? And what would be the point of such a "discipline," given that (*ex hypothesi*) there can be no such thing – that the knowledge-of-the-philosophers is so construed that *ex vi terminorum* it is subject to conditions which render it necessarily inapplicable.

As we have seen, discourse regarding issues of objective fact is inherently such that there is a standard, inevitable, and perfectly manageable evidential gap between the assertive *content* of our claims and the evidential criteria that define the requisite *supporting evidence* at our disposal for making them (appropriately and justifiably). But there is a bridge across this gap, a bridge erected by the mechanisms of our language and the governing conditions of its mode of operation. This state of things is implicit in the very ground-rules of rational discourse. To abandon or impugn it is to cast aside the practice of verbal communication as we actually carry it on. Learning these inbuilt principles of presumption and plausibility is an integral part of learning the language itself. To reject the ground-rules of operation is in effect to resign from the community of rational users of language. The sceptic who insists on a negative answer to the question "Do we ever really know anything?" because he adopts a conception of "knowledge" according to which the operative conditions for the application of the terminology of knowing is seldom if ever met is guilty of what had aptly been characterized as an "*ignoratio elenchi* by redefinition."[19]

In opposition to such a line of thought Arne Naess has written as follows:

[19] Paul Edwards, "Russell's Doubts About Induction," *Mind*, vol. 68 (1949), pp. 141–163. To be sure, a deep problem lurks in the background here, because the mere existence of a linguistic usage does not establish the reality of phenomena (think of the "evil eye").

This issue of the legitimation of our cognitive instruments is a perfectly legitimate one. For the author's position with regard to it see his *Methodological Pragmatism* (Oxford, 1976). Where scepticism is merely an instrument for raising questions of cognitive validation – rather than a device for erecting supposedly insuperable barriers in the way of any attempt at such validation – it serves a useful and constructive purpose.

> If I hesitate in, or abstain from, saying "I know it" because I see (am sure I see) a *remote possibility* of being wrong, this does not necessarily violate any explicit or implicit rules of ordinary language. It may be a symptom of overcautiousness, hypochondria, hyperactivity of the imagination, or inability to square up to some formidable responsibility, but . . . I am still a member of my language community.[20]

Nevertheless, this seems quite wrong. For in the specific regard at issue I have (to this extent) *withdrawn* from the community in abandoning the standards that govern its practices. To refuse to countenance what *they* call knowledge as *my* "knowledge" is as serious – and deviant – as to refuse to countenance what *they* call dogs as deserving of this appellation from my variant point of view. I can (in the appropriate circumstances) no more avoid responding "yes" to a "Does he know?" question without a (temporary) exit from the communicative arena than I can when a "Is it a dog?" question is at issue. If the praxis of language-use is such that certain sorts of remote possibilities do not contravalidate knowledge-claims (as is indeed the case), then this is not something about which I can choose to be more scrupulous than the language-using community without thereby entering (to this extent) into a self-imposed exile from it.

A further objection might be considered:

> Your contentions do not really defeat the sceptic. After all, you do not actually maintain that our knowledge claims are true. You only maintain that we are rationally warranted in making them. This approach does not do justice to the difference between (1) There is *adequate rational warrant* for claiming that x knows that p, and (2) x *actually knows* that p (i.e., it is true that x knows that p). Your epistemology is a theory of warranted assertability, not a theory of knowledge.

The fact, however, is that present discussion has *not* ignored this difference. It is in fact crucial to our purposes, and importantly operative in the distinction between truth-conditions and use-conditions. The epistemic fact of life is

[20] *Scepticism* (London, 1968), p. 124.

that we have to proceed to (2) via (1), that our only effective route to truth-claims is via warrant-claims.

What does the objector here really want? Does he insist that we somehow *demonstrate* (by way of a logically conclusive proof?) the truth of our knowledge claims in ways that *go beyond* adequate rational warrant? This is clearly impossible in the nature of the case – as the sceptical objector himself is the first to insist. Accordingly, we have no alternative but to reject the demand at issue as inherently absurd.

And much the same must be said to the objector who complains as follows:

> You claim to know that *p* and I will even concede (for the sake of argument) that the circumstances are such that you have adequate justification and due warrant for your making this claim. But nevertheless it is clear that the question remains: Do you *really* know that *p*?

Of course the question remains! Adequate warrant does not *prove* truth with demonstrative infallibility: truth conditions outrun assertion conditions.

What, once again, can it be that the objector wants? If challenged "Do you know that *p*?" the best that one can possibly do is to establish one's rational warrant for claiming to know that *p*. Whichever doubt remains is now of that neurotic kind that nothing doable will allay – the hobgoblin that remains a threat under the bed no matter how often and how carefully one verifies its absence. Given that one has done all that is needful given the very nature of the case, this is all that can rationally be asked for. Once we are properly entitled to claim knowledge, there is (*ex hypothesi*) nothing further *of any available sort* that need be provided. And to say this is not to say that it is unimaginable that we could turn out to be wrong, but simply that there remains no *realistic* possibility of this.

4. THE *ULTRA POSSE* PRINCIPLE

This difference between *factuality* and *warranted assertability* is pervasive. There is no choice but to recognize and admit the difference between

$$p \text{ is justifiedly held by } x \text{ to be true}$$

and

$$p \text{ is actually true.}$$

Clearly the first does not entail or require the second (as sceptics are the very first to insist). For the evidence-in-hand that suffices to justify someone in holding a thesis to be true need not provide a *deductive* guarantee of this thesis. And a strictly analogous situation obtains with the pair:

$$p \text{ is justifiedly held by } x \text{ to be known (by } x)$$
$$p \text{ is actually known by } x.$$

Here too we cannot move unproblematically from the first statement to the second. And this is simply an instance of the general fact that we do *not* have the principle that justification entails factuality – not in general, and not in the special case of knowledge-claims either.[21] The standard gap between the epistemic, warrant-oriented issue of what one justifiedly holds to be and the ontological issue of what is the case, objectively speaking, again comes to the fore.

The ground-rules of rational discourse are such that when factual claims are at issue the thesis:

(1) I am rationally warranted to assert p

does *not* entail (or presuppose or otherwise require) the thesis

(2) I have rational control (of a certificatory or confirmatory character) over each and every constituent part of the assertive content of p.

---

[21] See Keith Lehrer, "Knowledge, Truth, and Evidence," *Analysis*, vol. 25 (1965), pp. 168–175, where it is (quite properly) maintained that "a person may be completely justified in believing something that is in fact false" (p. 168). Here as elsewhere the issue of *justification* does not preempt that of *correctness*.

The constituting conventions that govern discourse are such that we become rationally entitled to make our descriptive claims *notwithstanding* the literally endless implicative ramifications of their content, ramifications over whose obtaining we in fact have no rational control without making specific verificatory checks. And these checks, no matter how far elaborated, still remain incomplete – mere samples drawn from an infinite range. (Cf. pp. 25–29 above.)

One must be willing to admit in general the existence of a gap between *warranted assertability* and ultimate *correctness*, admitting that on occasion even incorrect theses can be maintained with due warrant. And there is no good reason for blocking the application of this general rule to knowledge claims in particular. Justification does not entail truth here, with knowledge, any more than it does any place else. To be sure, appropriate justification does *guarantee* truth, not hyperbolically – and certainly not through logical necessitation – but in the only realistically pertinent sense of the term, extending an assurance qualified by considerations of realism rather than being categorical in some unrealistic manner.[22]

Entitlement to claim knowledge is just that – a matter of being rationally warranted in staking a claim to knowledge. And with knowledge claims the question of the *truth* of the claims inevitably poses issues over and above that of their rational entitlement. Yet while theoretically separate, the issues are not in practice separable *for us*: I myself cannot consider the question of the truth of *p* independently of the issue of my rational entitlement to claim the truth of *p*. I cannot deal with the truth of specific theses in detachment from the question of what I am to hold to be true. (Though this circumstance certainly does not mean that "*p* is true" and "I hold that *p* is true" are content-equivalent assertions.)

To be sure, the questions "Is *p* true?" and "Is there ade-

[22] This approach thus bears some similarity to that of Keith Lehrer's book on *Knowledge* (Oxford, 1973). He describes his position by saying "We avoid scepticism by constructing a theory of justification without a [*logically* airtight] guarantee of truth. . . . We affirm that there is no [absolute] security against failure or [unqualified] guarantee of success in our search for truth" (p. 241). Subject to the bracketed additions our present approach shares this salient feature of Lehrer's theory. But for a crucial difference in the approaches see pp. 48–49.

quate warrant to assert p (i.e. to claim that p is true)?" are different and distinct. But if asked the former, I clearly have no way of responding except via the latter: we cannot decide about the truth of something independently of considerations regarding issues of its warrant. And when x says "I know that p," we for our own part cannot accept this at face value (people are not infallible!); we must construe the situation as tantamount to "x *claims* to know that p" and – granting to x the usual presumption of competence and veracity – we may well supplement this with the addendum "x is rationally warranted in making this claim (that he knows that p)." But of course warrant does not preempt factuality: the rational entitlement at issue does not *guarantee* with logically demonstrative force that p is so in actual fact.

And we must, of course, expect our own knowledge claims to be construed in just this same light. There is no alternative to recognizing that our only epistemic route to the truth of p runs via the issue of its warranted assertability. The Genesis account of man's fall from grace has its epistemological counterpart in the fact that we have no road to truth about the world save via the epistemic route of empirical inquiry. We have no telephone line to the all-knowing Recording Angel – we have (and can have) no direct, immediate, warrant-independent access to the truth. To state this is not to espouse scepticism, but to recognize a conceptually inevitable fact of life. Here again we have an instance of the sceptic's penchant for denying the prospects of claims to knowledge because some inherently *unmeetable* condition has not been met.

Yet we must be cautious in invoking the implications of this fact. "I cannot tell you what *is* so, I can only tell you what I *think* (hold) to be so" is true but not strictly speaking correct. It puts the situation into too pessimistic and sceptical light. What is crucial is something like "I cannot tell you what *is* so as apart from (and without thereby) telling you what I think to be so." This gets the thing straight: in telling you what I (responsibly) think to be so, I *thereby* tell you what [in my best judgment of the matter] actually is so. Now my best judgment may, alas, be wrong (such is the nature of the human condition) but *ex hypothesi* I have no way of telling that it is so, and once it is (*ex hypothesi*) my "best judgment" there are no further safeguards or assurances that can reasonably be asked of me.

In the context of our knowledge, as elsewhere, the old Roman legal precept applies: "Obligation does not transcend the limits of the possible" (*Ultra posse nemo obligatur*). This *ultra posse* principle comes down to the injunction: You must not ask for what is *in principle* impossible to obtain. The imposition of a requirement that is in principle unmeetable is improper and unjustified: it makes no sense to set up as a necessary condition for something (be it knowledge or anything else) a demand which it is in the nature of things impossible to meet. Put in Kantian terms, the precept "*ought* implies *can*" applies. Only if the conditions posed *can* be met – with "can" construed in a realistic and implementable sense – will it ever be appropriate to recognize these conditions as reflecting proper and legitimate requirements.

5. THE SPECTRE OF PROBABILISM

It remains to deal with the sort of probabilism at issue in the line of thought of an objector who reasons as follows:

> The outright acceptance of objective factual contentions is never warranted – as a consideration of the evidential gap shows. Here only probabilistic contentions have a due rational entitlement. We are never justified in asserting an objective factual claim as true, but only as more or less probable.[23] Our cognitive horizons are limited to the sphere of "mere probability".

Such a probabilism is itself a drastically sceptical position – one must make no mistake about that. It involves giving up any attempt to describe the world. For given a probability-distribution across the range of possibilities, we can make no

---

[23] This position is typified by Rudolf Carnap's stance towards general assertions in *Logical Foundations of Probability* (Chicago, 1950; 2nd ed. 1962).

inference at all about the descriptive nature of the thing at issue. Thus consider the question of the color of a thing in the face of the following probabilistic data:

Violet	Blue	Green	Yellow	Red
.1	.2	.3	.3	.1

Note that one can now say nothing definite at all about the color of the object at issue. (And this would continue to be so even if some of the compartments had a probability value of 0.) A probabilism of the sort in question would constrain us to give up the endeavor to secure descriptive information about the world. We would have to abandon the whole effort to give answers to questions as to how things stand.

It is thus fortunate in the extreme that circumstances do not really compel us to this desperate pass. The assertion-authorizing conventions governing our employment of descriptive language – its use-conditions – afford all the authorizing warrant we need for our descriptive claims. In some cases no doubt the evidential situation is sufficiently murky that probability-claims are the best that can be warranted. But there is no compelling case for holding that this situation is general. After all, probability-assertion is a special case governed by warranting conventions of its own. To realize how they work is also to realize that they don't apply in all circumstances. The same sorts of considerations that make them appropriate in its apposite cases makes outright assertion appropriate in its apposite cases. To allow either to become so aggrandized as to annex the whole range of cases across the board is to do violence to the way our language actually works.

6. ON HUMAN LIMITATIONS

Renaissance sceptics from Erasmus to Montaigne harped unstintingly on the theme of man's inherent incapacity and his human limitations in the cognitive sphere.[24] For example, in his influential treatise *Quod nihil scitur*, the 16th century Spanish physician Francisco Sanchez maintained that our faculties just are not sufficiently reliable to yield knowledge of the real nature of things.[25] This theme of human limitations has recently come to the fore once more. Its latter-day exponents argue roughly as follows:

Man's sensory and cognitive equipment is the idiosyncratic product of setting-correlative evoluationary pressures that adjust *homo sapiens* to its peculiar ecological niche. The resultant faculties encapsulate what is biologically advantageous to creatures of a certain kind. But there is no basis for claiming that *the real truth* of things will emerge from so parochial and peculiar a basis.[26]

We are led back to that deep and old sceptical worry: What entitles us to claim "*our* truth" as "*the* truth"? What reason is there to think that, in the cognitive sphere, the best we can do is good enough?

But of course the pivotal issue is: *good enough for what*? And the answer must be: for us to have justification for holding something to be true, for staking a warranted claim to knowledge of a fact. But of course here, in answering our questions and substantiating our claims, as in anything else, the best that can be done is *eo ipso* the most that can reasonably be demanded. There just is no rationally viable alterna-

---

[24] For the scepticism of this period see Richard H. Popkin, *The History of Scepticism from Erasmus to Descartes*, 2nd ed. (Assen and New York, 1963).

[25] See *Ibid.*, Chap. 2.

[26] The position that the practical demands of survival-promotion and the theoretical demands of knowledge-acquisition may even be antithetical has been vigorously argued by Herman Tennessen in his essay "Knowledge *versus* Survival," *Inquiry*, vol. 16 (1973), pp. 407–414; and also in "On Knowing What One Knows Not," in J. Royce and W. Roseboom (eds.), *The Psychology of Knowing* (New York, 1972), pp. 111–160. See also Gilbert Harman, "Sellars' Semantics," *The Philosophical Review*, vol. 79 (1970), pp. 394–419 (see especially pp. 409–410 and 417–419). The stance underlying Harman's position is neatly depicted by Richard Rorty as follows:

The accident of which glimpses of the world our senses have vouchsafed us, and the further accidents of the predicates we have entrenched or the theories whose proportions please us, may determine what we have a right to believe. But how could they determine the *truth*? ("The World Well Lost," *The Journal of Philosophy*, vol. 69 [1972], p. 660.)

tive to accepting the best as good enough. (Back to this-or-nothing!)

To complain that even the best that we can come up with in the cognitive domain might fall short of some unattainable absolute – some Ideal laid up in a Platonic heaven, some God's-eye view of things – is to make an ultimately senseless complaint. It is not senseless because "the best we can do to realize the truth" is something that is necessarily *identical* with "the real truth" itself, for this is by no means the case. Rather, it is senseless once we have done the best we can do in the circumstances in which we do and must work we come *to be entitled – and rationally and appropriately entitled – to claim this as the truth of the matter*. What, after all, would a complaining sceptic have us do? What lies *ultra posse* cannot be asked of us: it is (to repeat) senseless to establish qualifying criteria for warranted truth-claims that cannot possibly be met. The whole issue of justified claims to truth and knowledge has to be kept within the domain of human power.

For in the final analysis it is no more a "miracle" that the human mind should give us a good working insight into the nature of things than that the human eye should provide useful information. In both cases, the information at issue is underwritten by Darwinian considerations.

The major criticisms of evolutionary theories of epistemic validation have all proceeded by dwelling heavily on the distinction between the cognitive/intellectual side of human affairs and their affective/physical side. They insist that there is no decisive reason of theoretical principle why conceptions and beliefs conducive to the welfare of man must be theoretically valid. The question is pressed: How – in the face of counterexamples of the sort readily constructed – can one validly maintain a necessary linkage between practical advantage and theoretical truth.[27] Survival-conducive beliefs are

---

[27] Bertrand Russell's criticisms of the pragmatists give many quaint examples, among them this: "Dr. Dewey and I were once in the town of Changsha during an eclipse of the moon; following immemorial custom, blind men were beating gongs to frighten the heavenly dog, whose attempt to swallow the moon is the cause of the eclipses. Throughout thousands of years, this practice of beating gongs has never failed to be successful; every eclipse has come to an end after a sufficient prolongation of the din." "Dewey's New Logic," in P. Schilpp (ed.), *The Philosophy of John Dewey* (New York, 1939), pp. 143–156.

surely not *invariably* (and perhaps not even *generally*) correct; nor need correct beliefs necessarily prove survival-conducive. This objection poses a serious difficulty for any program of evolutionary epistemology.

Such considerations have a by now familiar ring. They mount an attack against linking the survival-conduciveness of beliefs and their correctness in a way which parallels exactly the usual attacks against linking the practical utility of beliefs and their theoretical truth (as with the pragmatism of William James). And essentially the same weakness indeed affects both these doctrines: their orientation towards *theses*. But the telling force of such criticisms of evolutionary epistemology is blunted once we take the methodological turn. For considerations of survival-conduciveness are then no longer asked to militate for the adequacy (i.e., truthfulness) of specific beliefs or belief-systems, but rather for the adequacy of *methods* of inquiry.

Consider again J. S. Mill's contention (advanced in his famous essay *On Liberty*) that the competition among schools of thought is akin to that between biological varieties: the rivalry among ideas for acceptance amounts to a struggle for existence (i.e., perpetuation or *continued existence*), a struggle in which those beliefs which are the fittest – viz., those that represent "the truth" – must finally prevail. The survival of beliefs within an intellectual community is viewed as parallel with biological survival.

It is perhaps unnecessary to dwell, at this stage, on the shortcomings of this unduly optimistic view. Acceptance of theses is all too often governed by extra-rational factors: mere entrenchment, faddism, social pressures, band-wagons, propaganda ("thought control"), etc. And there can be no secure assurance that such perturbations will inevitably or even usually be eliminated in the course of time. The view that the inherent attractions of the truth assure its ultimate victory in a struggle for acceptance among the beliefs of imperfect humans is thus overly hopeful. However, its most serious shortcomings stem from its operation *at the thesis level*. An evolutionary approach seems to have substantially greater promise at the more general level of *methods* where the force of the above-mentioned disabilities is removed or attenuated.

The generality and open-endedness of an inquiry-method furnish it with a capacity to wash out the influence of these fortuitous and extraneous factors.

To be sure, action which proceeds on *beliefs* that are false and fail to capture "what is actually the case" can on occasion – or even frequently – eventuate as pragmatically successful, due to chance or good luck or kindly fate or whatever. However, the situation must be different when what is at issue is not an isolated action or a particular believed thesis (or even a cluster of them), but rather a general policy of acting based on alignment with a *methodologically universalized standard* of belief-validation. Individual these may well manage to slip through the net of disconfirmation singly or in groups. But *methods* for factual inquiry operate across a very broad and extensive front, and this feature of across-the-board systematicity renders them much more vulnerable. Their flaws and deficiencies are bound to manifest themselves in the vast multiplicity of their applications.

Methods function at a wholesale rather than retail level. As was stressed above, the success of a cognitive method must be construed in *systematic* terms: working on one occasion – or on some limited number of occasions – does not entail working in general, and failing on one or more occasions is not necessarily completely invalidating. Success hinges on how the method fares *in general* over the entire – infinitely varied – gamut of its applications. It is on such a generic and systematic plane that instrumental justification must be sought. These considerations, operative at the level of methodology-in-general, apply with special force to cognitive methodology in particular. The range and versatility of an inquiry procedure is too obvious to need much elaboration. Generality is here tantamount to open-endedness; a methodology of *inquiry* has to operate across the board of an enormous variety of areas of application and a literally innumerable proliferation of particular instances. In its case, above all, success is strongly indicative of adequacy or appropriateness. Here all of the safeguards built into the statistical theory of the "design of experiments" come into play with respect to the probative significance of the number and variety of instances. It is inconceivable that a *systematic* success across so broad a range should be gratuitous. We cannot reasonably look on nature as a friendly collaborator in our human efforts, systematically crowning our cognitive endeavors with wholly undeserved successes.

As these deliberations show, the evolutionary pressures that underly and condition our cognitive operations so function that we are warranted in treating the products attained through our mechanisms of inquiry as representing what is, for us, the very best that can be done to realize "the real truth" with respect to factual matters regarding the world we live in. In thinking about science – as in reasoning within science itself – we must have recourse to the principle of inference to the best explanation, and the best explanation of the substantial successes the scientific method has engendered is that it leads to results which afford some at least rough indication of "the way it is."[28]

[28] The arguments of this section are set out in fuller and more developed detail in the author's *Methodological Pragmatism* (Oxford, 1976).

VI

The "No Correction" Argument

SYNOPSIS

(1) Although a (correct) claim to knowledge must indeed be "incorrigible," all that is necessary to warrant a claim to knowledge is to exclude every *realistic* – rather than every *conceivable* – possibility of error. (2) The incorrigibility at issue in our knowledge claim is thus a matter of the realistic "practical politics" of the cognitive situation. (3) A *real* prospect of error turns on the presence of case-specific considerations: To claim knowledge is not to gainsay a "purely hypothetical" or "merely logical" possibility of error. Genuine doubt must be supported by realistic, concrete, detailed, case-specific considerations rather than fanciful conceivabilities and "general principly" considerations. (4) The absolutism of knowledge claims is accordingly the qualified absoluteness of "having as much security against the prospects of correction as it is reasonable to ask for in circumstances of the sort at issue." (5) A view that admits the potential fallibility of our altogether warranted claims to knowledge – and other comparable qualifications of their absoluteness – is accordingly feasible. The idea of "potentially fallibilistic knowledge" is *not* a contradiction in terms. (6) Accordingly, cognitivism does not entail dogmatism. And this nowise contravenes the KK-thesis which has it that in claiming knowledge one claims also to know that one knows.

1. INCORRIGIBILITY AND DEFEASIBILITY

The history of science – and of human inquiry in general – teaches the extreme fallibility of our claims to factual knowledge. The vaunted knowledge of one generation all too often becomes the rejected error of the next. There is a splendid opening for scepticism here. Our putative knowledge turn out to be something far removed from the genuine article with discouraging frequency.

Accordingly, the sceptics' "No Correction" Argument turns pivotally on the idea that knowledge must be incorrigible. It runs essentially as follows:

1. Genuine knowledge can only be claimed in circumstances where every possibility of error has been eliminated.
2. But the possibilities of error can never be eliminated totally and completely in the domain of factual claims.

∴ Genuine knowledge cannot be attained in the factual domain.[1]

The argumentation seems unexceptionable. If what we maintain to be "our knowledge" is indeed to be genuine knowledge, it must of course be free from error – all possibility of mistake must be precluded. And so the sceptics urge upon us time and again that "x knows that p" is never true because in the relevant contexts x is never in a position to rule out decisively every possibility that p is false.[2] But this argumentation will not do. Its talk of chances or possibilities is too facile. It ignores the fact that there are possibilities and possibilities, and that only some of these play a determinative role in relation to the propriety of claims to knowledge.

We may call p an *incorrigible belief* of x's if p is such that x's really believing it excludes any possibility that p

---

[1] Among the more recent instances of this line of argument is Keith Lehrer, "Why Not Scepticism?," *Philosophical Forum*, vol. 2 (1972), pp. 283–296; and Peter Unger, *Ignorance* (Oxford, 1975). See also William Roseboom, "Why I Know So Much More Than You Do," *American Philosophical Quarterly*, vol. 4 (1967), pp. 281–290 (see especially pp. 286–287).

[2] Note again, however, that "decisiveness" must here be taken in its *logical* sense.

may prove false. But given this formula, the question remains: What *sorts* of possibility are to be at issue here. Clearly, if the only admissible possibilities are of the logicoconceptual kind, then the only plausible candidates for incorrigible beliefs will be purely subjective (along the lines of "I have a headache"). When objective claims are at issue, the appropriate mode of incorrigibility will clearly have to be correlative with the *real* possibilities of error. It is emphatically not the case that our knowledge claims are inherently untenable because their validation would require the elimination of possibilities apart from those we can ever actually deal with.[3]

In his interesting book on *Scepticism* (London, 1968), Arne Naess distinguishes between "remote possibilities" for cognitive error like the machinations of evil demons, malicious Cartesian deceivers, wicked and powerful scientists operating from distant galaxies, etc., and "proximate possibilities" like the sources of error of everyday life. The characterizing key difference is that in the latter case we can secure evidence of a more or less straightforward sort to eliminate the potential pitfalls at issue, but no manner of obtainable evidence can suffice to remove the remote possibilities. In Naess' view, our knowledge claims are inherently flawed, because – as he sees it – the achievement of knowledge requires the prior removal of *both sorts* of possibilities, as well as the merely proximate ones. This, of course, leads straightaway to the sceptical conclusion that the attainment of knowledge becomes in principle infeasible. Thus Naess writes:

[The] incorrigibility claims [inherent in our pretentions to knowledge] are essentially based on convictions that in the particular case there could not be any source of error, both in the usual sense of "source of error worth mentioning" *and in the sense of no source of error even of the more remote kinds that we neglect in daily life.*[4]

[3] On this issue see the important essay by Norman Malcolm on "The Verification Argument" in Max Black (ed.), *Philosophical Analysis* (Englewood Cliffs, 1950), reprinted in R. M. Chisholm and R. J. Swartz (eds.), *Empirical Knowledge* (Englewood Cliffs, 1973), pp. 155–202.

[4] *Op. cit.*, p. 133; italics supplied.

But the italicized passage clearly makes an inappropriate addition. Given the fact that our knowledge-discourse is an instrumentality within the communicative program of our workaday daily life, the idea of "no possibility of error" must clearly be construed as "no *real* possibility of error." Those possibilities that are so remote and far-fetched that they can be ruled out as "just not worth mentioning in the setting of our workaday purposes" are irrelevant to knowledge claims as the conception of knowledge figures in actual discourse. The italicized addendum exhibits the penchant of sceptics to inject hyperbolic unrealism into our conception of knowledge – a conception to which such unrealism is quite foreign. The linguistic machinery we use has been designed through the evolutionary processes that have guided its development to serve our communicative purposes. And this elemental fact indicates that it is altogether improper to saddle our communicative mechanisms with implicit requirements that are inherently unsatisfiable.

Knowledge claims impose no inherently infeasible demands. The "incorrigibility" of our knowledge claims requires no more than that every *realistic* prospect of error has been eliminated. To be sure, it is not merely *logically* possible that any belief of ours regarding some matter of objective fact could prove wrong – there is always "a genuine chance" that it might be so. Its being false is "conceivable." But the pivotal question is: What *sort* of possibility would have to be realized in this case: is it a *merely hypothetical* possibility or a *real* one? In this connection, no more is asked than we do what can *realistically* be asked of us to preclude any *genuine* prospect of error. It is a matter of eliminating every possibility of slippage that is worth mentioning, recognizing that some possibilities – viz. the remote and purely hypothetical ones (human fallibility, Cartesian deceivers, and the like) – can *and should* be passed by in silence.

C. I. Lewis has written that:

No matter how fully I may have investigated this objective fact. ["A piece of white paper is now before me"], there will remain some theoretical possibility of mistake; there will be further consequences that must be thus and so if the judgment is true, and not all of these will have been determined. The possibility that such further tests, if made, might have a negative result, cannot be altogether precluded; and this possibility marks the judgment as, at the time in question, not fully verified and less than absolutely certain. . . . This character of being further testable and less than theoretically certain characterizes every judgment of objective fact at all times.[5]

But it is clear that whatever sort of *"theoretical* possibility" of mistake and whatever sort of *"absolute* certainty" may be at issue here must prove irrelevant to the conception of knowledge that actually figures in our real-life discourse. The scholastic formula got the matter just right: An appropriate claim to knowledge can properly be staked on a basis that is "sufficient to exclude all *prudent* fear of error" – *neurotic* fears are beside the point.[6]

And there is certainly no shortage of things that we know beyond any *realistic* possibility of error. G. E. Moore in "A Defense of Common Sense" manages to inventory many of them: statements about one's body, like "This is a body (hand, leg)"; about one's experiences, like "I am looking at a body (hand, leg)"; about the bodies and experiences of others, etc. These, as Moore rightly insists are "truisms, every one of which . . . I *know* with certainty to be true."[7] Nor need one be that homocentric about it. "Lead is heavier than water" or "Dogs have teeth" will do just as well. There is no real possibility of our being mistaken in matters of this sort. Wittgenstein puts the point well:

> In certain circumstances a man cannot make a *mistake*. ("Can" is here used logically, and the proposition does not mean that a man cannot say anything false in those

---

[5] *An Analysis of Knowledge and Valuation* (La Salle, 1946), p. 180. Compare Rudolf Carnap, "Testability and Meaning," *Philosophy of Science*, vol. 3 (1963), pp. 419–471, vol. 4 (1937), pp. 2–40 (see especially p. 425 of vol. 3).

[6] Compare D. J. Mercier, *Critériologie Générale* (8th ed., Louvain, 1923), pp. 6–15; and P. Coffey, *Epistemology*, Vol. I (London, 1917), chap. I.

[7] George Edward Moore, "A Defense of Common Sense" in *Contemporary British Philosophy*, 2nd series, ed. by J. H. Muirhead (London, 1925), pp. 193–223; reprinted in Moore's *Philosophical Papers* (London, 1959), pp. 32–59 (see pp. 32–33).

circumstances.) If Moore were to pronounce the opposite of those propositions which he declares certain,
we should not just not share his opinion: we should
regard him as demented.[8]

The only emendation that needs to be made here is that the
"can/cannot" at issue is not that of *logical* conceivability but
that of *real* possibility, of possibility in the proximate
domain rather than that of the sphere of unfettered conceivability.

The dichotomy of near/remote in relation to possibilities
of error is in fact imprecise: we can ask for more and more
assurances, imposing an ever greater weight of demands: the
standards can be raised higher and higher. But they cannot
be raised to infinity. Ultimately a point is reached where it is
absurd to ask for more. To be sure, this point cannot be
specified precisely – but it is there all the same. (Precision in
such cases is often unavailable: one cannot specify down to
the last hair the point at which a man becomes bald.) The
point is that the existence of remote possibilities of error
simply *does not count* as an appropriate objection to applications of "know" in the ordinary, standard use of the term.

We thus arrive at a fallibilistic theory of knowledge, one
which sees a fully legitimate, appropriate, and justified claim
to knowledge as compatible with a recognition – when based
solely on abstract general principles – that some possibility
of error (albeit only of the "remote" variety) does indeed
remain open.

On such a fallibilistic epistemology, all claims to knowledge in the factual area are inherently defeasible *in theory*.
But by their very nature knowledge-claims purport to be in-
fallibly correct and *incorrigible*. The very idea of "defeasible
knowledge" seemingly embodies an inner inconsistency. The
fallibilist who, following Peirce, is prepared to tolerate (or
even insist upon) the view that our knowledge is in some
manner provisional – and so accepts the idea of potentially
corrigible knowledge – is apparently forced into a problematic, nay untenable position. For he seemingly construes
"knowledge" in such a way that the truth, and indeed the

[8] *On Certainty* (Oxford, 1961), sect. 155.

certainty of *p* is not seen as a necessary condition for knowing that *p*. To speak of *defeasible* knowledge is thus to all appearances to be in conflict with the basic conditions and conventions governing our knowledge-oriented discourse.

The present position is perfectly orthodox on this issue, however. It insists that to be warranted in making a knowledge claim one must be warranted in maintaining the truth and indeed the certainty of the matter at issue by placing one's claim beyond the possibility of error. But the possibilities of error are the realistic not the transcendental ones. The point is that a rationally *warranted claim* to truth is not the same as a *failproof guarantee* of truth. (The fact that *x* has adequate rational warrant to claim *Kxp* neither entails nor presupposes *p*.) It is quite possible to reconcile a fallibilism on the basis of the "theoretical principles" with an infallibilism on the basis of the "practical politics" of the epistemic realm.

2. MORE ON CORRIGIBILITY

What one knows is, in an important sense, *incorrigible*. For "*X* knows that *P* but he might possibly prove to be wrong" is clearly not a tenable locution. What is indeed *known* cannot be abrogated – it cannot become unstuck as knowledge by some added knowledge that comes along. That is, it must prevail "come what may." If anything really *is* an item of knowledge, then it is incorrigible – no *further* knowledge can possibly upset it. No additional evidence or information can possibly undo what is indeed known: it represents an issue on which the books can be closed.[9] But how can we ever be sure that this is so? (As was observed at the outset, if the history of science has taught us any one thing, it has shown that the claimed knowledge of one era becomes the rejected error of the next.)

To accommodate this train of thought it becomes necessary to differentiate also between *effective* and *theoretical* incorrigibility. The critical point is that *effective* certainty precludes any *real* possibility of error, and that this sort of real possibility must be determined through case-specific

---

[9] Note, however, that the "indeed known" hypothesis makes this contention less significant than it at first sight appears. Compare p. 113 below.

considerations. The key idea of *realism* with respect to possibilities crops up once again.

The incorrigibility at issue with our rationally warranted claims to knowledge is, like their certainty, a practical ("effective") rather than purely theoretical matter. J. L. Austin has argued this point perhaps more emphatically than any other modern epistemologist, pressing such cases as: "if I watch for some time an animal a few feet in front of me, in a good light, if I prod it perhaps, sniff, and take note of the noises it makes, I may say 'That's a pig;' . . . [then this claim] will be 'incorrigible,' nothing could be produced that would show that I had made a mistake."[10] To be sure, the "nothing could [possibly] be produced" in establishing a mistake here has a view to the *real* possibilities of the situation, and not to merely *hypothetical* (or purely logical) possibilities. That is, it is "unthinkable" – though not, to be sure, in theory impossible – that in normal circumstances (e.g. when we are in the farmyard rather than, say, on the magician's stage) an error could be turned up to force us to revise our claims.

In view of these considerations I would (in anything like normal circumstances) be completely warranted in being certain that (as I write these words) I am awake, am sitting in my study in Pittsburgh, am holding a pen in my hand, etc. To be sure, the question of our entitlement to regard the case as a normal one arises and must be faced. But the answer here is straightforward. The circumstances are normal when "there is every reason to think them to be so" and moreover "there is no reason to think them otherwise." Normality is a matter of presumption – a presumption that can be defeated, but whose defeat requires definite information.

Arthur Danto has remarked that while "If *x* knows that *p*, then *x* cannot be in error regarding *p*" seems acceptable, its contrapositive "If *x* can be in error regarding *p*, then *x* does not know *p*" seems problematic.[11] But the difficulty lies in the slide regarding "can/cannot" as between these two implications. In the first case "cannot" bears the hypothetical sense of *ex hypothesi* supposition, in the second "can" de-

---

[10] John L. Austin, *Sense and Sensibilia* (Oxford, 1962), p. 114, but see the whole context on pp. 114–118.

[11] *Analytical Philosophy of Knowledge* (Cambridge, 1968), p. 51.

mands a categorical interpretation. If we insist on a *uniform* construction of the term, the two theses are indeed equivalent. And specifically, if both involve the "can" of the real possibility (in the proximate or realistic sense of the term) then both implication-theses are flatly false.

The "incorrigibility" of knowledge must be so construed that appropriate knowledge claims do indeed preclude any possibility of mistake. But it is not any "merely hypothetical" prospect of mistake that is excluded, but any *real* possibility of being mistaken. This distinction between *hypothetical* and *real* possibilities of error is reflected in a parallel distinction between what might be termed *categorical* certainty on the one hand and *practical* or *effective* certainty on the other. The operative idea here is that of taking "every *proper* safeguard," or of doing "everything that can *reasonably* be asked" to assure the claim at issue.

The evidential basis for such effective certainty need not be "all the evidence there conceivably might be," but simply "all the evidence that could reasonably be asked for under the circumstances."[12] It envisages that a stage could be reached when, even though further evidence could possibly be accumulated, there is no point to this because there are no counterindications to suggest that this theoretically feasible prospect is practically desirable: there is *no reason* to think that further accumulation might be fruitful and *no reason* to believe that additional evidence might alter the situation.[13] And by "reason" here we must understand not some synoptic, wholesale, across-the-board consideration of the sort favored by sceptics since antiquity, but case-specific considerations that bear in a definite and *ad hoc* way upon the particular case in hand.[14]

[12] This indicates that the operative standard will be to some extent case-variable. We cannot obtain evidence regarding Alexander the Great that bears comparison with that which we can gather for Napoleon. And this means that knowledge-claims in the latter context must fall subject to rather more stringent standards.

[13] This "absence of counterindications" within the available evidence was indicated by the ancient Academics in speaking of the "concurrence" (*syndromē*) of this evidence.

[14] To some extent, a fundamentally economic line of consideration is at issue here – viz., that a juncture will be reached when it would be *pointless*, under the circumstances, to dedicate further efforts (i.e., devote further resources) to the securing of a claim.

To be sure, we cannot appropriately claim something as an item of knowledge and in the same breath acknowledge its liability to error, its defeasibility. This would involve an inconsistency – albeit of a pragmatic rather than logical nature.

There is no gainsaying the thesis:

(I) If p is actually true (or certain or known) then no other truth can undo the truth (or the certainty or the being known) of p.

But the acceptability of its epistemically qualified counterpart

(II) If p is warrantedly thought to be true (or certain or known) then no other truth can undo the being warrantedly thought true (or certain or known) of p

stands on an altogether different footing. What is true (or certain or known) must *ex hypothesi* be so, but what is warrantedly thought to be so might turn out to be false – the realities of cognitive life being as they are. Actual knowledge is incorrigible and indefeasible, but what is reasonably and – in the circumstances – *justifiedly* thought to be known is not so.

These considerations falsify the contention that

(III) When someone's duly warranted knowledge claim is based on evidence, then his evidence must justify this knowledge claim regardless of what further (true) evidence is introduced.[15]

Actual, honest-to-goodness knowledge cannot be undone by further evidence – even as truth cannot be undone by further

---

[15] For a discussion of this principle and its cognates see Douglas Odegard, "A Knower's Evidence," *American Philosophical Quarterly*, vol. 15 (1978), pp. 123–128.

truth.[16] But this fact by no means shows that our *justified* (contrast *correct!*) claims to knowledge cannot become unstuck in the light of ampler information.

Sceptics sometimes talk as though one could only know p if one also knew the falsity of any and every *logically* possible hypothesis which could render p false:[17]

$$Kxp \rightarrow (\forall q)([L\text{-poss}(q) \ \& \ (q \rightarrow \sim p)] \rightarrow Kx \sim q)$$

On the basis of such a principle one could not claim knowledge unless one were in a position to rule out the whole gamut of knowledge-defeating possibilities – evil demons, powerful wicked scientists, and the rest.[18] But the principle at issue imposes an absurd and hyperbolic demand, having among its consequences (*inter alia*) that to know anything we must know an infinite number of things. The key point, however, is that we need *not* be able to rule out every LOGICALLY *possible falsifier*, but only every REALISTICALLY *possible falsifier*, which always range over a limited and manageable family of possibilities indicated by the characteristics and circumstances of the specific case at issue.

To be justified in a claim to know p, x must be *justified* in holding that there is no further truth q that might conflict with p. But his being justified in holding a thing to be so does not make it so. A claim to *knowledge* extends an assurance that all due care and caution has been exercised to ensure that any *real* possibility of error can be written off: it issues a guarantee that every proper safeguard has been exercised. It is exactly for this reason that the statement "I know p, but might be mistaken" is self-inconsistent. For the man who

---

[16] Risto Hilpinen has offered an interesting discussion of this principle that "Knowledge cannot be 'lost' simply as a result of learning something new" and refers to this as the *extendability thesis*. See his essay, "Knowledge and Justification," *Ajatus: Yearbook of the Philosophical Society of Finland*, vol. 33 (1971), pp. 7–39 (see especially p. 25). Compare Roderick Chisholm, *Theory of Knowledge* (2nd ed., Englewood Cliffs, 1976), pp. 114–116.

[17] Note that this thesis is a slight weakening of

$$Kxp \rightarrow (\forall q)([p \rightarrow q] \rightarrow Kxq)$$

whose untenability was considered in the preceding chapter.

[18] Compare Keith Lehrer, "Why Not Scepticism?," *Philosophical Forum*, vol. 2 (1971), pp. 283–298 and Peter Unger, *Ignorance* (Oxford, 1975).

claims to know that *p* thereby issues a guarantee which the qualification "but I might be mistaken" effectively revokes. What is established by the self-defeating nature of locutions of the type "I know that *p* but might well be mistaken" is thus *not* that knowledge is inherently indefeasible, but simply that knowledge claims offer guarantees and assurances so strong as to preempt any safeguarding qualifications. On strictly "pragmatic" grounds, claims to knowledge preclude abridgment of the sort at issue in a protective rider like "I might well be wrong." A knowledge claim puts its author's authority on the line beyond the point of no return as concerns any hedging on his part.[19]

The fact is that the sceptic here draws the wrong conclusion from a correct premiss. He correctly recognizes that our objective knowledge-claims are in theory fallibilistic, but he misjudges that this fallibilism is at odds with justified claims to knowledge. Here the sceptic misreads the situation. Granted, we can never have *theoretical* certainty that our *purported* knowledge is *actual* and so will ultimately and forever prove itself correct. We can never do better than the best we can: The only knowledge *we* can ever deal with – and thus the only knowledge at issue in our discussions – is (*ex hypothesi*) "*our* knowledge" which we recognize to be in principle fallible. We have no direct line to the Recording Angel. But this does not mean that our claims to knowledge are by their very nature necessarily unwarranted and inappropriate. The lesson to be drawn from the fallibilistic argumentation dear to the sceptic is not the *unattainability* of knowledge, but the potential imperfection, the theoretical *defeasibility* of the knowledge we can obtain.

3. A CLOSER LOOK AT THE IDEA OF A "REAL POSSIBILITY" OF
ERROR: G-DOUBT *vs.* S-DOUBT

In the face of these deliberations, a sceptic may well object as follows: How can you reasonably hold something to be incorrigible in the face of a recognition of *any* sort of possible

[19] Compare John L. Austin, "Other Minds," in *Philosophical Papers* (Oxford, 1961), pp. 44–84.

error – however remote this prospect of a "slip between the cup and the lip" may be?

The sceptic here misreads the "logic" of the situation in his usual way. Infallibility is unquestionably inherent in our claims to knowledge. But this infallibility is not of such an absolute, hyperbolic sort as to lie – as a matter of general principle – beyond the pale of feasible realization. Knowledge is indeed "incorrigible" – that is, duly secured against any *realistic* prospect of error. If a knowledge-claim is to be made appropriately there must be no specific indication that there is anything in view – or even dimly visible on the horizon – which would require this to be abridged or corrected or withdrawn.

This line of consideration opens the way to a further objection:

> How can you (defensibly, reasonably) claim certainty for something if you hold only that your evidence for this is "virtually" or "effectively" conclusive? If the evidence isn't actually *conclusive*, then you surely can't claim certainty. It's as simple as that.

This objection calls for a closer look at the idea of "conclusiveness." How is "conclusive" warranting evidence to be construed? It must, of course, be taken in its straightforward sense: conclusive reasons can only exist when there is "no possibility of slippage." Someone only has conclusive reasons when he could not be wrong; when, given these reasons, it is false that he might be mistaken in the matter at issue. There can be rational warrant for maintaining that I know that *p* only if there is "no possibility" that not-*p*. But the crucial question remains: *what sort of possibility* is to be at issue here?

Is it logical possibility? Philosophers sometimes talk as though the sort of certainty correlative with knowledge is such that an assertion is certain only if the logical possibility of its turning out false can be excluded.[20] But this is just

---

[20] "If knowledge is justified true belief, we can legitimately claim to know only those beliefs whose truth we can logically demonstrate." O. A. Johnson, *The Problem of Knowledge* (The Hague, 1974), p. 105; or again "To qualify a belief as know-

wrong. The necessitarianism of *logical* possibility is simply beside the point in a discussion of the epistemology of *factual* knowledge.[21] In contemplating the "possibilities" of mistake, we must look to the idea of *real* possibilities – to what can be expected with some semblance of plausibility, and not to what can be thought of when we let our imaginations run riot. If we grant even a chance of someone's being incorrect in his acceptance of a thesis, then we must indeed concede that he does not *know* this thesis.[22] But the point is that one must distinguish between *genuine* chances and possibilities and *merely conjectural* ones.

In this context, the position of Descartes at the outset of his *Meditations on First Philosophy* affords a good basis for deliberation. He writes:

> [I] had accepted, even from my youth, many false opinions for true . . . and from that time I was convinced of the necessity of undertaking once in my life to rid myself of all the opinions I had adopted. . . . But to this end, it will not be necessary for me to show that the whole of these are false – a point, perhaps, which I shall never reach; . . . *it will be sufficient to justify the rejection of the whole if I can find in each some ground for doubt. Nor for this purpose will it be necessary even to deal with each belief individually*, which would be truly an endless

---

ledge we must offer reasons in its support which demonstrate it to be true (*ibid.*, p. 116). We are thus offered a knock-down, drag-out proof of scepticism in the factual domain:

> So long as the belief . . . is formulated in a contingent statement, there is some chance that the belief is wrong, and consequently, one does not know for certain that it is true. (Keith Lehrer, "Skepticism and Conceptual Change" in R. M. Chisholm and R. J. Swartz (eds.), *Empirical Knowledge* [Englewood Cliffs, 1973], pp. 47–58 [see p. 55].)

[21] This point is well argued in Fred Dretske, "Conclusive Reasons," *The Australasian Journal of Philosophy*, vol. 49 (1971), pp. 1–22; reprinted (with some deletions) in G. S. Pappas and M. Swain (eds.), *Essays on Knowledge and Justification* (Ithaca and London, 1978), pp. 41–60.

[22] "Consider a statement like 'I know I have a brain.' Can I doubt it? Any grounds for doubt are lacking: everything speaks in its favor and nothing against. To be sure, it is *imaginable* that my skull should turn out empty in an operation. [But what is merely imaginable is irrelevant to those 'possibilities of error' that can invalidate claims to knowledge.]" (Ludwig Wittgenstein, *On Certainty* [Oxford, 1961], Sect. 4.)

labor; but, as the removal from below of the foundation necessarily involves the downfall of the whole edifice, I will at once approach the criticism of the principles on which all my former beliefs rested. *All that I have, up to this moment, accepted as possessed of the highest truth and certainty, I received either from or through the senses. I observed, however, that these sometimes mislead us; and it is the part of prudence not to place absolute confidence in that by which we have even once been deceived.*[23]

Let us consider more closely the rational warrant of such "Cartesian doubt" founded, not upon specific investigation of the individual merits or demerits of particular propositions, but upon the wholesale calling into question of entire groups of propositions on the basis of generic considerations, such as those regarding their subject-matter or their source.

To begin with, it is necessary to recognize such doubt for what it is, namely as an instance of a *generic warrant for doubting*. For it involves a procedure by which the claim of the doubtfulness of some particular proposition 'p' is supported by a highly generalized argument of the paradigm:

Statements evidenced by considerations of the type T are sometimes false.
'p' is evidenced by the considerations C, which are of the type T.

∴ 'p' is dubious (i.e., might well be false).[24]

It is clear that Descartes' line of reasoning in the above-cited passage is of precisely this kind, the "type T" at issue in his discussion being those statements which are based upon the evidence of the senses. Other forms of doubt-justification also fall under this paradigm. For example, the "type T"

---

[23] Everyman's Library edition, tr. by John Veitch (London, 1912); my italics.

[24] This generic argumentation for doubtfulness goes back to the ancient Sceptics' assault on the Stoic conception of decisive impressions (*katalēptikē phantasia*), arguing that it would suffice to show that a single decisive-seeming impression proves erroneous to establish that this whole group is not absolutely reliable.

might be determined with reference to a particular *source*. Again, the "type *T*" might also be defined in terms of the subject-matter content of the statements in question, or in some other way. The important point, however, is that any one of these ways of warranting doubt involves the *wholesale* justification of doubt and thus constitutes an instance of what may be termed *generically warranted doubt*, "G-doubt" for short, based on "general principles" alone. What is at issue with such G-doubt is the adducing of universal or at any rate highly generalized indicators of the possibility of error: human fallibility, the generic liability to error of our sources of knowledge (sense, observation, reasoning, calculation, memory, etc.), the deceiver hypothesis, or the like.

It is helpful and clarifying to contrast this sort of doubt-justification with doubt based upon some sort of direct evidence regarding the possible or probable falsity of the particular statement in question. In these cases we have a specific warrant for doubting a statement '*p*', in that we have good reason to accept some statement '*q*' which constitutes evidence specifically against '*p*'. This I shall term *specifically warranted doubt*, "S-doubt," which is based on case-specific considerations relating to particular considerations in the particular case in hand. Such doubt is not founded on the oblique procedure of placing a statement within a group of statements some of which are false, but upon direct evidence for its falsity. In S-doubt, our warrant for doubting a statement '*p*' is such as to address itself specifically and particularly to the statement in question, in that we have evidence which bears directly (and negatively) upon the truth-status of '*p*' itself. By contrast, G-doubt is only oblique, and does not furnish evidence of doubtfulness directly, but only "by association," as it were.[25]

---

[25] It will generally be the case that when we indicate a specific doubt-warranting consideration about a proposition '*p*', this indication may take the form of remarking that '*p*' has some feature Φ, so that this procedure is assimilated to the generic type, with "possessing the feature Φ" in the role of "being of the type *T*." But this assimilation is a purely formal maneuver. What is crucially at issue is the *character* of the type *T*, viz., whether it has to do with something abstract and general such as the generic source or generic content of the proposition or whether it *descends to detail* with reference to the specific epistemological properties of this proposition. In short, while S-doubt may, like G-doubt, rest upon typological

With G-doubt, the recognition of potential error is collective in character, but not distributive – error is seen to be present at the global (wholesale) level, not at the local (retail) level. This sort of thing is too weak a reed on which to rest the weight of the real doubtfulness capable of destroying knowledge. The recognition that some of our knowledge claims may be unwarranted just is not a sufficient reason for withdrawing them *en masse* and *in toto*. The theoretical or generic defeasibility of knowledge claims need *emphatically not* be taken to countervail against the propriety and justifiability of our advancing them.

Just as we cannot on the sole basis of general principles or generic considerations advance claims for the truth or falsity of a statement when direct, *ad hoc* evidence is at hand, neither can we so establish its doubtfulness. It follows that G-doubt is an acceptable and valid approach only in those cases in which no direct evidence is to be had regarding the truth or falsity of the assertion being considered.[26] Cardinal

---

considerations relating to the propositions at issue, this *formal* fact does not abolish the distinction based on the *material* nature of the specific features of the typological considerations at issue. In the case of G-doubt these pertain to some highly general source or type, and largely or wholly ignore the specific claim at issue, whereas with S-doubt they descend to the level of concrete detail.

[26] A largely analogous situation obtains with regard to the statistical assessment of probabilites. Probability in its statistical form is invariably determined with respect to a reference-class (type T). Thus in general we reason:

$$X\% \text{ of objects of type } T \text{ have the property } P.$$
$$A \text{ is an object of type } T.$$

$$\therefore \text{ the probability that } A \text{ has } P \text{ is } X/100.$$

Or, in a specific case:

$$90\% \text{ of dentists are male.}$$
$$A \text{ is a dentist.}$$

$$\therefore A \text{ is very probably male.}$$

But we cannot defensibly reason in this way if in so doing we ride roughshod over some available item of direct evidence. For example, we cannot justifiably employ the last-named inference if we happen *also* to know that A is a member of the American Association of University Women. Exactly this is the point of Carnap's "Requirement of Total Evidence" for probabilistic inference (Rudolf Carnap, *Logical Foundations of Probability* (Chicago, 1950; 2nd ed., 1969), some version or varia-

Newman got to the heart of the matter: "[W]hat is abstract reasoning to a question of concrete fact? To arrive at the fact of any matter, we must eschew generalities, and take things as they stand, with all their circumstances."[27]

The only possibilities of error that need be eliminated when factual claims are at issue are those which are realistic. One need not rule out all *conceivable* counterpossibilities, but only those which are plausible, those which some sort of case-specific consideration indicates as "being worth taking account of" in the circumstances. We need only worry about securing our claims against plausible, case-specific considerations, and not necessarily against those which – like Cartesian demons – are purely fanciful and altogether unrealistic.

The inadequacy of such generic considerations for establishing a real doubt of any sort can also be brought out by more formalized deliberations. For the reasoning at issue has the following structure:

Some claims evidenced by type-T considerations are false
The claim at issue (*q*) is evidenced by type-T considerations

---

∴ The claim at issue (*q*) might be false

A more precise construction of the reasoning which must be taken to be at issue here may be set out symbolically as follows:

$$\frac{(\exists p)[p \in T \ \& \ f(p)] \ \& \ q \in T}{\therefore \ \Diamond f(q)}$$

where '$\Diamond$' represents real (rather than "merely logical") possibility. (The "might be false" here is, of course, to be con-

---

tion of which is unavoidable in this context. In basing my probability-judgment regarding *A*'s sex on *A*'s profession, I (tacitly) presuppose that this argument "by association" is the best that I can do (in the light of the information available to me). But if some further and more direct information is available to me, this presupposition is violated, and the inference becomes inappropriate. Here again, a type-founded inference is only justified when it represents the best use that can be made of the information at our disposal. If our information empowers us to improve upon such a generic, type-founded inference, we cannot defensibly abstain from doing so.

[27] J. H. Newman, *A Grammar of Assent* (Chap. 8, Pt. 2, sect. 2).

strued in a sense that could plausibly be taken to block the prospect of knowledge.) Now this argument would only be valid if the following argument were valid:

$$\frac{(\exists p)[p \in T \ \& \ f(p)]}{\therefore \ (\forall p)[p \in T \supset \Diamond \ f(p)]}$$

But it is clearly inappropriate to argue that a feature that *does* belong to SOME individual of a certain set *might* belong to ALL individuals of that set. This argumentation from *some* to *possibly-each-and-every* is not very plausible. The fact that some integers are less than ten does not yield that every one might be, nor does the fact that some citizens of a country are female yield that every one might be. The reasoning at issue in a generic warranting of doubt is accordingly not convincing.

The key point is that a generic warranting of doubt is too feeble to reverse the presumption in favor of our standard cognitive resources. To be effective against specific knowledge claims that are duly attested, an objection cannot rest on such general principles but must be able to reverse the burden in favor of appropriately warranted claims. And here we need a detailed evidential linkage between the general prospect and the specific case – a particularized indication why the generic prospect should be of specific concern to us in the concrete case we have in hand. We require a case-specific indication of why the general prospect of error at issue in the G-warrant constitutes a specific threat on the particular case at hand. To call the testimony of a Cretan into doubt it is not sufficient to establish that *some* Cretans are liars, we must establish a more particularized case for denying the credibility of the specific Cretan before us. J. L. Austin put the key point at issue with characteristic incisiveness:

> If you are aware you may be mistaken, you ought not to say you know. . . . But of course, being aware that you may be mistaken doesn't mean merely being aware that you are a fallible human being [or indeed any such universalized consideration]: it means that you have some concrete reason to suppose that you may be mistaken in this case. . . . It is naturally *always* possible ("humanly"

possible) that I may be mistaken . . . but that itself is no
bar against using . . . "I know" . . . as we do in fact use
[it] . . .[28]

Universalized prospects of mistake and remote possibilities
of error (human frailty, Cartesian deceivers, etc.) do not
constitute a ground of suitable strength to defeat the appropriateness of knowledge claims as actually made in the
communicative framework of real-life discourse.

An illustration may help to bring home a recognition of
the appropriateness of the foregoing line of reasoning as to
the limited applicability of G-doubt. Consider a hypothetical
machine which produces a sequence of statements, some of
which are false, and some true. Consider a particular statement 'q' which emerges from the machine. Is 'q' dubious –
that is, are we justified in doubting 'q'? On the principle of
G-doubt, our answer must be an unqualified affirmative, for
is not the statement 'q' one of a sequence ($=$ type T) which
includes false statements? It is easy to see, however, that
such an *unqualified* answer is entirely unwarranted. The
appropriate answer obviously depends on our total body
of information regarding 'q'. Thus if 'q' is in actuality
"$2 + 2 = 4$," we would even be justified in ignoring entirely
its machine-output origin in considering the matter of its
dubiousness. Nor need we ever know the specific content of
'q'; its dubiousness (or lack thereof) may depend upon the
manner in which the machine functions. For example, if our
statement-generating machine provides alternatingly true
and false statements, then 'q' must again be judged on the
basis of all of the information known about it, *including its
place in the order*; its dubiousness cannot defensibly be asserted simply on the grounds of a link "by association," solely
because it is a member of a group in which false statements
also occur.

Consider another example. Our arithmetical calculations
do sometimes fall into error (perhaps, alas, only too often).
But this does surely not serve to show that we might be mistaken in the most obvious and elementary calculations, such
as $2 + 3 = 5$. Correspondingly, it is, to be sure, an undeni-

[28] J. L. Austin, "Other Minds," *op. cit.*, p. 66.

able fact that our senses do sometimes mislead us. But this – as G. E. Moore has argued so forcefully and persuasively[29] – simply does not show that we are entitled (let alone obliged) to doubt even in certain particularly blatant instances of clear sense perception in commonplace situations such as our present perception of our own hand in ordinary circumstances. Moore's analysis is entirely correct – the generic fact that we *actually are mistaken in some* sense-judgments or in calculations is wholly inadequate to entail the conclusion that we *possibly might be mistaken in all* such judgments. In these spheres, dubiousness-by-association in the Cartesian manner is not legitimate.

Such examples serve to render vivid the fundamental fact, already argued on general grounds, that G-doubt represents a justifiable approach *only* under certain rather far-fetched conditions, namely when no specific *ad hoc* information about the statement at issue is available – a circumstance seldom, if ever, realized. Whenever we are fortunate enough to have some direct evidence regarding its truth-status, over and above its being of a certain type that also includes false statements, we must judge the dubiousness of a statement solely on the grounds of our direct evidence, leaving indirect considerations entirely aside. It would be unjustifiable and logically indefensible to inject generic or indirect considerations into the evaluation of the truth, falsity, dubiousness, etc., of a statement when direct evidence is at hand. G-doubt is, at best, justifiable only as a *faute de mieux* procedure. Its employment would be warranted only in those cases where such an oblique appraisal represents the best use of our entire body of information.[30] To base a charge of doubtfulness against an otherwise duly attested thesis solely upon such generic considerations is to transgress the boundaries

[29] See G. E. Moore, "The Refutation of Idealism" in *Philosophical Studies* (London, 1922).

[30] Note that these conditions are never satisfied with respect to sensory propositions. When I look at the tree outside my window, I have at my disposal a whole host of relevant information (I feel wide awake and keenly aware of my environment, my glasses are on and my vision is clear, I have often seen that tree before, etc., etc.). To neglect this evidence and to argue "My sight has misled me before and might therefore be misleading me in this case" is an instance of illegitimate use of G-doubt, because it moves heedlessly past a whole mass of other and more direct evidence that is at hand.

which separate a real and warranted doubt from one that is far-fetched, inappropriate, and sometimes even crazy.

The reason for all this is simple. All our reasonable knowledge-claims have some sort of source-induced or evidential warrant that creates a presumption in their favor. And such presumptions – while indeed defeasible – can only be defeated by case-specific counterindications, and not by consideration of general principles like human frailty, the fallibility of the senses, conceivable Cartesian deceivers, etc.

There are, to be sure, some modes of reasoning in the neighborhood of G-doubt argumentation that have substantial plausibility. One such inference is

1. The fact of its membership in S is the *only* consideration that supports us in claiming the truth of *p*.
2. No known truth-relevant considerations are available to differentiate *p* from the remaining S-members (S is a truth-relative *infimum species* for *p*).
3. Some S-members are false.

∴ *p* might well be false.

But this reasoning is a weak instrument of doubt-generation because of the difficulty of putting this form of argumentation effectively to work. In applications of the sort in view, it is rarely if ever the case that premisses (1) and (2) can be made plausible, let alone established.

One important lesson of these considerations regarding the illegitimacy of G-doubt is that in cognitive contexts one must not visit the sins of the whole upon its constituent parts. And this has important consequences. We realize full well – the history of science constantly reiterates the fact – that the putative truth of one era differs from that of another and that, accordingly, one must distinguish with care between *the* truth (the real truth) on the one hand and *our* truth (our putative truth, what we think or maintain to be true) on the other hand. But this is a realization with which we can only operate at the abstract or wholesale level, and cannot implement at the concrete or retail level of putative judgments. (Cp. the Preface Paradox at p. 245.) We cannot so implement it simply because an item would not (*ex hypothesi*) be *our* truth if we did not regard it as *the* truth. The effect of the distinction is not to undermine our acceptance of particular truths but only to place us into a certain posture *vis-à-vis* the whole domain of what we accept as true – a regulative posture of nondogmatism based on a recognition of fallibility. Our ability to proceed in this way hinges crucially upon the pivotal fact that G-doubt and S-doubt are distinct and that the former just does not suffice to provide a basis for the latter.

4. THE DIALECTICS OF ARGUMENTATION AND THE WEAKNESS OF GENERIC CONSIDERATIONS

It deserves stress that our standard cognitive resources (the senses, memory, etc.) exert such weight that a burden of proof inclines in their favor. Admittedly, they often go amiss, and it would be quite inappropriate to claim for them an invariable and automatic correctness. But their deliverances enjoy a *presumption* of veracity: they must be allowed to stand until set aside by appropriate counterindications. And here, considerations of general principle (human frailty and the rest) do not count – the presumption at issue can only be undone by particularized and case-specific considerations. Generic considerations of the G-doubt sort do not serve. In giving up all claims to infallibility from the sources of our knowledge – by merely maintaining their *presumptive* veracity – we have already conceded that they are not always veridical and thus have put G-doubt (based on occasional failures or generic imperfections) out of consideration. The setting aside of the residual weight of presumption requires considerations of case-specific detail.

Descartes' justification of wholesale doubt misses attainment of its objectives because, taking the form of G-doubt, it constitutes a procedure which cannot properly be maintained in the face of the direct evidence which may (and generally will) be available in a particular case. Given the way the idea of "knowledge" operates in the conceptual scheme that is its natural home, the considerations of general principle at issue in G-doubt are impotent to reverse the presumption of certainty regarding the established sources of knowledge such as sight, memory, etc. The generic recognition that "some of our knowledge claims may be mistaken" at the collective level does *not* preclude our making these claims at the specific, case-by-case level. A specific knowledge-claim is not to be invalidated on grounds of general principles above – invalidation can only appropriately be based on case-specific considerations.

The sceptic rightly realizes that once embarked upon an omnium-gatherum doubt based on general principles alone we can never extricate ourselves by rigorously defensible moves. If G-doubtfulness destroys knowledge, the sceptic automatically wins the day. But an omnium-gatherum doubt based on general principles alone is itself an improper and indefensible proceeding. The correct lesson here was drawn by C. S. Peirce:

> We cannot begin with complete doubt. ... A person may, it is true, in the course of his studies, find reason to doubt what he began by believing; but in that case he doubts because he has a positive reason for it, and not on account of the Cartesian maxim. Let us not pretend to doubt in philosophy what we do not doubt in our hearts.[31]

Peirce puts his finger on the key issue: real doubt must issue from a positive reason, a definite, concrete, case-specific indication that something is amiss; considerations regarding general principles just will not serve.

Consider again the dialectical aspect of the cognitive situation. *A* says that there are some apples in the fruit bowl. *B* asks him if he is sure. *A* replies that he is quite sure – he sees them clearly with his own eyes, and recognizes them as the very apples he himself placed there a short time ago. *B* challenges that his eyesight is rather poor and his memory has been somewhat erratic lately. *A* might then go to the bowl, look more closely, touch, smell, even taste the objects in question. He then insists "These are indeed apples." If *B* were to keep on with doubts and challenges, pressing objections

[31] *Collected Papers*, Vol. V, sect. 5.265.

wholly devoid of any case-specific bearing (human frailty, Cartesian deceivers, the endless variety of yet unverified consequences, etc.), then *A* would no doubt abandon the discussion in disgust and anger. And quite rightly so. For *B* has now gone beyond the limits of what can reasonably be asked for and has thus managed to put himself outside the pale of rational discussion and inquiry.

Consider, in this light, the following interchange between the sceptical objector (S) and his cognitivist opponent (C):

S: What entitles you to claim that there is "no chance or error" with regard to this item of purported knowledge?

C: I have taken steps to rule out every possibility of error – that is, all of the *realistic* possibilities.

S: But do not some prospects of error still remain – is error not still conceivable?

C: Only conjecturally (or hypothetically) so, but not realistically.

S: But have you not in fact erred in the past in various cases where all these "realistic" possibilities of error had been eliminated?

C: Certainly, but this consideration affords no valid reason for abstaining from a claim to knowledge in *this* case. For it is only a generic consideration (sufficient to underwrite G-doubt) but indicates no case-specific basis for any S-doubt regarding the contention at issue.

To be sure, the sceptic is quite right in insisting that the usual (accepted or socially established) standards of certainty and incorrigibility do actually fail from time to time. (The medically dead do sometimes come back to life.) But this generic reflection just does not carry the weight to countermand knowledge claims in specific cases. In the ordinary or normal circumstances of everyday-life situations (and in the absence of case-specific counterindications all situations must be presumed normal), certain sorts of claims (those instanced by G. E. Moore, for example) must be allowed to pass as certain. Whatever possibility of mistake there may be in such

6. THE KK-THESIS AND THE CHARGE THAT COGNITIVISM ENTAILS DOGMATISM

John Dewey said that, since knowledge gives us a right to be sure, it "terminates inquiry" – if someone *knows* a contention to be true, then he may regard inquiry as closed with respect to it: "That which satisfactorily terminates inquiry is, by definition, knowledge; it is knowledge because it *is* the appropriate close of inquiry." [34] This is, in a way, perfectly true and correct. But it does need to be interpreted and qualified. A valid claim to knowledge terminates inquiry in that "everything has been done that need be done in the circumstances at hand." But one is never entitled to close his mind and simply disregard all further evidence. Cognitivism is not dogmatism. A fallibilist view of knowledge combines the entitlement to knowledge claims with a recognition of their fallibility in principle – their liability to upset in the light of unexpected and – in the circumstances – *unexpectable* developments.

In claiming to know that *p*, I do indeed "anticipate" the results of future inquiry as being in *p*'s favor – I take the stance that by all present indications the undertaking of further inquiry is pointless because its outcome is a foregone conclusion. [35] But in taking this stance that further inquiry is unnecessary we take a practical position within what Peirce called the "economy of research" – holding that the investment of time and effort in seeking out further information is counterindicated by the information at hand. [36] We have reached a point where there is, in the circumstances, no point in going on and no justification for the investment of further time and effort. But we certainly do not insist on ignoring such further evidence as may unsolicitedly come our way.

To be sure, we accept as a fact of the "logic" of knowledge

[34] John Dewey, *Logic: The Theory of Inquiry* (New York, 1938), p. 8. Dewey here leans on the ideas of C. S. Peirce.

[35] On the pointlessness of further inquiry in the face of knowledge see Jaakko Hintikka, "'Knowing that One Knows' Reviewed," *Synthese*, vol. 21 (1970), pp. 141–162.

[36] Cf. Chapter IV of the author's *Peirce's Philosophy of Science* (Notre Dame, 1978).

the principle that: If *p* is indeed known, then it will *eo ipso* be known that there is no decisive reason for rejecting *p*, no true *p* falsifier:

$$Kxp \rightarrow Kx \sim (\exists q)[q \ \& \ (q \rightarrow \sim p)].^{37}$$

Accordingly, when one claims to have adequate warrant for knowledge, one thereby claims to have adequate warrant for maintaining the nonexistence of a falsifier. However, such adequate warrant is not itself tantamount to knowledge: it does not – and need not – logically *entail* truth nor *assure* the nonexistence of a falsifier. It requires no more than that there be no real possibility of error – that no case-specific counterindications are in hand or on the horizon. But to take this stance is not to deny the prospect that circumstances may alter, to claim failproof foreknowledge that circumstances cannot possibly so eventuate as to call for abandonment of the no-falsifier claim, and thus also of the knowledge-claim itself. Given the recognition that circumstances may alter, one has to be prepared to examine new data that may come to hand.

And so even when we justifiedly claim to know something, we are *not* committed by this claim to "play ostrich" and refuse categorically to look at counterindicative information that might come along. The claim to knowledge is appropriate when we have done everything that need reasonably be done in the circumstances to ascertain the point at issue. To repeat: circumstances can alter. The fact that at one stage *there is no reason to think* that further evidence might alter the situation does not mean that further evidence cannot in fact alter it – no doubt to our surprise, chagrin, and embarrassment. There is nothing anomalous about the statement: "They thought they knew that *p*, and they were quite justified in thinking so, but it turned out that they were simply wrong."

The sceptic complains that knowledge claims engender an unhealthy dogmatism. As the sceptic sees it, the cognitivist

---

[37] Note that this is an immediate consequence of the principle [*Kxp* & *Kx*(*p* → *q*)] → *Kxq* plus the supposition that *p* → ~(∃*q*)[*q* & *q* → ~*p*)] is an "obvious implication" whose truth everyone recognizes.

must always argue in the following undesirably dogmatic way.[38]

> If I know that *p* is true, then I know that any evidence against *p* is evidence against something true. Therefore I know that any and all such evidence is misleading. I should disregard evidence which I know is misleading. Consequently, if I know that *p* is true, then I can "close the book" on inquiry and am in a position to disregard any future evidence which seems to tell against it.

The sceptic insists that to claim something as knowledge is to be prepared to dismiss out of hand whatever new countervailing data might come along.

But this view that cognitivism carries dogmatism in its wake is a misreading of the situation. To advance a warranted claim to knowledge one must "have good reason to believe that further evidence will not disestablish my claim," but one need not be in a position to rule this prospect out completely and absolutely – as lying not just outside the sphere of *real* possibility but of *theoretical* possibility as well. A theory of defeasible knowledge (i.e., defeasible but rationally-warranted claims to knowledge) is, as we have argued, perfectly viable and would provide a basis for avoiding a blinkered approach towards unforseeable counterindications. The fallibilism of our analysis blocks the complaint that claims to knowledge are inherently dogmatic.

The sceptic likes to charge, in season and out of season, that his cognitivist opponent is *eo ipso* a dogmatist – someone whose mind is closed, who refuses even to entertain any reasons against his commitments, and who denies flatly that there can be any evidence against what we claim to know. In claiming knowledge (so the sceptic insists) one closes his mind, turns a blind eye to the possibility of error, and ignores the inconvenient facts of human limitations and fallibility. And so, sceptical philosophers have often charged

[38] See Gilbert Harman, *Thought* (Princeton, 1970), p. 148. Compare also Peter Unger, *Ignorance* (Oxford, 1975), Robert Ackerman, *Belief and Knowledge* (New York, 1972), Keith Lehrer, *Knowledge* (Oxford, 1974), and Douglas Odegard, "A Knower's Evidence," *American Philosophical Quarterly*, vol. 15 (1978), pp. 123–128.

that cognitivism rationally entails dogmatism – that if someone who claims (warrantedly and correctly) to know something for certain, then there is nothing he would count as evidence proving its falsity. In claiming to know, so they argue, you claim that the books can be closed on the matter – that all further counterevidence can simply be dismissed.[39] As one writer puts it, someone who claims knowledge asserts absolute certainty and thereby avows: "I will not allow *anything at all* to count as evidence against my present view in the matter."[40] But surely few, if any, of those who use the word use it in this sense!

Cock-sure dogmatism must indeed be rejected as an unattractive and – more decisively – unwarranted approach. But as the present discussion has shown time and again, nothing in the nature of knowledge as this conception actually functions in our discourse involves one in such hyperbolic commitments that make pretensions to knowledge inherently absurd. An altogether realistic – and indeed fallibilistic – view of claims to knowledge is not only possible but appropriate. Our own position is emphatically fallibilistic and recognizes that even an adequately warranted claim to knowledge may in the end have to be withdrawn. For we deny that

$$\frac{x \text{ is warranted in claiming that } x \text{ knows } p}{\therefore \ p}$$

represents a valid inference.[41] An adequately warranted

---

[39] This line of thought can be found in John Locke, *An Essay Concerning Human Understanding*, ed. by A. S. Pringle-Pattison (London, 1924), p. 261. See also Norman Malcolm, "Knowledge and Belief," *Mind*, vol. 61 (1952), pp. 178–186 (see especially pp. 179–180). For a contemporary statement see Keith Lehrer, "Skepticism and Conceptual Change" in R. M. Chisholm and R. J. Swartz (eds.), *Empirical Knowledge* (Englewood Cliffs, 1973), pp. 47–58 (see pp. 51–53).

[40] Peter Unger, *Ignorance* (Oxford, 1975), pp. 122–123.

[41] Note, however, that since

$$\frac{x \text{ knows } p}{\therefore \ p}$$

is a valid inference, so is

$$\frac{x \text{ is warranted in claiming that } x \text{ knows } p}{\therefore \ x \text{ is warranted in claiming } p.}$$

claim to knowledge can prove false: what is purported to be real knowledge – and warrantedly so – is often spurious. To be warranted in claiming to know is one thing, actually to know that we know is another. (But to say this is certainly *not* to join the sceptic in dismissing knowledge claims as inappropriate and unwarranted.)

But what of the thesis that knowing entails knowing that one knows, the KK-thesis:

$$Kxp \rightarrow KxKxp.^{42}$$

This thesis, which stipulates the availability or the reflexivity of knowledge, seemingly qualifies as an appropriate principle of the "logic" of knowledge.[43] Knowing involves being certain of the fact at issue in a way that itself seems to demand suitable recognition. And does *this* aspect of the matter not enmesh our knowledge claims in dogmatism?

Perhaps this self-reflexivity of knowing can be simply dispensed with? One recent discussant writes:

> If his confidence in his statement is much less than it ought to be [given his epistemic posture], *he* will not say he knows it. But would *we* say that he knows it? We might say "He does not think that he knows it, but he really does know it."[44]

But this seems quite wrong. It is one thing to have information at one's disposal, and another to know the fact at issue. If *x* has the information that *p* but (for whatever reason) lacks confidence in its truth, the condition of "being certain of the fact at issue" – a condition crucial to the possession of knowledge – is simply lacking, and an accurate and consci-

---

But, of course, the inference at issue now makes the illicit move from *x*'s being warranted in claiming the truth of *p*, to the truth of *p* as such. We have another instance of "illicit strengthening."

[42] For a survey of relevant considerations see Jaakko Hintikka, *Knowledge and Belief* (Ithaca, 1962).

[43] Note that this thesis regarding ground-level knowledge does not commit us to a comparable contention regarding metaknowledge. That is, nothing commits us to allowing *p* to take the form *Kxq*. The KK-thesis itself does not embark us on an unending iteration leading *ad absurdum*.

[44] David Pears, *What Is Knowledge?* (New York, 1971), p. 14.

entious user of the language would feel himself constrained to withhold saying "he knows" and adopt some other, more guarded characterization of the situation.

But – it will be argued – the KK-thesis leads to unacceptable consequences. For it seems to imply that in claiming to know something we are cock-sure of it – that we must close our minds to any and all counterindications.

This seeming implication is not an actual one. It by no means follows from the KK-thesis that the person who maintains that there is adequate rational warrant for holding that p is known (certain, etc.) thereby asserts that it is known to be known. The deduction

x has adequate rational warrant for accepting "I know that p" (or "It is certain that p")

$\therefore x$ knows that "I know that p" (or "It is certain that p")

clearly does not work, owing to the fallacy of "consequence-inflation" that is committed. (See pages 53–54.) No untoward consequences by way of unacceptable dogmatism inhere in the stipulation that in claiming to know we claim to know that we know.

On the other hand, the case stands very differently with the related thesis that not knowing entails knowing one doesn't know:

$$\sim Kxp \rightarrow Kx \sim Kxp.$$

According to *this* thesis, what is unknown is known to be unknown. One is held to be omniscient with respect to one's ignorance in that whenever q takes the form "$\sim Kxp$" then we have it that: $q \rightarrow Kxq$. This contention is patently unacceptable. It would clearly make the life of the antisceptic unfairly simple to transmute ignorance into knowledge in this way. The sceptic would insist – and quite rightly so – that such a device for extracting knowledge *ex nihilo* must be rejected.[45]

But let us return to the KK-thesis itself. Note that it follows from the thesis that if x has adequate rational warrant

[45] Accordingly, no principle of the "logic" of knowledge can take the general form $\sim KxA \rightarrow KxB$.

for *Kxp*, then *x eo ipso* has adequate rational warrant for *KxKxp*. But of course it does *not* follow from this that *KxKxp* must be true. (Indeed, it does not even follow that *Kxp* or *p* itself will be true.) To be sure, in claiming *Ksp* (with *s* = myself), I become committed – via the KK-thesis – to the claim that *KsKsp*. But this fact – viz. that I claim to (or indeed even that I do actually have) adequate rational warrant for *KsKsp* – does *not* mean that I am (or take myself to be) entitled to close the book with respect to any and all further evidence regarding *p*. The sceptic's charge that our claims to knowledge entail an unjustifiable lapse into dogmatism is simply unfounded.

VII

Mundane Knowledge

SYNOPSIS

(1) The sceptics' view of the inherent unattainability of knowledge embodies a mistaken and unrealistic construction of what "knowledge" is. The concept of knowledge is a mundane conception developed for a certain range of real-world utilizations and any construction of it that totally blocks its applicability is an unrealistic one. (2) The need for realism: it is absurd to think that the use-conditions of such a conception can impose requirements that are *in principle* unmeetable. (3) A fuller exploration of the contrast between mundane and hyperbolic approaches to the idea of knowledge-defeating possibilities. (4) This mundane conception of knowledge is indeed a conception of *knowledge* – we are not changing the topic to "reasonable belief," but endeavoring to expand the conception of knowledge as it actually works in the linguistic setting that is its natural home. (5) A rebuttal of the charge that such a view amounts to "relativism" in regard to knowledge. (6) Our scientific knowledge too is potentially fallible and merely mundane, but this does not undo its cognitive standing – our claims to knowledge are not to be invalidated by the imposition of standards that cannot in the nature of things be met.

1. BRINGING ABSOLUTENESS DOWN TO EARTH

The aim of the cognitive enterprise as a realistic human endeavor is *to obtain the best available answers to our ques-*

tions about the ways of the world. Now here, as elsewhere in human affairs, it transpires that while we indeed aim at the very best ("the truth, the whole truth, and nothing but the truth"), we must be prepared to settle for less than the absolutely ideal. And this is something the rules of the conceptual game certainly provide for.

The concept of knowledge is a human contrivance – evolved with a view to its real-life applications. As with other concepts, we ourselves determine the rules of its applicability – the Protagorean dictum "Man is the measure of all things" must be applied in this context. The sceptic regards certainty, and accordingly also knowledge, as reflecting an ideal that is unattainable in this dispensation. The common-sense cognitivist replies that *this* sort of "knowledge" is a phantasm of the sceptic's own devising, cut off from the conception of knowledge as it actually figures in established discourse – the knowledge that is actually at issue in the language we employ in the real-life communicative exchanges of everyday affairs. Given this fact that the conception of knowledge *as we use it* is indeed *made* for the end – i.e., is made for our use of it through the historical course of developments that has led to its institution as part of our conceptual praxis – it would be gravely mistaken to think of this conception as subject to a set of standards that could block its applicability from the very outset and as a matter of abstract general principles.

The idea of knowledge, as we actually work with it, represents a conception that is in use and has, in fact, been *designed* for use through the process of its historical evolution as an instrument for communication and for the coordination of human action. Like the other conceptual instruments operative in our everyday-life discourse, it represents a conception built for employment in this world, and is not something transcendental and extramundane. It is not just incorrect but foolish to think that knowledge claims are automatically inflated beyond the range of reachability. There would *be* no concept of knowledge if the sort of thing that is at issue with "knowledge" were in principle never realizable. It would be little short of absurd to construe the elements of absoluteness – which are, undoubtedly, present in our knowledge claims – in such a way as to allow them to 'pull the rug out" from under this very conception by precluding any prospect of its warranted application.

As the "evidential gap" of Chapter II indicates, it is *in principle impossible* to establish full confirmatory control over each and every element of the content of an objective factual claim. It is accordingly unjustified – indeed absurd – to establish it as a requirement for the achievement of objective knowledge that such control should be established.

The sceptic's perfectionistic argumentation here runs roughly as follows:

Knowledge must be absolutistically perfect in nature
Whatever we can actually obtain is not absolutistically
 perfect in nature
_____

∴ We cannot attain knowledge.

Conceding the formal validity of this syllogism, we ourselves argue so as in effect to stand the argument on its head:

We can attain knowledge
Whatever we can actually obtain is not absolutistically
 perfect in nature
_____

∴ Knowledge is not absolutistically perfect in nature.

The sceptic's perfectionism sees the path to knowledge blocked by the inconsistent triad at issue. Our own analysis sees the sceptic's perfectionism as itself invalidated. The "absoluteness" of knowledge claims is not one of unrealistic perfectionism.

Rather than establishing the unattainability of knowledge, the sceptic's argumentation merely brings to light the unacceptability of the hyperbolically perfectionistic conception of knowledge that he chooses to operate with. For sceptics insist upon construing knowledge in such a way as to foist upon the cognitivist a Sisyphus-like task by subjecting all knowledge claims to effectively unmeetable standards. Scepticism involves the hypertrophy of our cognitive standards: the usual criteria of knowledge become exaggerated and inflated beyond any feasible prospect of satisfaction. But this hyperbolic standard separates the sceptic from the concept of knowledge as it does actually function in common-life and should function in philosophical discussions as well.

To be sure, the sceptic may say: "My construction of knowledge is the correct one; your mundane, absoluteness-abating standard of 'knowledge' violates the proper ground-rules of our knowledge-talk." Against someone minded to complain that the King's English requires a hyperbolic construction of the term one may invoke the authority of those masters of the language who Englished the King's Bible: "And if any man think that he knoweth anything, he knoweth nothing yet as he ought to know." (I Corinthians 8, 2.) We do indeed know things in this imperfect dispensation, albeit suboptimally if a wholly idealized standard of optimality is applied: we know things, yet not perhaps as we ideally might.

The sceptic, however, sets up standards upon "knowledge" that are so unrealistic and perfectionistic as to move outside the range of considerations at work in the conception as it actually functions in the language.[1] He holds that our beliefs never (or hardly ever) constitute knowledge, precisely because the standards he imposes on the assessment of knowledge claims are much more rigorous than our own. But this will not do. If it is in fact our conception of knowledge the sceptics wish to discuss and to argue about, then they must accept the standards that are part and parcel of this conception.

2. THE IMPETUS OF REALISM

The truism that knowledge must be certain requires critical scrutiny and analysis in the light of the preceding considera-

[1] The hyperbolically demanding "knowledge of the philosophers" goes back to Plato and his insistence that no genuine knowledge can be had regarding the affairs of this irregular and imperfect world of ours. The theory of "mundane knowledge" goes back to Aristotle's *Topics* which develops a fairly elaborate theory of realistic knowledge – a "knowledge" capable of doing the work of everyday life, subject to the criteriology of general acceptance (*endoxa*) by the relevant experts and belonging to well-established disciplines. (See 101b5 ff.) However, it was the neo-Platonists of the Middle Academy (especially Carneades) who gave this Aristotelian approach its fullest and most developed articulation. (See Charlotte L. Stough, *Greek Scepticism* [Berkeley and Los Angeles, 1969], pp. 50–64.)

tions. To say of a thesis that it "is certain" is to say no more than *it is as certain as, in the nature of the case, a thesis of this sort reasonably could be rendered.* And this does not, and need not, preclude *any* possibility of error – however hypothetical and far-fetched – but rather merely any *real* or *genuine* possibility of error. G. E. Moore put the key point well: "There is no reason why we should not, in this respect, make our philosophical opinions agree with what we necessarily believe at other times. There is no reason why I shall not confidently assert that I do really *know* some external facts. . . . I am, in fact, as certain of this as of anything, and as reasonably certain of it."[2] As Austin stressed, the claiming of knowledge represents a performance which extends a promise or guarantee – an assurance that all that needs to be done to establish the matter has indeed been done.[3] The preclusion of error (imprecision, inaccuracy, etc.) that is implicit in a claim to knowledge is always a matter of precluding the *real* prospects of slippage, and not those which are "merely theoretical" or "purely conjectural" or the like.

It is sometimes offered as a decisive objection to scepticism that the sceptic is unable to tell us what would satisfy the conditions he takes to govern knowledge – that he is unable to specify what sorts of conceivably available support he would be prepared to accept in validation of a knowledge claim. But this *ad hominem* argumentation does not do full justice to the needs of the situation. For against this sort of objection the sceptic can simply reply:

> I cannot say in advance just exactly what sort of grounding would exact my concurrence to a knowledge claim. Just go ahead and try to convince me. I am not going to help you out by specifying just what will do – that's your problem. The burden of proof lies with you – you, after all, are the one for whom knowledge is available, not I. All I can say is that when you've come to the

---

[2] G. E. Moore, *Philosophical Studies* (London, 1922), p. 163.

[3] J. L. Austin, "Other Minds" in *Philosophical Papers,* ed. by J. O. Urmson and G. J. Warnock (Oxford, 1961), pp. 44–84.

point where I am actually persuaded that the knowledge claim is in order, I'll be candid enough to tell you.

But this sort of exchange simply confuses the dialectic of the situation. The key point is not that the sceptic is unable to say in advance just what will do to validate a knowledge claim but that he is prepared to argue on general principles that nothing will do. He espouses a conception of knowledge according to which nothing by way of conceivably available substantiation is sufficient to validate a claim to knowledge. And it is this fact that leads him afoul of *ultra posse* considerations.

*   *   *

The sceptic constantly insists that what we vaunt as "our knowledge" has two features:

(1) that it contains an admixture of merely *purported* "knowledge" which is in fact plausible error.
(2) that real and spurious truth (plausible error) are *contempotaneously* indistinguishable and can only be discriminated (if at all) with the wisdom of hindsight – and even then only imperfectly, since past error is only determinable as such in terms of present "knowledge."

Accordingly, we are in fact "color blind" with regard to the authentic/spurious distinction insofar as our own *current* particular claims to knowledge are concerned. This useful distinction can at best render us a merely retrospective service.

These basic facts of cognitive fallibility are – broadly speaking – agreed upon between the sceptic and his cognitivist opponent. The quarrel centers about the question of what inference can be drawn from them. The sceptic holds that where knowledge is at issue, we cannot ever here and now discriminate with certainty the real thing from a counterfeit article, and concludes that it makes no sense to advance any authenticity claims here. The cognitivist holds that such claims make perfectly good sense provided we recognize in making them that they are defeasible and may eventually have to be abandoned. A. J. Ayer has put this point in his characteristically trenchant way:

> The discovery of . . . error refutes the claim to knowledge; but it does not prove that the claim was not, in the circumstances, legitimately made. The claim to know . . . [a] statement is satisfied only if the statement is true; but it is legitimate if it has the appropriate backing. . . .[4]

The realities of human fallibility do *not* block the way to justified claims to knowledge. For they serve merely to define the limits of the possible and *ultra posse nemo obligatur*.

3. EPISTEMIC POSSIBILITY AND ITS RAMIFICATIONS

In his search for knowledge-defeating circumstances, the sceptic places great stress upon his favored contention that "even the bare *possibility* of falsity suffices to defeat knowledge." But matters are not quite so simple. For, of course, the principle "possible falsity defeats knowledge" must *not* be construed in the sense:

$$\Diamond \sim p \rightarrow \sim Kxp.$$

This would at once yield the idea that only the necessary can be known:

$$Kxp \rightarrow \Box p.$$

And this is obviously unacceptable in its across-the-board proscription *a priori* of any prospect of knowledge of contingent truth.[5]

As has been insisted time and again, only a *real* possibility of falsehood can defeat knowledge. Thus let us define "being a real possibility given x's epistemic posture" as "obtaining

[4] *The Problem of Knowledge* (Harmondsworth, 1956), pp. 43–44.
[5] Note that this principle will arise either by "inflation of consequences" from $Kxp \rightarrow p$, or else by a modal fallacy with respect to $\Box(Kxp \rightarrow p)$.

for all that x knows" – that is, as "being compatible with everything that x knows":

$$\Diamond_{x!}p = Df \quad (\forall q)(Kxq \rightarrow \text{compat}[p, q]).[6]$$

Accordingly, if $\Diamond_x p$, then p is "a real possibility within x's epistemic horizons."

Given *this* construction of "being a real epistemic possibility for x", one arrives straightforwardly at the result that a real possibility of falsehood defeats knowledge:

$$\Diamond_x \sim p \rightarrow \sim Kxp.$$

For this is equivalent with

$$(\forall q)(Kxq \rightarrow \sim[\sim p \rightarrow \sim q]) \rightarrow \sim Kxp$$

which in turn is equivalent with

$$Kxp \rightarrow (\exists q)(Kxq \text{ \& } [q \rightarrow p]).$$

This thesis is an evident truth that obtains on logical grounds alone (obviously so, since p will itself do for the q at issue). The principle that "possible falsity defeats knowledge" is compatible with – indeed *invites* – a realistically nonhyperbolic construction of the possibilities at issue.

This idea of epistemic possibility has associated with it a concomitant notion of epistemic necessity

$$\Box_x p = Df \sim \Diamond_x \sim p = (\exists q)(Kxq \text{ \& } [q \rightarrow p])$$

This mode of necessity is what is necessary given what x knows; it represents necessity relative to x's knowledge. What is at issue here is epistemic "necessity" in a realistic sense of this term. Now it is readily seen that whatever is known is epistemically necessary in just this sense:

$$Kxp \rightarrow \Box_x p.$$

For this thesis is tantamount to

$$Kxp \rightarrow (\exists q)(Kxq \text{ \& } [q \rightarrow p])$$

---

[6] Note that compat(p, q) could and should be construed as $\sim (p \rightarrow \sim q)$, provided $\rightarrow$ is *strict* rather than merely *material* implication.

which, as we have already seen, is an evident truth. This thesis that $Kxp \to \square_x p$ stands in striking contrast to the clearly unacceptable principle $Kxp \to \square p$, which arises from it by an illicit strengthening of the consequent.

As these considerations indicate, the contrast between the acceptable theses

$$\diamondsuit_x \sim p \to \sim Kxp$$
$$Kxp \to \square_x p$$

and their inappropriately absolutized congeners

$$\diamondsuit \sim p \to \sim Kxp$$
$$Kxp \to \square p$$

sharply highlights the distinction between the mundane and the hyperbolic construction of the knowledge-defeating possibilities.

4. REASONABLE BELIEF AND THE CHARGE OF TOPIC-ABANDONMENT

It becomes necessary to deal also with the following line of sceptical objection:

> In insisting upon what you call the "usual ground-rules" and the *accepted* standards that govern our common-language discourse about knowledge you espouse a conception of *mundane* knowledge which is in fact nothing other than merely *reasonable belief.* Now it is one thing to maintain that what you accept is espoused rationally ("reasonably believed") but something quite different to say that it is actually *known.* The conception of mundane knowledge you adopt here simply blurs this important distinction.

But this objection is based upon a falsification of our position. We are not concerned with "reasonable belief" in the sense of a thesis to the effect that, "it is reasonable to believe (hold, maintain) that p" (where p is a claim about the world).

Insofar as we are concerned with reasonable belief at all, it is in the context of a specifically *cognitive* claim of the form: "It is reasonable to believe (hold, maintain) that *one knows* that *p*." It is – we must insist – not reasonable belief but *knowledge* that is the focus of these deliberations. Yet a claim to knowledge – like any other factual claim – can appropriately be based upon adequate grounds that fall short of *logical* conclusiveness.[7]

It is helpful in this connection to reconsider the idea of the ancient Academic sceptics that since we cannot really attain authentic Knowledge (*epistēmē*) we must settle, *faute de mieux*, for something less. Thus the Academic Sceptic Arcesilaus (315–241 B.C.) held that since genuine knowledge (*epistēmē*) in unavailable, the rational man must, at the theoretical level at any rate, maintain a strict suspension of judgment (*epochē*). But, he maintained, this agnosticism need not paralyze action, for rational action need not rest on certain knowledge but can rest on the mere appearances of things.

Carneades (*c*. 187–129 B.C.), the most important successor to Arcesilaus as head of the Academy, held a very different position. He carved out a new epistemic category, "the *plausible* or *probable*" (*to pithanon*) as intermediate between certain knowledge (*epistēmē*) and mere appearances. And he taught that this sort of plausibility is not merely good enough as a guide to reasonable action, but provides a basis of reasonable belief as well. We must thus distinguish between the absolute assent involved in genuine knowledge (*epistēmē*), which can never be warranted in matters of empirical fact, and the qualified assent appropriate in situations where claims attain to plausibility. Alone among the sceptics of antiquity, Carneades conceded the rational appropriateness of actual assent in some circumstances – viz., those relating to matters of *praxis*.[8] And Carneades went on to develop, in the special case of perceptual knowledge, a complex criteriological theory with respect to this mode of

[7] The transition from "(justifiedly) believes" to "(justifiedly) believes that he knows" is *not* a matter of the accumulation of more and more evidence. These cognitive circumstances do not lie along a uniform evidential spectrum of increasing certainty (or increasing anything else). Altogether different sorts of things are at issue.

[8] Cf. Cicero, *Academica*, Bk. II, sect. xxi.

qualified assent. Where Pyrrho and Arcesilaus had the view that assent must always be withheld, Carneades held that duly qualified assent can actually be justified (though not that absolute assent which the Stoics demanded for cataleptic perceptions).

But this line of approach does *not* reflect our own position. We are not concerned here to espouse an idea of the plausible and of reasonable belief distinct from – and falling short of – genuine knowledge. It is, of course, one thing to say that a belief is rationally held or a claim rationally made, and something very different to say that what is at issue is actually *known*. This distinction between "knowledge" on the one hand and "reasonable belief" on the other must be recognized and honored. To know is one thing and to have some basis of rational warrant for claiming it to be so another. But this distinction is nowise violated by noting that there is such a thing as *a rationally warranted claim to* KNOWLEDGE, and that it is exactly this issue with which epistemology has traditionally concerned itself and whose prospects divide the sceptic and his cognitivist opponent.

It is accordingly necessary to reject – flatly and categorically – the contention that the mundane conception of knowledge espoused here represents a distinct *sort* of "knowledge" contradistinguished with the actual, truly authentic Knowledge that should concern philosophers. For – so we insist – the mundane sort of knowledge that is governed by our ordinary standards *is* authentic knowledge – the only sort of knowledge worth discussing. The "knowledge of the philosophers" subject to the hyperbolic standards insisted upon by sceptics is "something else again," something whose unavailability in principle is *irrelevant* to discussions about knowledge as this concept actually figures in the conceptual scheme that is its home.

The standard use of knowledge-talk is governed by the characteristic conventions of a language that has evolved as an instrument for use in "the real world." The sort of justification needed to warrant a knowledge claim is inherent in the communicative practices that constitute the ground-rules of our language. These practices are fallible, to be sure, and are recognized as such, but nevertheless – as matters actually stand in the communicative domain in which they function – *they do in fact* DEFINE *the range of proper and appropriate uses of knowledge claims.* For knowledge-talk, as for all other varieties of talk, the rules of language are the rules of the game, affording the definitive norms of our communicative practices. Only at the cost of sacrificing the relevancy of our discussion can we turn our back upon these norms.

5. THE CHARGE OF RELATIVISM

Someone might object to this approach as follows:

> If what counts as knowledge is (as you say) subject to the proprieties of language-use and the ground-rules of communication and of probative reasoning, then surely knowledge (or what can qualify as such) will be relative to time and place and culture.

But this conclusion misses its mark. One cannot but take the stance that what "knowledge" is is to be determined entirely in the context of *our* discussions, for this, after all, is what *our* deliberations are all about and is the decisive consideration *for us.* When *we* deliberate about knowledge it is (*ex hypothesi*) the case that what counts as such is to be fixed by the frame of reference at issue with our language and our probative rules. (To talk about something else is – as we have seen – simply to change the subject.)

Of course, to say this is not to deny the truism that what is justifiedly and plausibly accepted as knowledge (i.e. *thought* to qualify as such) in *one* time or place or culture can differ from another. The ancient Greek astronomers thought they knew that the earth was positioned in the center of the cosmos, but we realize they were wrong. This sort of "relativity of knowledge" is not under dispute – the question here is not what is held to be knowledge, but what knowledge is held to be. The relativism that the objection attributes to our approach does not in fact characterize it at all. Our discussion is emphatically not committed to the idea that there is no viable distinction between what is knowledge and what is merely thought to be such.

6. THE DEFEASIBILITY OF SCIENTIFIC KNOWLEDGE

It must be recognized and stressed that scientific knowledge falls squarely within the framework of the preceding analysis. The "scientific knowledge" of yesterday more often than not turns into the error of today. Accordingly, the scientific context makes it particularly important to have a conception of potentially fallible knowledge – knowledge subject to a theoretical but not a real prospect of error.

The exactness of scientific claims makes them especially vulnerable – despite our most elaborate efforts at their testing and substantiation. There is safety in vagueness: a factual claim can always acquire security through inexactness. Just here lies the basis of the security of our ordinary-life claims, a security that makes it difficult to envisage their defeat. Take "There are rocks in the world" or "Dogs can bark." It is near to absurd to characterize such contentions as fallible. Their security lies in their indefiniteness or looseness – it is unrealistic and virtually perverse to characterize such common life claims as "defeasible." They say so little that it is "unthinkable" that contentions like that should be overthrown.

Science scorns this sort of safety, and stands in a significant contrast with our "ordinary, everyday-language discourse" in this respect. These are in a position to gain (relative) security by vagueness and imprecision. But in science we do not say "There are lions" or "Lead has a melting point" – we endeavor always to say just exactly when, where, and how. Science aims at saying not only that a certain eventuation occurs in *roughly* these-and-these circumstances, but in *exactly* such and such circumstances, and in such circumstances only, or maximally or minimally or in some other exactness-introducing way.[9]

The fact is that science makes greater epistemological demands than everyday life. In science we don't just want to be *adequately* precise for "all practical purposes" we want to

[9] Vagueness constitutes a context in which we trade off *informativeness* (precision) against probable *correctness* (security), with science moving towards the former pole, and "everyday knowledge" towards the second. The relevant issues are considered in tantalizing brevity in Charles S. Pierce's short discussions of the "logic of vagueness" which he laments as too much neglected. (See *Collected Papers*, vol. V, 5.446–450, 5.500–506, and passim.)

be *optimally* precise for "all cognitive purposes." Hence vulnerability and defeasibility are (if anything) *more* characteristic of scientific than of everyday generalization. Claims to scientific knowledge are subject to more rigorous justificatory procedures than those of our ordinary affairs, but these procedures too are fallible and are recognized by all concerned as being so.

In science, too, we operate with a mundane conception of knowledge – one that is committed to the attainability of knowledge but is realistic about what this involves. And accordingly, one must resist any temptation to reason as per the chain:

(1) Every earlier stage of "our knowledge" has contained errors
(2) This stage is in principle no different from earlier stages

∴ (3) This stage of "our knowledge" contains errors
(4) This particular theses under consideration – whichever one it be – is one of this stage

∴ (5) This thesis might be in error
(6) If this thesis is possibly in error, then we do not actually know this thesis

∴ (7) This thesis is not genuine knowledge.

One mis-step occurs at stage (5) – one which commits the error of an overly glib slide from generic considerations to the specific case.[10] For it commits the mistake of inferring that a feature which *does* belong to *some* single individual of a certain group *might* belong to every individual of that. And a further mis-step occurs at stage (6). For the "is possibility" at issue here is purely theoretical (generic) and not a matter of practical politics: it is based on considerations of *hypothetical* rather than *realistic* defeasibility, and is accordingly unable to sustain the implication at issue.[11] Collective doubtfulness at the generic, wholesale level surely does spill

[10] Compare §2 of Chapter VI above (pp. 103–107).
[11] See pp. 94–100 above.

over into distributive doubtfulness at the level of specific, retail considerations.

Consequently one cannot appropriately move along the route (3) to (5) to (7) to derive a sceptical conclusion from the presumptive truth of (3). For as we have already seen in other contexts, a realization on the basis of general principles (only!) that a claim to knowledge may ultimately have to be withdrawn does *not* invalidate it as such: this would be so only if case-specific considerations so indicated. As was insisted above (pp. 100 ff.), only case-specific indications of (realistically) possible error can invalidate our knowledge claims.

The mundane, down-to-earth aspect of all human endeavors comes to the fore once again. Our scientific knowledge too is mundane (fallible, defeasible). But this does not mean that the claims at issue are not perfectly proper and appropriate claims to knowledge. It is worth reiterating the key point that possible imperfection "on general principles" does *not* entail inappropriateness; the idea of altogether warranted but yet potentially fallible knowledge claims does *not* involve a contradiction in terms.

In scientific inquiry, we seek to determine the truth about things; this is beyond question our goal and our desire. But, of course, though we aim at this target, we fully realize that we often miss the mark. How, then, is one to characterize the relationship between our cognitive efforts and the truth at which they are directed, given that outright *identification* is out of the question here?

What we manage to do in inquiry (as far as our warranted claims about the matter stand) is neither to *attain* nor *approximate* the truth but to *estimate* it – to form, as best we can, a reasoned judgment of where the truth of the matter lies. With the progress of inquiry these estimates become better based. Given the ongoing augmentation in our data and the improvement in our methods for their utilization, it is rational to prefer the new estimate to the old one. But the basis of this rationality does *not* lie in some purely theoretical consideration like "getting near to the truth" – in a content-oriented sense akin to that in which a picture made with a better camera is more accurate. Rather it rests on the fact that all the indications on the side of application and praxis are such that there is every available reason which indicates the preferability of the new estimates over the old.

The need for such an estimative approach is easy to see. Pilate's question is still relevant. How are we men – imperfect mortals dwelling in this imperfect sublunary sphere – to determine where "the real truth" lies? The consideration that we have no *direct* access to the truth regarding the world is perhaps the most fundamental fact of epistemology. We have no lines of communication with the Recording Angel. We live in a world not of our making where we have to do the best we can with the means at our disposal. We must recognize that there is no prospect of assessing the truth – or presumptive truth – of claims in this domain independently of the use of our imperfect mechanisms of inquiry and systematization.

> You do not claim actually to have the truth here and now – not only at present but for *any* here and now. Do you not thereby abandon the whole traditional conception of science as the pursuit of truth? And does this not at once lead to a scepticism that rules out any claim to truth or to the attainment of knowledge.

This objection fails to reckon appropriately with the standard gap between aspiration and attainment. In the practical sphere – in craftsmanship, for example – we may *strive* for perfection, but cannot ever claim to have *attained* it. And in inquiry the situation is exactly parallel. On the side of aim and aspiration "the truth" is indeed what we're after. But of course in matters of theoretical science we're never in a position to claim with dogmatic certainty that we've actually got it. The most we can ever realistically do is to claim what we do have as being the very best that one can possibly obtain in the circumstances – as affording a best estimate of the truth.

This is something we must accept realistically and have no right to lament. Simple realism forbids us to regret that "we can't get outside our thought and experience to compare it with reality." We have and can have no "direct access" here and it is foolish to hanker after this. *Of course* we have to come by our view of reality via the epistemic route – not "direct inspection." It is a fallacious mis-analogy of picture-thinking to suppose that only in somehow direct or intuitive apprehension could we ever really know what things are like. The lesson here is not that there is no difference between 'what we think we know" and "the real truth," but just that we are never entitled to do more than to view the former as our best estimate of the latter, where "best estimate" means that estimate for which the best case can be made out according to the established standards of rational cogency.

We thus cannot simply follow the sceptic here and drop the reference to the truth. Our estimate is still and ineradicably an estimate of *the true answer* to the question. Without a reference to the truth we would lose our hold on the teleology of the aims that define the nature of the enterprise of inquiry, which is, after all, to obtain answers to our questions about the world and to secure information about it. And we would also lose our hold on its methods, since if one is not prepared to claim the premises to be true one cannot use logic to draw any conclusions from them (the definitive characteristic of the rules of logic being that they lead from truths to truths). The pursuit of truth is the name of the game, the definite object of the whole project of inquiry. And the rules of the game enable us to stake a claim to knowledge once we have done everything needful in this direction.

But what are we to reply to the moderate sceptic who argues as follows:

> I do not for a moment deny that people may well stake warranted claims to knowledge. What I do deny is that one can ever be sure that any of these well-warranted claims to knowledge are actually *correct* – that we ever have sufficient reason for characterizing our knowledge claims as *true*.

To see how a suitable reply can be developed, compare the situation of the sceptic who says:

> I do not for a moment deny that people may *think* that certain theses are true. What I do deny is that one can

ever be sure that any of the things one thinks is *actually* so.

The reply here is straightforward. I can never exit from the sphere of what I think to be so. No matter how much I investigate, no matter how elaborately I base my conclusion, no matter how loudly I assert it, no matter how extensively I exploit the available evidence and the vicarious testimony of the authorities – all I can ever manage to achieve in my assertions made *in propria persona* is to articulate what I think to be the case. But the very fact that this is and must be so – that it is *inevitable* that my approach to what *is* so proceeds via what *I think* to be so – means that any complaint about this situation as being cognitively unsatisfactory is simply absurd. And an analogous response is in order with respect to the initial complaint. If a limitation is indeed inevitable, we cannot reasonably be asked to transcend it.

What does the moderate sceptic of our preceding pseudo-quote want? What is he asking for? Before he concedes that our claims to knowledge are appropriate, does he ask us to somehow step outside ourselves to check our accepted knowledge-claims against reality *an sich* – a reality outside of and beyond the reach of our warranted knowledge-claims. It is plain on the very face of it that this is an absurd demand. The sceptic at issue is clearly involved in setting up unworkable requirements for knowledge-attributions – a violation of the *ultra posse nemo obligatur* principle. We can never grasp the truth direct, but only through the mediation of the epistemological procedures that warrant our claims with regard to it.

The quarrel between the sceptic and the cognitivist takes place in the no-man's land between the assertions

(1) *p* is true as best we can tell through the cognitive resources at our disposal (= is part of "the truth as we see it")

and

(2) *p* is true (= is part of "the truth as it is *an sich*").

The sceptic maintains that there is a gap here that we are simply unable to close, and takes this to be a proper basis for

Mundane Knowledge

complaint regarding the status of "our knowledge." The cognitivist admits the gap but insists that there is no earthly reason why the closing of this gap should be asked of us: seeing that there is *just no way* of avoiding the gap, its existence is no occasion for justified complaint. Granted: no claim to infallible accuracy can be advanced on behalf of "our knowledge." But no harm ensures from this realization – our claims to knowledge cannot be invalidated as somehow improper by the imposition of standards that themselves cannot in the very nature of things be met.

VIII

The "No Right" Argument and the "Ethics of Belief"

SYNOPSIS

(1) A formulation of the "No Right" Argument to the effect that it is wrong (in a moral or quasi-moral sense of the term) to claim knowledge in matters of objective fact. (2) A critique of W. K. Clifford's contention that the acceptance of a thesis on "insufficient evidence" is *wrong*. No such moral derogation is appropriate in the cognitive sphere. (3) A cognitive mistake as such is – at worst – *irrational* (rather than *immoral*). To be mistaken in one's claims to knowledge is contrary to one's best interests – certainly one's *intellectual* (or *cognitive*) interests, and presumably one's *practical* (or *material*) interests as well. (4) However, in general, the making and accepting of knowledge claims – even at the risk of error – is by no means irrational; *au contraire* it can be a sensible and prudent move, one that is indispensably necessary relative to our aims and objectives in the cognitive domain.

1. THE "NO RIGHT" ARGUMENT

The sceptic's "No Right" Argument runs roughly as follows:

1. Because of their inevitable transcendence of the evidence-in-hand, the assertive content of objective factual claims will always outrun the supportive warrant at our disposal.

2. It is irresponsible to the point of moral turpitude to make claims that outrun their supportive warrant.

∴ It is wrong to claim knowledge of matters of objective fact.

This argument in effect supplements the "No Entitlement" Argument by endowing it with the coloration of moral disapprobation.

To evaluate this line of argumentation it becomes necessary to consider more closely the propriety of such a moralistic approach with regard to the acceptance of factual theses.

2. IS ACCEPTANCE IMMORAL? CLIFFORD'S THESIS

The whole area of rational inquiry and discourse is governed by epistemological ground-rules: principles regarding rules of evidence, rules of presumption and burden of proof, etc. Why should we obey them? When the appropriate standards and norms are violated in argumentation or inquiry, a person "has no *right*" to be persuaded because "a *proper* case" has not been made out. What is the force here of *right* and *proper*? What sort of obligation or "duty" is at issue? Do these terms here bear their familiar ethical or moral sense? Does the acceptance of factual theses about the ways of the world fall within the province of ethics and moral philosophy? Is it perhaps the case – as C. I. Lewis has maintained – that "cognitive correctness is itself a moral concern, in the broad sense of 'moral'"?[1]

In his classic 1877 essay on "The Ethics of Belief" (to which William James' even more famous 1895 essay on "The Will to Believe" offered a reply), the English philosopher W. K. Clifford maintained his famous thesis that:

---

[1] C. I. Lewis, *Values and Imperatives*, ed. by J. Lange (Stanford, 1969), p. 163. This work canvasses various issues relevant to our deliberations, and its ultimate upshot does not differ greatly from that of the present discussion, since Lewis' broad sense of "morality" actually encompasses prudence. For Lewis, the moral or ethical sphere is one unified whole comprising what is usually regarded as morality proper on the one hand, and prudential issues on the other. Our present approach envisages a sharper separation between prudence and morality.

[I]t is wrong always, everywhere, and for anyone, to believe anything upon insufficient evidence.[2]

Clifford's words must be construed with care here. If
"wrong" were altered to "mistaken" the thesis would
become transformed into an unproblematic platitude. Presumably that's exactly what we *mean* by speaking of *"insufficient* evidence" – evidence whose employment as a proper
basis for credence would be a mistake. But given this re-
placement, the thesis would no longer bear the moral over-
tones which Clifford unquestionably intended it to have (as
is shown by his talk of "duties" and of "guilt" in this connection). A violation of the rules of rational procedure in the
cognitive domain was seen by Clifford as an *ethical* transgression. Clifford's discussion thus gave rise to a new project,
the "ethics of belief," and some writers even go so far as to
push this approach to its logical conclusion by pressing it
towards the boundaries that separate the morally reprehen-
sible from the legally criminal. For example, in Janet Chance's
ardent little book on *Intellectual Crime,* one finds "the
making of statements that outstrip the evidence" prominently enrolled on the register of this category of "crimes."[3]

[2] *Lectures and Essays* by W. K. Clifford, ed. by L. Stephen and F. Pollock
(London, 1879; 2nd ed. 1886); originally published in the *Contemporary Review,*
vol. 30 (1877), pp. 42–54. In actual fact, Clifford did not adhere to this hyperbolic
standard throughout his epistemology. Rejecting the prospect of certainty in the
area of *scientific* knowledge, he took the line that man's scientific "knowledge" of
nature rests on various principles that are not in the final analysis justified on cognitive grounds at all, but must be accounted for in terms of natural selection. The
principle of the uniformity of nature is a prime example, and "Nature is selecting
for survival those individuals and races who act as if she were uniform; and hence
the gradual spread of that belief over the civilized world." (*The Common Sense of
the Exact Sciences* [London, 1885], p. 209.)

[3] Janet Chance, *Intellectual Crime* (London, 1933), pp. 33–34. This tendency of
thought is also found in John Locke. There is, he wrote, "one unerring mark by
which a man may know whether he is a lover of truth for truth's sake," namely *"the
not entertaining of any proposition with greater assurance than the proofs it is built
upon will warrant."* (Quoted in John Passmore, *A Hundred Years of Philosophy*
[Harmondsworth: Penguin Books, 1968], p. 95. Locke is sometimes cast in the role
of the founder of the "ethics of belief." (See, for example, H. H. Price, *Belief* [London,
1969], pp. 130 ff. and cf. fn. 3 above.) But Locke hinges the matter wholly on "the
mind, if it will proceed rationally, ought to [do]." (*Essay Concerning Human Understanding*, Bk. IV, chap. 15.) He sees the imperative at issue as strictly instrumental
vis-à-vis rationality. Later on, however, the situation changes in this regard. Passmore speaks of the "striking degree of moral fervor" by which this precept was
espoused by agnostic thinkers in nineteenth century England.

We must examine this doctrine that it is wrong – and in effect *morally* wrong – to accept anything that has some tincture of fallibility about it, and accordingly that it is wrong to accept any objective factual claim.

3. VIOLATING THE PROBATIVE RULES IS IRRATIONAL RATHER THAN IMMORAL

William James quite properly argued against Clifford that the enterprise of inquiry is governed not only by the negative injunction "Avoid error!" but no less importantly by the positive injunction "Achieve truth!" [4] And, in the domain of objective fact – where the "evidential gap" means that the assertive *content* of our claims unavoidably outstrips information we can ever gather by way of supportive *evidence* for them – this goal of achieving truth inevitably demands (so James insisted) running a risk of error. There is nothing irra-

---

[4] James wrote "*We must know the truth*; and *we must avoid error* ... are two separable laws. ... We may regard the chase for truth as paramount ... or we may, on the other hand, treat the avoidance of error as more imperative, and let truth take its chance." (*The Will to Believe and Other Essays in Popular Philosophy* [New York, 1899], pp. 17–18.) The situation in ethics as between a negative morality ("Avoid evil!") and a positive morality ("Promote good!") is of course a parallel. For a useful outline of the James-Clifford controversy and its background see Peter Kauber, "The Foundations of James' Ethics of Belief," *Ethics*, vol. 84 (1974), pp. 151–166, where the relevant issues are set out and further references to the literature are given. And see also *idem*, "Does James' Ethics of Belief Rest on a Mistake?" *Southern Journal of Philosophy*, vol. 12 (1974), pp. 201–214. For a particularly interesting recent treatment see Roderick Chisholm, "Lewis' Ethics of Belief" in *The Philosophy of C. I. Lewis*, ed. by P. A. Schilpp (La Salle, 1968), pp. 223 ff., and compare Roderick Firth, "Chisholm and the Ethics of Belief," *The Philosophical Review*, vol. 68 (1959), pp. 493–506. See also: Peter Hare and Edward Madden, "William James, Dickinson Miller and C. J. Ducasse on the Ethics of Belief," *Transactions of the Charles S. Peirce Society*, Autumn 1969, No. 3, pp. 115–129, and Bernard Williams, "Deciding to Believe" in Howard Kiefer and Milton Munitz (eds.), *Language, Belief, and Metaphysics* (Albany, 1970), pp. 95–111. More recently, see Peter Hare and Peter Kauber, "The Right and Duty to Will to Believe," *Canadian Journal of Philosophy*, *IV*, No. 2, December 1974, 327–343; James Muyskens, "James' Defense of a Believing Attitude in Religion," *Transactions of the Charles S. Peirce Society*, Winter 1974, Vol. X., No. 1, 44–54; and A. E. Johanson, "'The Will to Believe' and the Ethics of Belief," *Transactions of the Charles S. Peirce Society*, Spring 1975, Vol. XI, No. 2, 110–127. For various ramifications of the James-Clifford controversy regarding the ethics of belief see the interesting essay by Alex C. Michalos, "The Morality of Cognitive Decision-Making," in M. Brand and D. Walton (eds.), *Action Theory* (Dordrecht and Boston, 1976.

tional – let alone *wrong* – about accepting this risk. Quite to the contrary: "a rule of thinking which would absolutely prevent me from acknowledging certain kinds of truth if those kinds of truth were really there, would be an irrational rule." [5] Only by being willing to run in the race do we stand a chance – however slim – of winning it: "Nothing ventured, nothing gained." Running the risk of error is the most fundamental requisite of the cognitive life.

H. H. Price has put the key point at issue here very well:

> But "safety first" is not a good motto, however tempting it may be to some philosophers. The end we seek to achieve is to acquire as many correct beliefs as possible on as many subjects as possible. No one of us is likely to achieve this end if he resolves to reject the evidence of testimony, and contents himself with what he can know, or have reason to believe, on the evidence of his own first-hand experience alone. It cannot be denied that if someone follows the policy of accepting the testimony of others unless or until he has specific reason for doubting it, the results will not be all that he might wish. Some of the beliefs which he will thereby acquire will be totally incorrect, and others partly incorrect. In this sense, the policy is certainly a risky one. ... But it is reasonable to take this risk, and unreasonable not to take it. If we refuse to take it, we have no prospect of getting answers, not even the most tentative ones, for many of the questions which interest us (for example "What is the population of London?" "Did London exist 300 years ago?" "If it did, what was its population then?"). [6]

As James cogently argued, if we want to engage in the cognitive enterprise – if we want to obtain answers to our questions about the world – we have no choice but to accept a risk of error, a risk which we cannot evade altogether, however ardently (and rightly!) we strive to reduce its magnitude.

[5] *The Will to Believe and Other Essays in Popular Philosophy* (New York, 1899), pp. 27–28.

[6] H. H. Price, *Belief* (London, 1969), p. 128.

The James-Clifford controversy emits a lesson of profound importance for epistemology. It constrains us to recognize that as regards the theory of knowledge (as in other ways) we live in an imperfect world. The ultimate ideal of absolute perfection is outside our grasp: the prospect of proceeding in ways wholly free from the risk of error is not attainable in this epistemic dispensation.

Errors can be of two kinds:

(1) A type I error that arises when *p* is in fact true, but is not accepted.
(2) A type II error that arises when *p* is accepted, but is not in fact true.

Type I errors reject truths, type II errors accept untruths.

Now in the imperfect epistemic dispensation in which we live and move and have our being there is an inherent trade-off between these two kinds of error. They stand in inseparable coordination: any really workable mechanism of cognition can only avoid errors of the first kind (excluding truths) at the expense of incurring errors of the second kind (including untruths). The situation is as portrayed in Figure 1. As the placement of point (1) indicates, if we insist upon adopting an epistemic policy that allows no type II errors – admitting no untruths at all – then we are constrained to all-out scepticism: we can accept nothing and are thereby involved in a total exclusion from the whole realm of truths. The placement of point (3), on the other hand, indicates that, as we insist with increasing stridency upon reducing the exclusion of truths and curtailing type I errors, we are compelled to an increasingly gullible policy that allows the goats to wander through the gate alongside the sheep.

What we have in hand is clearly a minimax problem: the object of the enterprise is to minimize a quantity of the type $F(x,y) = ax + by$ or some comparable but more complex (nonlinear) formula of coordination. We want to allow the optimal balance of truths attained relative to errors excluded. The total idealization of achieving the whole truth (no type I errors) and nothing but the truth (no type II errors) is simply not part of the practical politics of the situation. In the conduct of our cognitive affairs – as in other departments of life – we must do the best we can in the circumstances: what one might *in abstracto* think of as the absolute ideal is simply not attainable in this mundane dispensation.

FIGURE 1
HOW A COGNITIVE MECHANISM INVOLVES
A TRADEOFF BETWEEN THE TWO KINDS OF ERROR

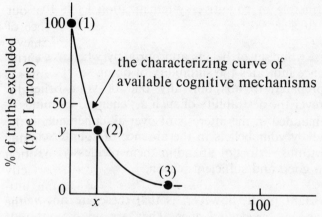

Agreeing with James as to the irrationality involved in neglecting the commandment to "Achieve truth!" we maintain, however, that no specifically *ethical* or *moral* obligation is operative in the epistemic injunctions against the acceptance of inappropriate claims to truth (or to knowledge). The issue is one of self-deprivation rather than one of moral turpitude – of prudential losses rather than ethical transgressions. One must avoid the temptation to construe all uses of right/proper in a specifically moral sense. For this fails to do justice to the vast range and scope of rule-governed activity, and slurs over the distinction between importantly different types of rules and norms. These, after all, encompass not only the moral and prudential and legal, but logical, linguistic, and cognitive – as well as the constituting rules and the efficiency rules of every sort of human praxis from games playing to carpentry. To break a rule is not necessarily to commit a *moral* transgression or something approximating thereto; a very different sort of sanction can be at issue.

The enterprise of rational inquiry into the nature of the world is governed by a sizable complex of cognitive imperatives, all of which are subject to the ruling injunction: Adapt your beliefs to your experience – and that of others – as efficiently and "economically" as possible. This fundamental principle of cognitive systematization leads to such corollary rules as:

1. Revise your set of beliefs appropriately whenever experience indicates the suitability of doing so.
2. Be prepared to abandon any one of your beliefs wherever the desirability of such a "change" of mind is demanded in the interests of over-all coherence.
3. Stand by your beliefs in the absence of counter-considerations – do not abandon them recklessly, without a good and sufficient reason.

The important point, however, is that these are not *moral* injunctions, but *prudential* ones. They are injunctions that convey the principles of cognitive rationality – rules of art (the art of right reasoning), and not rules of morality. They do not deal with unconditional ends but with purpose-relative means. They relate to teleological considerations of purpose realization, specifically, in the case of inquiry, falling subject to the ruling cognitive goal of securing the optimal answers to our questions about the world. The issue is one of prudence, not of morality.

A claim to knowledge undoubtedly proclaims an entitlement-to-assent – a "right to be sure." But the entitlement at issue is not a *right* in the specifically moral sense of the term. For the obligation to be rational is not a *moral* obligation, and lapses from rationality are not *moral* lapses. They do not violate the valid claims of others but involve the frustration of one's own objectives as a member in good standing within the community of rational inquirers.

In the light of such considerations, Clifford's ethico-moral interpretation must be rejected. The goals relevantly operative in the cognitive sphere relate not to our moral ends but to our prudential means in the proper management of rational inquiry, exposition, discussion, and argumentation. The sanctions of erroneous cognition are not those of *morality* but those of *rationality* – of intellectual rather than ethical standards.[7] The rules of ethics and morality are correlative with the purpose of avoiding damage to the rights and interests of people – preeminently *other* people. By contrast, the person who violates the evidential standards simply manages to reason badly. The probative ground-rules of inquiry are correlative with certain specific purposes: the acquisition of truth in the endeavor to achieve intellectual and physical control over nature. The interests that the man who departs from the norms of cognitive appropriateness damages are in the first instance his own – in falling away from the principles of right reason into irrationality, he frustrates his own *cognitive* objectives of getting at the truth of things (and presumptively his *practical* objectives of successfully goal-realizing action as well). The resultant sanctions fall directly and immediately upon him himself, and upon others (if at all) more or less incidentally. The irrationality at issue is a matter not of *immorality*, but one of *imprudence* – of comporting oneself so as to impede the very objectives (theoretical and practical alike) of the cognitive enterprise on which one is engaged.

To be sure, the person who sets out *deliberately to deceive others* by means of improper assertions or deceptive reasonings is morally culpable, just like the person who makes a false promise or who sets out to offend others deliberately by boorish behavior.[8] But it is not possible to insist too emphatically that there is nothing inherently deceptive about knowledge claims made in appropriate conditions and circumstances. Admittedly, there is no gainsaying the evidence-transcendence of objective factual claims. But no deceitful

---

[7] John Locke was already quite clear on this issue. Cf. n. 3 above.

[8] This role of knowledge claims as extending assurances and guarantees to others is stressed by J. L. Austin in "Other Minds." It is clear – and unproblematic – that insofar as *I* seek to induce *you* to believe and act on the basis of my knowledge claims a moral issue is operative.

exaggeration is involved here – no improper guarantees are intended or extended. Everyone in the linguistic community can be presumed to have learned the warranting rules for our knowledge-claiming assertions. The "rules of the game" are known to everybody – or must be presumed to be so. No one (among those duly informed) will think that claims formulated in the language of knowledge thereby extend improper and unrealistic assurances.

To be sure, someone might be tempted to object as follows:

> Cognitive rationality is surely not wholly a matter of prudence, to the entire exclusion of moral considerations. After all, man has a moral or quasi-moral duty to make the most of his natural endowments. And making the most of our natural endowments calls for adherence to the rules of right reason. Accordingly, adherence to these rules becomes a matter of duty as well.

But this line of argumentation is mistaken. A circumstantially necessary condition for the discharge of a moral duty does not itself thereby become a moral duty. (I may have a moral duty to honor my promise of being in a certain place at a certain time, and it might, in the circumstances, be a necessary condition thereof that I drive beyond the speed limit, but that does not make my driving beyond the speed limit a matter of moral duty.)

Again, somebody might object as follows:

> Even if you are right in holding that what is at issue is a matter of the procedural principles of rationality, does this not still generate an ethical aspect through the higher-level principle that *People ought to be rational*?.

The reply here is straightforward. Of course, people *ought* to be rational – this is something that one must admit and indeed insist upon. But this "ought" is not at bottom one of a specifically ethical orientation. For people ought also to be perceptive, sensitive, intelligent, open-minded, healthy, handsome, etc. The "ought" here is not, however, a *moral* ought, but one of the cosmic fitness of things. It does not indicate an operative principle of human action, but represents an idealized vision of the optimal arrangements of the world.[9] The world *ought* to be a place where things go properly. But people have no more a *duty* to be good believers than they have a *duty* to be good rememberers or good learners, however desirable it may be in the larger scheme of things for them to be so.[10]

Yet is there not a moral duty to do what we can to realize the good – to enhance the actualization of positive value in the world? Of course there is! But this holds for *every* sort of good or value. It does not establish these goods or values as specifically ethical ones, and it does not establish failures to realize these goods (save when motivated by malice) as *moral* failures.

The person who is defective in point of rationality – who reasons inadequately, thinks poorly, and argues badly – is akin to the person who is defective in point of intelligence. His failings are not *sins* but *defects*, not offenses but disabilities. They are more to be pitied than censured. (Of course, the case of *deliberate* transgression is a very different one.) Insofar as reckless assertion beyond the available evidence may, when given credence, cause others to have and act on mistaken beliefs, it can also, of course, be a matter of wrong-doing – certainly so when this results from faults of character [e.g., cupidity] rather than faults of intellect [e.g., stupidity].

The crucial point is that the rules of evidence are principles of rational argumentation which define what is "right and proper" in a *procedural* sense relating to the adequate conduct of inquiry, and this is something quite different from the "right and proper" of ethical evaluation or moral criti-

[9] Of course, whenever such an "ought" of cosmic fitness is operative, there is a correlative duty to cultivate and promote its realization. But this represents quite a different issue. People ought to speak correctly or do their sums properly. But that does not make departures from correct speech or correct arithmetic *ethical* transgressions.

[10] The "ought" at issue is what I have elsewhere called that of *evaluative metaphysics* in contrast with that of *normative ethics* – it is, if you like, the moral ought of a world-creator rather than that of a world-occupant. See "The Dimensions of Metaphysics" in *Essays in Philosophical Analysis* [Pittsburgh, 1969], pp. 229–254, where the relationship between these two modes of deontology is explored.

cism. And the governing factor with respect to this issue of procedural rationality is the teleology of the enterprise – its purposes and objectives, preeminently the achievement of intellectual and physical control over the world we live in. It is these purposes of the enterprise – including the acquisition of information about our common world and effective communication with one another about it – that determine the rules for its rational conduct, rules among which the established principles of plausibility and presumption play an important part. This controlling role of purposive efficacy renders the issue one of prudence rather than morality.

One issue should be made quite explicit in this connection. In the ethical case *"ought"* implies *"can."* But *can* we avoid accepting objective factual claims on less than *deductively* conclusive evidence: do we really have an option here? Clearly not – for as we have seen such claims are inherently evidence-transcending – as we have seen, they cannot just reflect the evidence actually at our disposal, a particularism that would destroy their communicative utility. (And our repeated recourse to the *ultra posse* principle once again comes into operation at this juncture.) Our *appropriate* cognitive claims do not "distort the evidence" – the evidential gap to the contrary notwithstanding. In implementing the use-conditions that are basic to the language we use they *fit* the evidence in the only way it is reasonable and realistic to ask for.

This, then, is how one can tackle the following sceptical argument:

> It is misleading, and perhaps even deceitful, ever to claim actual knowledge. At most, one can speak of one's "best estimate" of the truth, relative to the usual conditions and standards.

Now there is indeed *something* to this. In claiming knowledge we cannot do more than "the very best we can" to establish the item at issue. But the key point is simply that when this is appropriately done, then the ground-rules of the language do fully entitle us to stake knowledge claims. And the claims we stake (in the standard circumstances) will be both proffered and received in just this way, as issued under the aegis of the established conditions and standards that govern our talk of knowledge.

The key question of "the ethics of belief" is whether someone who stakes a claim to knowledge is thereby automatically being hypocritical and involved in making exaggerated assertions where (as common parlance has it), "he actually knows better"? Surely not! The way an assertion is standardly intended by its "sender" must be construed as correlative with the way it is to be construed by its "recipient." When I say "I know that *p*," I must expect *you* to construe this circumstance as "Rescher claims to know [or maintains he knows] that *p*." And if I am conscientiously concerned to preserve my credibility, I will only make such assertions in circumstances where I have good reason to believe them to be true. But their *actually* being true – as contradistinguished to my *holding* them to be true and having good (or excellent or effectively conclusive) grounds for making them – is not and cannot be a legitimate precondition of my rational entitlement to make such an assertion. For the only handle that I have on the issue of the actual truth of *p* proceeds via the issue of whether there is good (or excellent or effectively conclusive) reason for me to maintain *p*. To insist that the truth of *p* itself – independently of any justificatory warrant I may have to it – is a *precondition* of my rational entitlement to claim to know that *p* is to impose an illegitimate (because *in principle* unrealizable) condition. We have – and can have – no *independent* access to the truth-status of *p* save via the epistemological route of evidential warrant for claiming *p*.

4. IS ACCEPTANCE IRRATIONAL?

Yet even if it is granted that the making and accepting of claims to objectively factual knowledge – under the realistic conditions of cognitive fallibilism – is not *immoral*, is there nevertheless not someting *irrational* about it once the inherent defeasibility of such claims is recognized? If we recognize and admit that our acceptance-commitments "might be wrong" (even though we view this prospect as rather far-fetched), then why should we say that we *know* these things, thereby seemingly contradicting this realization?

The answer is simply that this line of objection is based on a misleading premiss. As we have seen, factual knowledge claims are *not* in fact so absolutistic as to gainsay any and all possibility of error whatsoever; they are not automatically inflated beyond the range of reachability. Quite the reverse. The issuing and accepting of knowledge claims just is not – as the sceptic has it – an illegitimate pretence to cognitive possessions to which we have no right, but a useful and legitimate part of the apparatus of communication in facilitating the transaction of our human affairs.

The key fact is that the issuing and accepting of knowledge claims – even at the risk of error – is by no means irrational. On the contrary, it is an eminently sensible and prudent move, in exactly the same sort of way that other things we do are sensible and prudent – namely as appropriate means towards the realization of our legitimate goals. Given the goals of the cognitive enterprise – the achievement of intellectual and physical control over nature and of effective communication with one another – the making and accepting of objectively factual knowledge claims should *and can* be something altogether prudent, reasonable, and above all) *justified*.

IX

The "No Foundation" Argument

SYNOPSIS

(1) The "No Foundation" Argument claiming that the validation of our knowledge must terminate in a bedrock of self-justifying claims, and that such perfectly sure theses cannot be had in the domain of objective fact. (2) A nonfoundationalist approach to cognitive validation via the mechanisms of plausibility and presumption affords the means for dispensing with the idea of a self-evidencing bedrock, and so averts the impact of the "No Foundation" Argument. (3) Scepticism heedlessly violates the standard probative ground-rules governing our use of language in the area of knowledge claims. (4) These ground-rules embody certain presumptions regarding the operation of the standard "source of knowledge," presumptions which cannot be brushed aside without violating the social contract that underlies our communicative discourse. (5) The "methodological turn" of a presumptist approach also makes it possible to avoid the infinite regress of justification envisaged in the sceptic's "No Proof" Argument.

1. THE "NO FOUNDATION" ARGUMENT

With a mixture of admiration and exasperation Leibniz said of the Electress Sophie of Hanover that she always sought to know the reason why behind the reason why (*Elle veut tousjours scavoir la raison de la raison*). The why/because cycle can be pushed on without end, and clearly no satisfactory validation can be obtained on the basis of an infinite regress. We cannot go on *ad indefinitum* doing the cognitive equivalent of putting earth on back of elephant on back of tortoise on back of alligator, etc. But how can the process of rational justification, once launched on its way, ever find a stopping-point?

The only resolution is seemingly afforded by terminating the justificatory regress at the ultimate stopping point of a *self-evidencing* foundation – an ultimate epistemic *ne plus ultra* that itself stands in no need of any sort of support or substantiation. It would seem that in the final analysis a point must be reached where the adversary's challenge is met with a stonewalling insistence that the end of the line has been reached. And then the sceptic's argumentation comes into operation once more, proceeding in a manner cogently set out in the following passage from Aristotle:

> Some hold that, owing to the necessity of knowing the primary premisses, there is no scientific knowledge. Others think there is, but that all truths are demonstrable. Neither doctrine is either true or a necessary deduction from the premisses. The first school, assuming that there is no way of knowing other than by demonstration, maintained that an infinite regress is involved, on the ground that if behind the prior stands no primary, we could not know the posterior through the prior (wherein they are right, for one cannot traverse an infinite series): if on the other hand – they say – the series terminates and there are primary premisses, yet these are unknowable because incapable of demonstration, which according to them is the only form of knowledge. And since thus one cannot know the primary premisses, knowledge of the conclusions which follow from them is not pure scientific knowledge nor properly knowing at all, but rests on the mere supposition that the premisses are true. The other party agree with them as regards knowing, holding that it is only possible by demonstration, but they see no difficulty in holding that all truths are demonstrated, on the ground that de-

monstration may be circular and reciprocal. Our own doctrine is that not all knowledge is demonstrated: on the contrary, knowledge of the immediate premises is independent of demonstration. (The necessity of this is obvious; for since we must know the prior premises from which the demonstration is drawn, and since the regress must end in immediate truths, those truths must be indemonstrable.) [1]

The sceptic steps in at this stage of the discussion, pressing a line of argumentation which may be set out in the following "No-Proof" Argument:

1. Adequate demonstration can only proceed from premises whose claims to acceptability have *already* been made good.
2. But the supporting premises cannot be made good, seeing that whatever evidencing considerations may be adduced in their support will not yield a cogent probative basis of support until they themselves have become established through the specification of adequate support of their own, so that we are launched upon a stultifying regress.

∴ A probatively adequate basis can never be devised for any claim to knowledge.

This historic and influential line of reasoning seemingly confronts the cognitivist with a stark alternative: Either find

---

[1] *Posterior Analytics*, Bk. I, chap. 3 (Oxford translation). The basic idea of this regress argument goes back to Plato's *Theaetetus* (209E–210B). In a recent restatement by Anthony Quinton, this line of thought is traced out as follows:

If any beliefs are to be justified at all, . . . there must be some terminal beliefs that do not owe their . . . credibility to others. For a belief to be justified it is not enough for it to be accepted, let alone merely entertained: there must also be good reason for accepting it. Furthermore, for an inferential belief to be justified the beliefs that support it must be justified themselves. There must, therefore, be a kind of belief that does not owe its justification to the support provided by others. Unless this were so no belief would be justified at all, for to justify any belief would require the antecedent justification of an infinite series of beliefs. . . . [Such "terminal" beliefs] are needed to bring the regress of justification to a stop . . . [and what] is required is that they should not owe their justification to any other belief. (Anthony Quinton, *The Nature of Things* [London, 1973], p. 119.)

a stopping-point in the regress of justificatory grounds for knowledge or else be prepared to recognize that your knowledge claims must be abandoned as vitiated by circularity or infinite regress.

Faced with this unpleasant choice, cognitivists have generally opted for the first alternative. We encounter here a long and distinguished tradition – a tradition beginning with the characteristic definitions basic to Aristotle's view of scientific knowledge, and continuing with the decisive ("cataleptic") perceptions of the Stoics, the "clear and distinct perceptions" of Descartes, the self-evidencing judgments of the school of Brentano, the protocol statements of Moritz Schlick, Rudolf Carnap, and the logical positivists of the Vienna Circle, the givens of C. I. Lewis, and the self-evident claims of Roderick Chisholm in our own day, which all exemplify the approach of this *foundationalist* school of thought.[2] The position at issue is "foundationalist" because it espouses the idea that there is some category of primary and immediate truths capable of providing the ultimate, certain, self-certifying propositions that provide the starting-point and ultimate basis of cognitive justification – a starter-set, as it were, of *basic* cognitions.[3]

This approach provided the motive for Descartes' search – basic to the whole Cartesian program of methodological scepticism – for a secure, Archimedean point to serve as fulcrum for the lever of knowledge-acquisition (the "clear and distinct" apprehensions of the mind). Throughout, the same fundamental idea is operative. There are two classes of cognitions, in that (1) there are basic and self-evidencing truths at which we arrive by some immediate, nondiscursive process of validation, and (2) there is the rest of what is known, all of

[2] See F. Brentano, *Wahrheit und Evidenz* (ed. O. Kraus, Leipzig, 1930). The most influential present-day advocate of an epistemological position along Brentano-esque lines is R. M. Chisholm (see this *Theory of Knowledge* [Englewood Cliffs, N.J., 1966]). Compare also R. Firth, "Ultimate Evidence," *The Journal of Philosophy*, vol. 53 (1956), pp. 732–739; reprinted in R. J. Swartz (ed.), *Perceiving, Sensing, and Knowing* (New York, 1965), pp. 486–496.

[3] As one recent commentator on C. I. Lewis puts it, such emphasis on the given aspect of sensory presentation "helps him to respond to the scepticism that would follow the grounding of knowledge in a merely probable base. If the structure of empirical knowledge cannot be built on certainty somewhere in experience, then empirical knowledge would not be probable but only probably probable." (M. G. Murphey and E. Flower, *A History of Philosophy in America*, vol. 2 [New York, 1977], p. 899.)

which is validated on the basis of the former by suitable discursive processes of deductive or ampliative reasoning.[4]

Modern epistemologists have continued remarkably faithful in their attachment to the central themes of this foundationalist model of cognitive systematization which can be described without exaggeration as the mainstay of Western epistemology. We are repeatedly told of the need for *immediate* or *basic* or *"protocol"* truths of fact to provide a secure foundation for the epistemic structure of our knowledge of truth: other items are made to rest upon them, but they rest upon no others: like the axioms of a deductive system they provide the ultimate support for the entire structure. In the order of cognitive justification some beliefs are epistemically prior to others, and some are such that no others are prior to them. With these we hit rock bottom, as it were – they provide the ultimate supports on which the whole structure is erected.

The sceptic turns this line of thought to his advantage. He attacks foundationalism by attacking its key requisite – the foundation. Where, he asks, are we ever to get absolutely certain and theoretically failproof theses about the real world. And he deploys arguments of which the sceptics' strictures against the senses are typical. When we are told that "Seeing is believing," the sceptics say *nonsense*! And he adduces such counterexamples as the straight stick that looks bent when held at an angle under water, the distorted color vision of the jaundiced man, etc.

The sceptic accordingly sets out the simple syllogism of his "No Foundation" Argument:

1. Knowledge demands an ultimate foundation in a family of basic, self-evident, absolutely certain claims.

[4] For an informative survey and critique of recent foundationalism see Anthony Quinton, "The Foundations of Knowledge" in B. Williams and A. Montefiore (eds.), *British Analytical Philosophy* (London, 1971), pp. 55–86. Various important recent papers on aspects of foundationalism are reprinted in Pt. V, "Does Empirical Knowledge Have a Foundation?" of R. M. Chisholm and R. J. Swartz (eds.), *Empirical Knowledge* (Englewood Cliffs, 1973). A comprehensive collection of papers on recent foundationalism and its critics is given in G. S. Pappas and M. Swain (eds.), *Essays on Knowledge and Justification* (Ithaca and London, 1978). This book also contains a useful bibliography of the subject.

2. In matters of objective knowledge about the world, there are no certain, self-evidencing propositions.

∴ No objective knowledge about the world can be attained at all.

The sceptic's reaction to a foundationalist approach to knowledge has always been at bottom the same: a denial that there is any such adamantine bedrock of absolutely secure contentions about the objective facts of the world.[5] In proceeding this way, the sceptic agrees (at least for the sake of the argument) that knowledge must be grounded and that such grounding can only be effective on a basis of foundational and somehow self-evidencing propositions. But he now goes on to insist that this requirement cannot be satisfied – that there just are no such foundational and self-evidencing (immediately certain, cataleptic) theses available to play this crucial role. After all – says the sceptic – even if we grant *in abstracto* the ancient Stoics' idea that *cataleptic* ("clear and distinct," "self-evidencing") perceptions automatically yield authentic knowledge, the difficulty always arises in each and every particular case whether this perception in hand is indeed cataleptic? Once this issue itself becomes a matter of contention, the capacity of the supposedly foundational propositions to serve this function effectively is seriously undermined.

This problematic issue of the special theses that are to provide the basic foundation by serving in the role of ultimate axioms of our knowledge has always proven to be a major source of difficulties for foundationalism. On the one hand, they must be very secure (certain, "self-evident" or "self-evidencing") to be qualified themselves to act as supports that can themselves dispense with all need for further substantiation. But on the other hand, they will have to be enormously content-rich, since they must carry on their back the whole structure of knowledge. These two qualifications stand in an irresolvable conflict with each other.

---

[5] The foundationalist, of course, uses this self-same syllogism, but he turns it on its head. Negating the conclusion, he simply negates the second premiss as well. (We ourselves, on the other hand, maintain the falsity of the *first* premiss.

Insofar as any statement provides information about the world (e.g., "I now see a cat there" which entails, *inter alia*, that a cat *is* there), it is not invulnerable to a discovery of error. But insofar as it is safeguarded (e.g., by some guarding-locution such as "I take it that . . .", so that we have "It now seems to me that I see a cat there" or "I am under the impression that I see a cat there"), a statement relates to appearance instead of reality and becomes denuded of objective content. Egocentric statements of phenomenological appearances may have the requisite security, but are devoid of objective information; claims regarding "external" reality are objectively informative, but are in principle vulnerable.[6] And so, the quest for protocol statements as a foundation for empirical knowledge has always foundered on this inherent tension between the two incompatible desiderata of indubitable certainty on the one hand and objective factual content on the other. This tension makes for a weak point which sceptics have always been quick to exploit.

The sceptic's key point is essentially this. To attain theoretical certainty we must draw back from making claims formulated in the language of objectivity ("That *is* an apple") to claims formulated in the language of subjective appearance ("I take that to be an apple," "That looks like an apple to me"). But in taking this step – a step which runs through foundationalism from the "clear and distinct perceptions" of Descartes to the "(self)evident perceptions" of Roderick Chisholm – we run into insuperable difficulties. For we cut ourselves off from the prospect of realizing objective knowledge about the world. There is – and can be – no certainty-preserving, failproof epistemological bridge from the realm of subjective appearances to that of objective reality. This is a point on which sceptics have always insisted, and one has little alternative but to concede it to them. The ensuing deliberations will endeavor to show that this "No Foundation" argument nevertheless fails to realize the sceptic's purposes

[6] Recognition of these and other weaknesses of foundationalism has in contemporary times not been spearheaded by coherentists – its idealistic advocates were ineffectual, and its positivist adocates (i.e., Neurath and his sympathizers) were unsuccessful. The only effective opposition has centered about the refuationism of K. R. Popper's *Logik der Forschung* (Vienna, 1935; tr. as *The Logic of Scientific Discovery*, New York and London, 1959; 2nd edn. 1960).

because it involves him in a profound misreading of the
probative situation in regard to burden-of-proof considerations.

2. DISPENSING WITH FOUNDATIONS

There are two possible ways of meeting the sceptical line of
argumentation at issue in the "No Foundation" Argument.
The first is to tackle Premiss 2 of the argument and to maintain that a perfectly secure and satisfactory foundation is in
fact available. This line is not open to us here, because of our
commitment to the view that the evidence-transcendence of
objective factual claims does indeed preclude the achievement of an utterly failproof and theoretically total security
on their part. Accordingly, we shall have to tackle Premiss 1,
rejecting the need in cognitive justification for any foundational bedrock of self-justifying theses.

The considerations of the preceding chapter provide the
materials needed to implement such an approach. For due
recourse to the principles of plausibility and presumption
shows that the validation of knowledge claims can perfectly
feasibly dispense with any recourse to self-validating ultimates. No one wants to deny the need for *inputs* into the
process of validating factual knowledge. But these inputs
need not – even ultimately – be of the *foundational* sort; they
need not be basic, ultimate, "immediate," self-evidencing, or
anything of that nature. Presumptions can provide a workable stopping point – a stopping point not in terms of absolute (self-evident, irrefrangible) truths, but in affording theses
that deserve to stand unless duly overthrown.[7]

A useful way of viewing scepticism is to regard it from
the perspective of the standard probative ground-rules – particularly the ideas of presumption and burden of proof. The

---

[7] Such a recourse to presumptions, *prima facie* truths, or theses of initial credibility, is sometimes called a *modest foundationalism*. (See, for example, Mark Pastin,
"Modest Foundationalism and Self-Warrant" in G. S. Pappas and M. Swain (eds.),
Essays on Knowledge and Justification (Ithaca and London, 1978), pp. 279–288. This
is quite misleading. A thesis whose status is so tentative that it needs supporting
more than it itself has any support to offer is scarcely of *foundational* status. Their
status as *inputs* into the cognitive process does not make a *foundation* of theses at
issue.

sceptic's traditional line is that burden-of-proof considerations operate decisively in his own behalf. Whenever a knowledge claim is made, the burden of proof against it is – so the sceptic maintains – effectively insuperable. The reasoning by which he supports this conclusion runs somewhat as follows: (1) *Agenti incumbit probatio*: the burden of proof always goes against one who takes a positive step in argumentation or reasoning. Now the acceptance of theses and the advancement of knowledge claims are clearly positive steps, so that the burden of proof always goes against one who takes this step at any given stage of the probative process. However, (2) *a thesis can only be justified from accepted premisses*. This being so, one cannot adequately justify any propositional acceptance at all. For no matter how far one carries the process back there still remain those further – i.e., yet undefended – assertions against which a burden of proof yet inclines. This is how the sceptic sees the matter. But he does not see it aright.

The pivot-point here lies in the simple but crucial fact that a legitimate "burden of proof" *must be capable of being discharged*. No rational argumentation or deliberation could ever get off the mark if the sceptics' view of an insuperable burden were correct.

The conception of "burden of proof" is standardly correlative in rational dialectics with the idea of *presumption* – i.e., of "presumptively true" theses that deserve the benefit of doubt in the absence of counter-indications.[8] Thus consider, by way of example, the following pattern of argumentation:

(1) S-members generally have ϕ
(2) There is no cogent reason to think that this particular S-member x differs from the rest in ϕ-relevant respects (i.e., there are not within our epistemic

---

[8] For some recent philosophical discussions of presumption see: Louis I. Katzner, "Presumptions of Reason and Presumptions of Justice," *The Journal of Philosophy*, vol. 70 (1973), pp. 89–100; James W. Lamb, "Knowledge and Justified Presumption," *The Journal of Philosophy*, vol. 69 (1972), pp. 123–127; J. E. Llewelyn, "Presuppositions, Assumptions and Presumptions," *Theoria*, vol. 28 (1962), pp. 158–172; and William Edward Morris, "Knowledge as Justified Presumption," *The Journal of Philosophy*, vol. 70 (1973), pp. 161–165. See also the author's *Dialectics* (Albany, 1977).

horizons any case-specific counter-indications to x's being ϕ).

∴ (3) x too may be presumed to have ϕ: that is, assumed to have ϕ "until further notice" – until some indication to the contrary is given.

Such reasonings illustrate the role of presumption in the context of the principles of rational inquiry.

The considerations at issue here require a deeper look at preconditions of rational inquiry and argumentation. The ruling purpose of communication is to convey information. And this entire process of information transmission is predicated on an inclination to give credence to the assertions of others – it presupposes the tendency to accept them as true and as duly warranted, at least as provisionally, that is as *presumptively* so, in the absence of any specifically problem-indicative data.

The processes of inquiry and of communication are subject to this idea that certain sorts of support entitle a claim to count as acceptable – at any rate provisionally and *pro tem*. In particular, our ordinary, standard probative practice in empirical inquiry stipulates a presumption in favor of sensory observation, of memory and records, of inductive reasoning, etc. The ground-rules that govern rational deliberation and discussion are such that we standardly accept the claims derived from these sources as veridical until proven otherwise. Here we may think back to the position of the Scottish school of "common sense" philosophy which maintained that, while our usual sources of knowledge are by no means infallible, a *presumption* of veracity nevertheless rests on their side – they are to be trusted in the absence of specific counterindications: they are "innocent until proven guilty."[9]

[9] See Thomas Reid, *Essay on the Active Powers of the Mind* in William Hamilton (ed.), *Reid's Philosophical Works* (London, 1895), p. 617. This approach goes back to the Academic Sceptic Carneades (fl. 170 B.C.), who rejected the Stoic idea that sense impressions are decisive ("cataleptic"), assigning them a merely presumptive veracity like that of the "witness" in a trial, the symptoms in medical diagnosis, or the messengers conveying a report. (Compare Charlotte L. Stough, *Greek Scepticism* [Berkeley and Los Angeles, 1969], p. 62.)

One way of establishing a rationale for the usual ground-rules of presumption and burden of proof is with reference to communication and its ultimate evolutionary rationale. Informative communication rests on the basic postulate or presupposition that people by and large "know what they're talking about." As H. H. Price has written in regard to the special case of the presumptive veracity of the assertions of other people:

> Let us try to imagine a society in which no one would ever accept another person's testimony about anything, until he had completely satisfied himself about the *bona fides* of that person, his powers of accurate observation and capacity for recalling accurately what he had observed. Such a society would hardly be a society at all. It would be something like the State of Nature described by Hobbes, in which the life of every man is solitary, poor, nasty, brutish and short.[10]

This perspective underlies the Principle of Trust, the principle which H. H. Price has formulated in the injunction: "Accept what you are told, unless you see reason to doubt it." He says regarding this principle:

> What our Lockean observer calls credulity is a necessary condition for social cooperation. What he calls credulity is not only in the long-term interest of each of us. It has a moral aspect too. If some people make a virtue of accepting testimony so readily, they are not wholly mistaken. Am I treating my neighbour as an end in himself, in the way I wish him to treat me, if I very carefully examine his credentials before believing anything he says to me? Surely every person, just because he is a person, has at least a *prima facie* claim to be believed when he makes a statement? This claim is not of course indefeasible. But it might well be argued that we have a duty to trust him unless or until we find pretty convincing reasons for mistrust, and even to give him "the benefit of the

[10] H. H. Price, *Belief* (London, 1969), p. 114.

doubt" if we have some reasons for mistrusting him, though not conclusive ones.[11]

And if this can be said for the testimony of others there is, *a fortiori,* bound to be no less strong presumption of veracity for the "testimony" of *our own* sources of information: memory, the senses, etc. And not only do such testimonial sources come into the picture, but also such discursive resources as the principles of inductive reasoning. Our probative practice of empirical inquiry as standardly conducted stipulates a presumption in favor of the senses, of memory, the inductive ground-rules, etc. We standardly do, and – given the nature of language as an instrument of communication – are rationally entitled to accept the claims derived from these sources as veridical until proven otherwise, as innocent until proven guilty.[12]

Of course there will be many situations where we must be sceptical, where doubt is appropriate and trust should be put into suspension; cases where we need to be convinced and must probe for grounds in the best "I'm from Missouri" tradition. But this distrustful stance – go ahead and convince me! – only makes sense in a contest of agreed probative ground-rules on whose basis the construction of a cogent case is in principle possible. A convincing case can only be demanded where one views its provision as in principle possible and is prepared to concede the mechanisms for its being made. And so the posture at issue presupposes the operation of suitable rules of presumption and burden of proof. These considerations indicate the rational inappropriateness of the stance that every cognitive circumstance requires a sceptical

---

[11] H. H. Price, *Belief* (*op. cit.*) pp. 114–15; see especially the chapter on "Belief and Evidence," pp. 92–129. Compare J. H. Newman, who speaks of certain sources as having a *"prima facie* authority" and suggests by way of illustration that, in particular, "tradition, though unauthenticated, being (what is called) in possession, has a prescription in its favor, and may, *prima facie,* or provisionally, be received." (*A Grammar of Assent,* Chap. 9, Pt. 3, Sect. 2.)

[12] Many epistemologists have taken this general line. Alexius Meinong, for example, rightly denies that "seeing is believing" and insists that senses yield only presumptive conclusiveness (*Vermutungsevidenz*). (See his monograph *Uber die Erfahrungsgrundlagen unseres Wissens* [Berlin, 1906].) Again, H. H. Price maintains that the senses yield only "prima-facie evidence." (*Perception* [New York, 1903]; see p. 148, and especially p. 185.)

abstention from assent.

And there is sound reason behind our standard of probative practice. The most elemental considerations of the
nature of rational inquiry indicate that the why/because cycle
of sceptical challenges cannot be pushed *ad indefinitum*, but
must come to a stop at some appropriate place. Just as we
must not explain the obscure through the yet more obscure
(expounding *ad obscurum per obscurius*) so we must not substantiate the questionable through the yet more questionable.
We must not be placed into a position where the only grounds
we can ever give for a contention are more problematic than
the contention itself.[13] The task of the standards of plausibility and presumption is to ensure that this illicit demand is
never put upon us within the setting of standard probative
practice.

Our actual probative standards are rooted in the conditions for making out a conclusive (probatively solid) case in
rational controversy. And these ground-rules of rational discourse and inquiry embody the standards and norms of presumption and burden of proof – with respect to knowledge
claims, *inter alia*.

On such a recourse to *presumptive* truths – themselves
always essentially defeasible – it transpires that questions
about truth and knowledge are not at all settled at the outset
of inquiry at the input level. The validation of claims as
genuinely known comes at the end of the process of analysis
and inquiry rather than at its beginning, and the claims that
are eventually validated emerge as true not in the first but in
the final analysis – on the basis of coherentistic best-fit

---

[13] As Ludwig Wittgenstein has it, "I want to say: my not having been on the
moon is as sure a thing for me as any grounds I could give for it." (*On Certainty*
[Oxford, 1969], sect. 111. Or again:

> When one says that such and such a proposition can't be proved, of course that
> does not mean that it can't be derived from other propositions; any proposition
> can be derived from other ones. But they may be no more certain than it is
> itself. (*Ibid.*, sect. 1.)

It is this general rule of epistemic argumentation that the premises must be no less
perspicacious than the conclusion that Hume has in mind when he says "To have
recourse to the veracity of the supreme Being, in order to prove the veracity of our
senses, is surely to make a very unexpected circuit." (*Enquiry*, Sect. XII, Pt. I, para.
120.) The ideas at issue go back to Aristotle's insistence in *Posterior Analytics* that
the premises must be "(cognitively) *prior*" to the conclusion.

considerations.[14] On this line of approach, *knowledge* is *always* a matter of output – the processing machinery from which it emerges needs no hard, certain, indefeasible *inputs* at all.[15] (We must reject the old idea that even as life must come from *life*, so knowledge must come from *knowledge*.) Inputs there must indeed be, but they can be frail and defeasible. They are of the order of claims by certain standard "sources": the senses, memory, inner perception (reflection), and the like, or again rest on the deployment of certain inductive mechanisms, such as appeals to analogy, simplicity, economy, or the like. The coherentism at issue takes the stance that knowledge does not originate in a foundationalist process of derivation from "basic knowledge," but in a process of extraction from a raw material that is less than knowledge because of its merely presumptive weight, an extraction whose *modus operandi* is afforded by a process of best-fit systematization.

While such an approach issues in questions of detail that pose complex issues – issues whose adequate resolution ultimately calls for the construction of a comprehensive theory of knowledge[16] – the fact remains that such a presumptivist strategy of approach does provide a means for averting the impact of the sceptics' "No Foundation" Argument for the unattainability of knowledge. In denying that cognitive validation must have the Euclidean structure of a system that terminates in an axiomatic bedrock – thus rejecting the first premiss of the "No Foundation" Argument – we remove the justification basis of its conclusion. A presumptivist strategy of cognitive justification thus makes it possible to avert the "No Foundation" Argument, and to do so even without taking on the unpalatable task of a *frontal* attack arguing that a foundation is indeed attainable.

[14] This is the key motivating idea of the so-called "coherence theory" of truth. For further information and for references to the literature see the author's *The Coherence Theory of Truth* (Oxford, 1973).

[15] This idea that all knowledge is certified as such only discursively – that all knowledge is ultimately inferential – is common to Carneades, Hegel, and Peirce (however differently they may implement this shared view).

[16] For the author's essays in this direction, see *The Coherence Theory of Truth* (Oxford, 1973), *Methodological Pragmatism* (Oxford, 1977), *Plausible Reasoning* (Assen, 1976), and *Cognitive Systematization* (Oxford, 1979), *Induction* (Oxford, 1980).

It warrants note that the operation of burden-of-proof considerations also invalidates the second premiss of the sceptic's "No Proof" argument. The regress of reasons is no stultifying entry upon an endless and vitiating retreat, but a reliance on the operative standards (assertion-conditions) of the very language by which we communicate with one another. The regress of reasons must indeed end, but it need not terminate in a *self-evident* contention (as the classical epistemologists were inclined to hold), but in one that merits the presumption of truth in that the burden of proof lies with one who would challenge this contention.[17]

3. SCEPTICISM AND BURDEN OF PROOF

One need not read long in the sceptical literature to see just how the sceptic runs afoul of considerations of burden of proof and presumption. Take perception-based claims: "That is a window" will do for an example. The sceptic immediately protests: "How can you be certain?" And he proceeds to deploy the whole Cartesian demonology with which we are only too familiar. How can we be so sure a deceitful spirit is not at work with lights and mirrors? How can we guarantee the whole of our cognitive life is not being staged for a pickled brain by a mad scientist playing a tape? How can we tell that the totality of our perceptions is not being arranged on another planet by clever beings affecting our brains with electrostatic discharges? In sum: What categorical assurances can be obtained that the whole stage of our experience is not merely one vast Potemkin village?

Burden-of-proof considerations sweep all such worries aside. They say in effect: "Do not plague me with these merely hypothetical possibilities. If you are in a position to adduce any positive, *case-specific*, indications that here and now, in the concrete circumstances of this particular claim, mirrors may be involved or evil scientists at work, well and good. Let us look into the matter more closely. But, given

[17] For further details regarding the workings of the principles of presumption and burden of proof see the author's *Dialectics* (Albany, 1977).

the standard mechanisms of presumption and burden of proof, purely conjectural hypothetical possibilities just don't count in probative situations. What does count is only what the available evidence indicates to be a genuine prospect under the circumstances."

When the sceptic refuses to grant the standing presumption in favor of our established cognitive resources – when he simply abandons the usual common-sense practice of granting a presumption of veracity to our senses, our memory, our practices of inductive reasoning, and the like – he thereby rejects the serviceability of the very materials from which alone our knowledge of the world is – or can be – constructed. Accordingly, the sceptic moves towards such positions as agnosticism regarding factual matters, solipsism in abstaining from belief in the existence of other people, cognitive isolationism in the rejection of the vicarious evidence of others, etc. All these positions are a direct consequence of rejecting the presumptive veracity of our standard cognitive resources.

When it comes to the validation of our empirical beliefs about the contingent arrangement of what goes on in the world, the sceptic in effect refuses to adopt the usual probative evidential rules of procedure. When we adduce the data of the senses, of memory, etc., in support of such beliefs, the sceptic simply denies their probative weight. "You admit," he says in a Cartesian tone of voice, "that these data-sources occasionally deceive you; so how can you be confident that they do not go amiss in the case in hand?" Given that the only sort of evidence we could possibly adduce in the specific circumstances will itself have to be of the very type whose probative weight the sceptic calls into question, we have no way of meeting his argument head-on. But scepticism profoundly misreads the dialectical situation in rational deliberation by insisting on taking the *initial* situation (viz., a burden of proof against the thesis maintained at the outset) as *ultimate* (viz., a burden of proof against *every* contention, even those introduced evidentially at later stages).

Throughout the sphere of empirical reason, the rules of probative praxis must be allowed to do their proper work of showing where presumptions lie and how the burden of argumentation can be shifted – one cannot be allowed to redesign them so as to cut one's opposition off from all further prospect of argumentation. After all, if it were simply a *request for justification* that were at issue, then this would have to be understood as itself subject to the appropriate ground-rules of evidence in the building up of a justificatory case. But in undertaking a blanket rejection of the usual principles of presumption and benefit of doubt, the sceptic renders it in principle impossible to provide the sort of case he demands. Accordingly, the sceptic's stance, in effect, begs the question (perhaps "begs the conclusion" would be better) by laying down conditions which block from the very outset the development of the case he challenges his opponent to produce.

On his home ground of theoretical argumentation regarding conjectural possibilities, the sceptic's position is thus no doubt secure and irrefutable. By refusing to accept the standard probative grounds *as grounds* – as capable of constituting a rational basis of warrant for acceptance – the sceptic assures the security of his position. He sets up a standard for "knowledge" so hyperbolic that he *systematically denies evidential weight to those considerations which alone could be brought to bear in making out a case to the contrary.* But surely, whatever victory the Pyrrhonian sceptic is able to gain by this sort of strategy will have to be altogether Pyrrhic. The victory won by one who systematically refuses to grant the evidential weight of considerations contrary to his position is at once inevitable and empty.

4. SCEPTICISM AND THE JUSTIFICATION OF OUR PROBATIVE STANDARDS

The sceptic simply turns his back upon the whole of our standard machinery of presumption and burden of proof. And it is all too understandable why he does so. For its guiding conception lies in the principle that in suitable circumstances *one needs grounds* to call into question the thesis on whose behalf the weight of presumption and burden of proof rest. And this idea that something positive may be needed to ground the appropriateness of calling a contention into question is anathema to the sceptic. The very idea of a presumption – of a thesis which must be allowed to stand until set aside by positive, case-specific considerations – is one which the sceptic has no option but to reject. For the sceptic wants to insist that a thesis can only be established if another thesis is already established, so that the whole process of validation cannot ever get off the ground. The idea that a positive claim must be established to set aside a duly qualified presumption throws the sceptic's whole program off the track.

However, a sceptical objector may well press the issue further, arguing as follows:

> The preceding line of reasoning shows the need – in interests of rationality – to admit SOME canons (standards, principles) of presumption and proof. But why should one accept *these* (that is, our actual) probative standards? *Quis custodiet ipsos custodes?* Upon what validating considerations do the probative standards of presumption and proof themselves rest?

This line of questioning is not without its merits. There will, to be sure, have to be some appropriate rationale of justification for our probative ground-rules. And if it were simply this legitimation that the sceptic is asking for, his demands would not be unreasonable, and could certainly (in principle) be met. But in transmuting the need to justify the principles for allocating benefit of doubt into a ground for distorting the nature of this allocation – turning it, in effect, against the theses it initially favored – the sceptic takes an unwarranted step that vitiates his position.

Still, one must grant that the sceptic is entitled to ask: "What gives you the right to impose *your* probative standards and procedures on *me*? How can you actually establish their propriety?" The answer is straightforward. If it is *knowledge* as the language deals with it that we wish to discuss – and not some artificial construct whose consideration constitutes a change of subject – then we must abide by the standards and norms of the conceptual scheme in which this concept is at home. And this simply is not a matter of playing the game by X's rules instead of Y's. It is not a conventional game that is defined by the rules we arbitrarily adopt, but an impersonal set of rules established in the public instrumentality of a language. We must not afford the sceptic the luxury of a permission to rewrite at his own whim the warranting standards for the terminology of our cognitive discourse. (He cannot substitute a more rigoristic standard for *counting as knowledge*, any more than he can substitute a more rigoristic standard for counting as a dog, say a standard that ruled chihuahuas out as just too small.) The probative standards of rational discussion cannot be brushed aside without violating the social contract that underlies our discourse. Rational discussion and inquiry and controversy could never come into existence but for the operation of certain rules of presumption – preeminently including the presumption that people say what they believe to be true and the presumption that they are generally right about this. In failing to make effective contact with the conceptual scheme in which our actual knowledge claims in fact function, the sceptic assumes an untenable posture in the setting of the debate he is endeavoring to conduct.

Here it is not morality but prudence that comes into operation – our shared self-interest of being able to acquire any information at all about the world. The crucial interest at issue is that of the community of rational inquirers, with its established rules of procedure and methodology. The sceptic cannot dismiss these rules without violating the social contract that underwrites the use of language in inquiry and discussion.

The sceptic has to negotiate the vessel of argumentation in very tight waters. For he presents himself as a devotee of "sweet reasonableness," seeing that he insists that it is always *unreasonable* to lay claims to knowledge. And here "unreasonable" must be construed in terms of the accepted norms of rational argumentation. For at *this* stage of the argument the sceptic cannot make recourse to some idiosyncratic standard of his own, but must conduct the discussion on "our" standards, that is, *everybody's* – the usual ones. Since he has taken a *rational controversy* into hand,[18] he just is not in a position to reject the pre-systematic doctrine-neutral reasonableness which he needs for the dialectical development of his own program. And at this stage, so we insist, his cause becomes lost, seeing that the reasonableness to which he must subscribe itself embodies the very standards for valid claims to knowledge that he proposes to reject.

5. THE METHODOLOGICAL TURN

But exactly how can such an approach based on a recourse to our probative methods get rid of the potential infinite regress of justification inherent in the "No Proof" Argument by which the sceptic assails the prospects of cognitive validation? Cannot the sceptic simply question the basis of our probative principles of plausibility and presumption, thereby launching another regress on the way?

The answer is: No. And its key lies in observing the essentially *methodological* status of plausibility and presumption as probative tools of inquiry. This methodological aspect reorients the issue in a new and different direction, a reorientation which makes a crucial difference to the structure of justificatory argumentation because different planes of consideration are involved. It is necessary to give a careful heed to the essentially Kantian distinction between substantative *theses* on the one hand and regulative *methods* on the other.

It is indeed ultimately unsatisfactory to adopt the purely discursive course of justifying theses in terms of further theses and so on until, perchance, we reach an unproblematic

---

[18] The obvious exceptions here are those among the ancient sceptics who looked on scepticism not as a *doctrine* but as a *mode of life*, declining to advance any theses and espousing no arguments but simply advocating (as *seemingly* advantageous on various grounds) a policy of life free from all cognitive commitments – and from any commitment to rationality as well. It is clear that this form of scepticism steps outside the arena of rational debate – one cannot carry on a rational controversy against the posture of the abandonment of rational controversy. Here one can at best point out the evident truth that the abandonment of the cognitive venture carries with it sanctions that – as best we can tell – more than offset any supposed advantages of this alternative course.

bedrock. But reflection on the structure of cognitive validation shows that this is not our only option. Rather, we can
justify our acceptance of certain factual theses because (ultimately) they are validated by the employment of a certain
method of inquiry (the scientific method in the case of objective factual knowledge). We thus break outside the cycle of
justifying thesis by thesis, thanks to the fact that a thesis can
be justified by application of a cognitive method. And then
we justify the adoption of this method in its turn in terms of
certain *practical* criteria. (With respect to *methodology*, at
any rate, the pragmatists were surely in the right – there is
certainly no better way of justifying a *method –any* method
– than by establishing that "it works" with respect to the
specific tasks held in view.) Exactly how "successful praxis"
is to be construed here is a large issue that can be left open
for present purposes. (Presumably it is to be construed in
terms of the traditional trinity of the aims of science –
success in explanation, prediction, and control over nature,
i.e., the various cognitively relevant sorts of problem solving.
And one would also join C. S. Peirce in imposing certain
structural criteria – general applicability, transcultural and
transtemporal range, self-correctiveness, etc.)

Such a dialectic of justification breaks out of the restrictive
confines of the sceptic's regress argumentation, and does so
without relapse into a dogmatism of unjustified ultimates.
For we now justify the acceptance of a thesis by reference to
the method by which it is validated, then justifying this
method itself in terms of the classical pragmatic criterion of
methodological validation. Such a line of approach blocks
the route towards scepticism by a complex, two-stage
maneuver, combining the method-utilizing justification of
the *theses* that embody our claims to knowledge with the
pragmatic justification of the cognitive *methods* themselves.
The sceptic's charge that the validation of knowledge always
presupposes *prior* knowledge, so that the justificatory enterprise cannot adequately get under way, can thus be defeated
by "the methodological turn" with its recognition of a dualism of propositional and procedural rationality. And this
methodological turn, with its reliance on the presumptions and
presuppositions of the practical sphere, accordingly also

makes it possible to avoid the infinite regress of justificatory argumentation envisaged in the sceptic's "No Proof" argument.[19]

[19] For a fuller working out of this general strategy of epistemological validation, see the author's *Methodological Pragmatism* (Oxford, 1977).

X

The "No Source" Argument

SYNOPSIS

(1) The sceptic's "No Source" Argument maintains that we have no sources competent to the authentication of knowledge. (2) An examination of the "Poisoned Well Principle" of Descartes to the effect that a source that is once wrong might well be wrong in this case. (3) Implications of the "Poisoned Well Principle" for the nature of cognitive sources: a source that is sometimes mistaken can never yield knowledge. (4) The inherent failings of the Cartesian approach. (5) A refutation of the "No Source" Argument: infallibility need *not* be demanded of an appropriate source of knowledge. A cognitively useful source need not be of unfailing accuracy – its *presumptive* veracity will adequately serve our needs. (6) What sort of work principles are called upon to do and how the presumption of the veracity of an established source operates.

1. THE "NO SOURCE" ARGUMENT

Descartes wrote that "In the matter of the cognition of facts two things alone have to be considered, ourselves who know and the objects themselves which are to be known. Within us there are four faculties only which we can use for this purpose, viz. understanding, imagination, sense, and memory . . ."[1]

---

[1] "Rules of the Direction of the Mind," in *The Philosophical Works of Descartes*, Vol. I, ed. by E. S. Haldane and G. R. Ross (London: Cambridge University Press, 1934), p. 35.

Most epistomologists agree with this general approach of granting a central place to the sources of knowledge. But the recognition of such "sources" as duly qualified leaves a problem. If the question "How can we decide, in any particular case, whether we actually know?" is seriously intended, then the reply "An ostensible item of knowledge is genuine if, and only if, it is the product of a properly accredited source of knowledge" is not likely to be viewed as sufficient. For such a reply leads at once to the further question: "How are we to decide whether an ostensible source of knowledge is indeed properly qualified as such?"

And so, yet another line of sceptical argumentation unfolds through a denial of the availability of any adequately competent sources of knowledge. Since classical antiquity, the reliability of such sources – the senses, memory, self-awareness (or "inner consciousness"), reason, etc. – has been called into question. Fastening on to such doubts, the sceptics have argued that any such imperfect and fallible "sources" cannot provide the assurance necessary for the authentication of actual knowledge. The sceptics' argumentation runs along the following general line:

1. To qualify as a proper source of *knowledge*, a source must be in a position to guarantee the security of its deliverances beyond any doubt or question – its reliability must be such as to preclude all prospect of error; it must, in sum, be infallible.
2. None of the so-called "sources of knowledge" that are actually at our disposal are infallible in this way.

∴ None of our so-called "sources of knowledge" are in fact able to qualify as genuine sources of knowledge.

Descartes himself is the philosopher who has given the widest currency and most emphatic emphasis to this line of thinking. Let us begin by examining his argumentation on this issue more closely.

2. THE "POISONED WELL PRINCIPLE" OF DESCARTES AND THE QUEST FOR INFALLIBILITY

In the *Meditations*, Descartes stage-managed his doctrine of doubt through a series of successively more radical theses and hypotheses, ranging from the standard ancient sceptical contentions about the fallibility of the senses through the life-but-a-dream argument to the hypothesis of the powerful deceitful demon who unfailingly misleads us into accepting error for knowledge. To be sure, the sceptical worriment induced by illusions, dreams, and demons is only one chapter in Descartes' story. His main aim and interest does not end at this negative stage, but looks beyond it to the foundation of a rational program of positive cognition to which scepticism is but a methodological preliminary. Nevertheless, despite his positive and constructive aims, a certain highly sceptical principle lies at the basis of Descartes' program, a principle which he articulated as follows in Book I of the *Meditations*:

> All that I have, up to this moment, accepted as posses- sed of the highest truth and certainty, I received either from or through the senses. I have observed, however, that these sometimes mislead us and IT IS THE PART OF PRUDENCE NOT TO PLACE COMPLETE CONFIDENCE IN THAT BY WHICH WE HAVE EVEN ONCE BEEN DECEIVED.

Let us designate this emphasized principle – the stricture to the general effect that the prudent man always avoids drink- ing from the well which once gave him indigestion – as the *Poisoned Well Principle*. What is at issue here is a principle of rational caution having the general structure:

once wrong → possibly wrong in any given case → possibly wrong in *this* case.

Using "$wr(S, c)$" to symbolize "The source S is wrong (mis- taken, in error) in the case c", we may represent this chain of reasoning as follows

$$(\exists c)wr(S, c) \rightarrow \lozenge (\forall c)wr(S, c) \rightarrow \lozenge wr(S, c^*)$$

where c^* is the particular case in question.

It is clear that the second of these entailments is not forth-coming on the basis of logic alone. The inference from $\Diamond(\forall x)\phi x$ to $\Diamond \phi y$ poses difficulties. To be sure, one can move unproblematically from $(\forall x)\Diamond \phi x$ to $\Diamond \phi y$, but the step from $\Diamond(\forall x)\phi x$ to $(\forall x)\Diamond \phi x$ hinges on the Barcan formula, which fails to hold in many sorts of situations. It is possible that all humans might have perished prior to 1800 (in a plague of some sort), but that certainly does not make it possible for little Johnny Smith (b. 1970) to have perished prior to 1800.

Moreover, the first entailment has its difficulties as well. It relies on a very questionable generalization step in reasoning from "Some sense-based propositions are false" to "All sense-based propositions might be false." The inference at issue has the form:

$$\frac{\text{Some } X\text{'s are } Y\text{'s}}{\text{Therefore, All } X\text{'s might be } Y\text{'s}}$$

But this pattern of reasoning is not, of course, valid in general. We clearly cannot move from "Some integers less than 10 are integers less than 5" to "All integers less than 10 might be integers less than 5." It is simply probatively in-sufficient – given the logic of the situation – to justify the conclusion that any and every sense-based proposition *might* be false by invoking the fact (however true) that some of them in fact *are* false. (Cf. pp. 103ff. above.)

Since the Cartesian inference in view is thus clearly not forthcoming on the basis of abstract logic alone, it is clear that a substantive assumption regarding the nature of "being wrong" must be at work here. This prospect needs closer scrutiny. The propriety of allowing retail errors to invalidate wholesale sources must be examined.

3. IMPLICATIONS OF THE POISONED WELL PRINCIPLE FOR THE OPERATION OF COGNITIVE SOURCES

Given the fact (which is not being controverted here) that we must make *certain* of what we know – that valid knowledge-claims preclude the concession of even *possible* error – the Cartesian position envisages the move from a single failure to a generalized fallibility. One may stress the general reliability of such a source as strongly as one likes ... "It goes amiss but once in 100 or once in 1,000,000 cases." Still, our pleas will be brushed aside with the response: "Even if the source goes amiss only once in a blue moon, the prospect still arises that this case is such a case. We therefore must not claim certainty for the case before us. And so the source cannot qualify as a source of *knowledge*." The consideration that anyone who does sufficiently many arithmetical calculations will eventually make *some* mistake would thus be used to support the fallibilist conclusion that no arithmetical calculations whatsoever – not even $2 + 2 = 4$ – are absolutely trustworthy. In its negative and sceptical bearing, the Poisoned Well Principle leads to the result that an error-admitting source of informative claims cannot possibly qualify as a source of *knowledge*. And "source" here can be construed very broadly to embody any sort of cognitive faculty, process, or principle.

The sceptical implications of such a position are obvious. For what sources of information do we mortals have that do not on occasion misfire? Where among our sources of information – be they mental or sensory, personal or vicarious, empirical or rational – is that Homer who does not occasionally nod? No cognitive source at our disposal can pass the test of *total* reliability. And then, we are told, no available source is actually a source of knowledge. The Poisoned Well Principle clearly commits us to such a result. It requires us to say with respect to our information-sources:

> ever wrong → *not* knowledge-producing.

Subjecting this thesis to contraposition we obtain

> knowledge-producing → *not* ever wrong.

And so it follows that the only way in which the quest for a source of knowledge can escape the destructive impact of the Poisoned Well Principle is by finding an absolutely *infallible* source – a wholly error-free knowledge source or faculty or process.

Given the Poisoned Well Principle, a source of knowledge must not only yield certainty so as to be a source of *infallible claims*, it must be an *infallible source* of claims as well. The margin of tolerance is zero; a source can afford no mistakes whatsoever without a decisive detriment to its standing as a source.[2]

4. THE CARTESIAN "DEUS EX MACHINA"

Once the Poisoned Well Principle is accepted, the quest for knowledge is immediately transformed into something far more difficult – a quest for infallibility. Purported knowledge can only qualify as real knowledge if it originates in an infallible source. The sceptical utility of this conclusion is obvious.

On the other hand, however, it now emerges that *even a single item* of authentic knowledge will at once bring us into the presence of an *inherently infallible general source of knowledge*. We are in the situation of the Archimedean lever. Give us but one single, solitary piece of knowledge and we are already in a position to move mountains in the epistemological realm. Exactly this is why the *cogito* is of such transcendent importance for Descartes. It yields nothing terribly exciting and informative in itself. But it provides the one thing we need to get the whole mechanism of Cartesian epistemology moving – an authentic item of knowledge, which then, in turn, becomes source-authenticating. The single knowledge-item represented by the *cogito* suffices to validate a general resource of knowledge, to wit, the "clear and distinct perceptions" of the mind. All seems well. But there are worms in the woodwork.

A serious problem lurks in the background of Descartes'

[2] J. H. Newman for one clearly saw the inappropriateness of such a Cartesian demand that only an infallible source can be the source of a failproof claim:

> If indeed I claimed to be infallible, one failure would shiver my claim to pieces; but I may claim to be certain of the truth to which I have already attained, though I should arrive at no new truth in addition as long as I live. (*A Grammar of Assent* [London, 1870], Chap. 7, Sect. 2.)

It is clear that item-certainty is one thing and source-infallibility something else, and that very different issues are involved here.

sceptical argumentation. For we have two Cartesian entailments:

$$\left[\begin{array}{l} \text{It is clearly and distinctly} \\ \text{manifest to me that } p \end{array} \right] \rightarrow \text{I know for certain that } p$$

and

[I know for certain that p] → It *is* certain that p.

When put together these yield:

$$\left[\begin{array}{l} \text{It is clearly and distinctly} \\ \text{manifest to me that } p \end{array} \right] \rightarrow \text{It } is \text{ certain that } p.$$

There is clearly a difficulty here. The antecedent of this entailment relates to the *egocentric* issue of what is (suitably) manifest to me. It deals with what I do, nay "must," think: what I cannot but accept. However, the consequent relates to the perfectly objective and impersonal issue of what is in fact the case (and indeed certainly so). There is a patent discontinuity here, a theoretical gap that must be bridged by some appropriate device. This is a difficulty whose resolution within the Cartesian program has, even from the outset, never managed to satisfy its critics.

Descartes' "clear and distinct perception" will, like any sort of *perception*, have to lie within the domain of the cognitive activity of a mind. Perception – no matter how cataleptic or clear and distinct – thus remains a fundamentally psychological and person-correlative process. As long as we remain in the domain of what is manifest to us (no matter how sharply, forcibly, etc.) we are locked into an egocentric sphere, the domain of what is uneliminably self-referential. The radius of our world goes to zero, its dimensions shrink to a single minuscule point – ourselves. There we are stuck. God help us! God help us indeed . . . for only God can get us out – as Descartes himself soon came to realize.

The plot of Descartes' *Meditations* is strikingly reminiscent of Goethe's *Faust*; the Evil One wins fair and square all along the line until in the final act he is cheated of his seemingly deserved victory by a hostile *deus ex machina*. The sceptic in fact carries everything before him until at last he meets the insuperable obstacle of divine intervention. This sort of story makes for better drama than philosophy. Where did things go wrong?

It is clear that things went wrong pretty much right at the outset – with the Poisoned Well Principle itself. It would appear to be a thoroughly ill-advised step to rule out the prospect of obtaining actual knowledge from imperfect sources. A workable epistemology must envision an effective role in the "production" of knowledge for potentially fallible sources of information. The cold and cruel fact is simply this, that imperfect sources are the only ones there are. If we cannot make do with them, we must retire and leave the sceptic in possession of the field.

But there is no reason for us to do so. For the Poisoned Well Principle is clearly untenable. It envisions an unrealistic and improper cognitive standard, and embodies an absoluteness that is simply unworkable. If we want to have a realistically workable theory of knowledge we must be prepared to reckon with the fallibility of man. J. L. Austin put the point well:

> The human intellect and senses are, indeed, inherently fallible and delusive, but not by any means *inveterately* so. Machines are inherently liable to break down, but good machines don't (often). It is futile to embark on a "theory of knowledge" which denies this liability: such theories constantly end up by admitting the liability after all, and denying the existence of "knowledge".[3]

The key difficulty of a Cartesian foundationalism is simply that it asks too much of its sources. They must be perfect and failproof – unlike any pope of this world they must always speak with *ex cathedra* infallibility. And this is altogether unrealistic. There is no need – and no justification – for asking our cognitive sources for more than they can ever deliver in this mundane dispensation. Here again we must operate within the orbit of the *Ultra posse nemo obligatur* principle. A source is not asked to guarantee the truth of its deliverances but just to establish a presumption of truth in its favor.

---

[3] "Other Minds" in *Philosophical Papers* (Oxford, 1961), pp. 44–84 (see p. 66).

In the present context of the Poisoned Well Principle, as so often with scepticism, we see that the sceptic arrives at his conclusion of the unattainability of knowledge through the hypertrophy of cognitive standards – through setting up a series of requirements for "genuine knowledge" that is *in principle* unrealizable in the circumstances of the case.

5. REJECTING THE "NO SOURCE" ARGUMENT

It emerges that what goes awry with the "No Source" Argument is its very first premiss, the claim that a source must be infallible to qualify as a source of *knowledge*. For what validates a claim as authentic knowledge is not – or need not be thought to be – determined purely and solely in terms of its *source*, but is, rather, a matter of its over-all standing in the cognitive scheme of things. The decisive thing is not the starting-point of the question "What is its source?" but the ending-point of the question: "What are its *over-all* credentials (the source being only one consideration here)?" A workable theory of knowledge must recognize that the decisive issue here is not that of provenience, but that of its systematic fit within the whole structure of cognition.[4]

A source is not something whose weight need of itself be final or decisive: its cognitive bearing need not be *conclusive* but merely *presumptive*. Indeed, the very fact that a source has become established as a source constitutes a presumption in favor of its deliverances. Admittedly, our sources are imperfect: all cognitive routes available to man are fallible. (The second premiss of the "No Source" Argument is quite correct.) But there is no harm in this, as long as we are content to ask of our sources not irrefrangible accuracy but merely presumptive veracity. What, after all, is the characteristic and appropriate work of a source? It is simply and merely to give some nonevidential support to a contention, some content-external basis for affirming its truth (as distinct

---

[4] This is a theme which the author has broached in various books: *The Coherence Theory of Truth* (Oxford, 1973); *Methodological Pragmatism* (Oxford, 1977); *Dialectics* (Albany, 1977); *Cognitive Systematization* (Oxford, 1979); and *Induction* (Oxford, 1980).

from giving *grounds* for what is being claimed). Accordingly, a cognitive source begins to render a useful service once it provides some tincture of presumption – it need make no pretences to invariable (and indeed not even to preponderant) correctness. We must simply reject the hyperbolic idea that a fallible source is thereby necessarily a contaminated and thus useless source.

The fallibility of our sources does *not* destroy their cognitive utility. Knowledge claims are not to be impugned through guilt-by-association. As we have seen, generic considerations (of the undiscriminating sort that we have characterized as G-doubt) are inappropriate as a basis for invalidation of knowledge claims. Only case-specific considerations (of the sort that validate S-doubt) can appropriately serve here. There is thus reason why an eminently useful and suitable "source of knowledge" should not be fallible and be allowed the luxury of an occasional error. For a cognitive source is never asked to bear – of and by itself – the whole burden of the claim that its deliverances are indeed knowledge. The "No Source" Argument relies on a quite mistaken premiss in this regard.

6. PRESUMPTION AND BURDEN OF PROOF

The crucial question is: just what is to be asked of a "cognitive source," what sort of work it can reasonably and properly be expected to do. And it lies in the very surface of the issue that we cannot reasonably expect them to be infallible, since this is something quite outside the sphere of practical politics in human affairs. As Alexius Meinong rightly stressed, the so-called "data" of sense, memory, etc. are (reasonable) *suppositions* (*Vermutungen*) which can lay no claims to automatic veracity, but only to *plausibility* (*Vermutungsevidenz*) – evidence which warrants no exaggerated confidence because "the justification of the supposition and its nonfulfillment are by no means incompatible."[5] Accordingly,

---

[5] Alexius Meinong, "Toward an Epistemological Assessment of Memory" in R. M. Chisholm and R. J. Swartz (eds.), *Empirical Knowledge* (Englewood Cliffs, 1973), pp. 253–270.

a cognitive source is not infallible but merely of presumptive veracity. All it can manage to do is to establish a presumption in favor of its deliverances – a defeasible presumption that can be upset in the light of countervailing developments.[6] And this, in the context of present purposes, is all that it *needs* to do.

The aim of a cognitivist theory is not, after all, to rule out doubt *per se* with respect to the knowledge-claims it views as warranted, but to rule out *appropriate* or *rationally warranted* doubt. Even when one has all the support one could reasonably ask for with respect to an item of knowledge, doubt may still be logically or even psychologically possible. The key point, however, is that the *realistic* basis for a *rationally warranted* doubt is no longer at hand.

Doubt, after all, is itself a positive and committal condition,[7] and once a thesis has any presumption on its side, however feeble, it requires the adducing of considerations of some positive weight to set it aside. To say that a contention is doubtful, after all, is not to say that it *can* be doubted (in some very hypothetical sense of "can"), but that it *should* be doubted.

Doubt is no more self-validating or self-warranting than is assent or belief. Rational doubt must have a rational foundation. To say that it is doubtful that *p* is to maintain that *p* *might well* be false, that it is possibly or even probably not the case that *p*, and thus to say that not-*p* is possibly or probably the case. A definite and positive *claim* is thus made, a claim falling into one of two distinct types: (1) that the available evidence supports the conclusion that not-*p*, or at least (2) that the available evidence does not support the contention that *p*. Doubt can correspondingly occupy one of two positions, the one stronger and contradictorily opposed to the thesis at issue, the other weaker and agnostic towards it. But clearly both the contradictory and the agnostic variety of doubt must have some *ground* or *basis*. In both cases, the

[6] Exactly as in law. A person missing for seven years is presumed dead, but that doesn't mean that this presumption cannot be upset – that the reawakened Rip van Winkle or the returned Odysseus cannot possibly reestablish himself as one of the living.

[7] On this important point see J. H. Newman's *A Grammar of Assent* (*op. cit.*).

positive contention is made: "So far as the available evidence goes, the thesis at issue may be false."

The rational man only doubts a proposition when he holds it to *be dubious* – i.e., to *merit* doubt. And such a posture involves a claim about the evidence for the proposition, exactly as would the contention that the proposition is certain. In both cases reasoned justification in the form of supporting grounds is required: assertions of doubtfulness must be supported – or at any rate supportable – just as assertions of certainty, probability, or the like. Once a thesis has some element of presumption in its favor, weak though it be, some sort of warranting considerations are needed for its overthrow. We cannot appropriately cast it aside on some idle whim.

We have to return here to the important medieval distinction between *rationes essendi* (our reasons for what is said) and *rationes cognoscendi* (our reasons for saying them). For our sources relate to *testimonial* grounds rather than *evidential* ones. "I remember it to be so" or "A learned scholar told it to me" no doubt afford an appropriate basis for my acceptance of a contention, but they afford no reasons for *it* (as distinct from reasons for *believing* it) – seeing that they afford no information whatsoever regarding its *content*. Testimonial grounds answer the question "Why do you (or somebody) say that it is so?" but not the question "What is the reason for its being so?"[8] Testimonial grounds, unlike evidential ones, provide no *logos*, no rationale, no reason in the sense of a *ratio essendi*. Sometimes we must simply settle for a *ratio cognoscendi*.

Nevertheless, testimonial grounding resembles evidential grounding in this important respect, that it too can provide the needed backing for our knowledge claims. And this

---

[8] Thus compare:

> I may claim to know that the Italian word *spigo* means "lavender" without being able to base my statement on any reason. If challenged, I should only be able to say "It just does mean that"; for, though this piece of factual knowledge is lodged in my mind, I cannot remember how or when it got there. Yet, if my memory for this sort of thing were good, it would be allowed that I really did have a piece of factual knowledge. . . . The human mind is a sort of recording instrument, and on certain occasions the only justification for a statement it will be able to produce is its own reliability. (David Pears, *What is Knowledge?* [New York, 1971], pp. 11–12.)

circumstance is very important in the epistemic scheme of things. For if (contrary to fact) the only supportive reasons one could ever give were of the evidential sort – were discursive-reasons – then the process of reason-giving could never come to an end. We would have to go on and on and on, and reason-giving would become a Sisyphean labor that can never be brought to an end. The crucial and indispensable role of testimonial grounding lies precisely in this, that it affords us the needed methodological device for grounding our knowledge claims outside the discursive domain. Ordinarily and usually we adduce evidential reasons for our judgments, but it is important – crucially important – that we have the option of a nondiscursive route to the grounding of knowledge (albeit its "grounding" as *merely presumptive*). The pivotal work of testimonial grounds is to place this resource at our disposal.

The attest of a duly qualified source manages to place the burden of proof on the other side. And this means that the opponents of a suitably source-warranted cognitive claim must do some positive work to set this claim aside. But work of exactly what sort? There remains the important issue: Just what is capable of defeating such a presumption?

The answer is that in these cases of reputable sources of established credit it takes a lot. And in particular it takes case-specific counterconsiderations. Generalized recourse to human fallibility and theoretical possibilities of error just will not do. Nor will those other "remote" possibilities of error near and dear to the sceptic's heart – powerful deceivers, wicked scientists, and the rest. It takes concrete and case-specific considerations. In these circumstances only considerations which themselves have cognitive weight can serve as counter-weights. (At *this* stage of the discussion, a sceptical approach does not augur victory, it assures defeat.)

In developing his sceptical argument, Keith Lehrer writes:

> [P]hilosophers of common sense . . . claim that we are warranted in saying that we know for certain that various statements expressing common sense beliefs are true. [That, for instance, there is a human hand before me, to take G. E. Moore's example.] The basic assumption

is that at least some common sense beliefs are to be considered innocent until proven guilty. We may then argue
that we know for certain that such beliefs are true until
some proof to the contrary is presented on the other
side. The reply to this . . . is that I have offered an argument on the other [i.e., sceptical] side, and the burden
of proof now rests with my [cognitivist] opponents.[9]

But the difficulty here is that the sceptical arguments offered
on the other side are all of the generic, universalized sort
involving theoretical possibilities of error and the other para-
phernalia of generic doubt. And such considerations are not
capable of annulling the presumption at issue with an established cognitive source. They simply are not in a position to
exert the weight needed to reverse the burden of proof at
issue.[10]

The distinction between generic *vs.* specific doubt (S-doubt
vs. G-doubt as per pp. 101ff. above) thus has a crucial
bearing upon burden-of-proof considerations. The presumption of veracity at issue with appropriately source-attested
claims is indeed defeasible, but only concrete, case-specific
considerations correlative with S-doubt have the firepower
necessary to enforce defeat. And this sort of enterprise – the
establishment of case-specific counterclaims is clearly not to
the sceptic's liking. Once he is forced onto this ground of
specifically warranting certain particular, case-specific considerations for use in the defeat of particular knowledge
claims, his over-all position is doomed. It there are cases in
which only knowledge can defeat a knowledge claim, the
sceptic's position becomes wholly untenable.

To be sure, cognitive sources are not only fallible in detail,
but they are defeasible *in toto*. In extreme cases, their very
status as sources can become unstuck. Our "sources of
knowledge" need not be regarded as something sacred and
sacrosanct. The evolutionary course of intellectual history is

---

[9] Keith Lehrer, "Skepticism and Conceptual Change" in R. M. Chisholm and R.
J. Swartz (eds.), *Empirical Knowledge* (Englewood Cliffs, 1973), pp. 47–58 (see p. 55).
[10] For further explanation of these considerations of presumption and burden of
proof, see the author's *Dialectics* (Albany, 1977).

strewn with the bones of the extinct dinosaurs of epistemology. For along with the senses and memory, such "sources"
as dreams, omens and astrological signs once held sway.
As these examples show, even the claims to merely presumptive truth can be made out for certain sources
can eventually come unstuck. But such overthrows can only
come about in situations of conflict where the stronger prevails over the weaker. And in such a conflict as is at issue
here it is not possible for *all* of the rival constituents to kill
each other off; that which prevails as the stronger will *eo ipso*
survive the competition. The idea that *all* of our cognitive
sources can become unstuck in this way can thus be dismissed out of hand. One cannot argue from the potential
defeasibility of *any* given source to the prospect that all of our
sources may become defeated *en bloc*.

One final point. The sceptic is not free simply to dismiss
the usual standards of presumption and burden of proof on
ground of their inconvenience for his position – at any rate
not without paying an unacceptable price. For the standards
of presumption and burden of proof serve as constituting
part of the very norms of reasoned deliberation and inquiry.
They represent *conditiones sine qua non* of this enterprise –
conditions under which alone probative cogency can be
realized. To reject these standards is to turn one's back upon
cognitive rationality itself by abandoning the defining standards of the enterprise. (We shall return to this issue in
Chapter XIII.)

XI

The "No Generalizing" Argument

SYNOPSIS

(1) A Formulation of the "No Generalizing" Argument which has it that experience cannot validate any universal knowledge claims. The bearing of this argument is even more far-reaching than appears on first view, because *all* objective knowledge claims embody an element of universality. This would mean that experience can never validate factual claims at all. (2) The incorrectness of the "No Generalizing" Argument is maintained on the grounds of its mistaken supposition that the validation of a universalized knowledge claim requires its *total* assurance by way of logically airtight guarantees. (3) The capacity of experience to provide objective factual knowledge can be maintained by means of this-or-nothing argumentation, and the bearing of this argument can be supported by a line of defense that is ultimately pragmatic (in the broad sense of being purpose-oriented).

1. THE "NO GENERALIZING" ARGUMENT

An influential line of sceptical argumentation runs as follows: Experience is always of the particular. On its basis, one can perhaps secure contentions like "This lion is tawny" or "Each member of yonder group of lions is tawny," but never contentions like "All lions are tawny" (save perhaps with those transitory species whose origination and extinction lie within the range of our experience). Experience never affords genuine universality. The following "No Generalizing" Argument implements this line of thought:

1. Experience can never provide total assurance for genuinely universal knowledge claims (i.e., logically airtight guarantees).
2. To validate universal knowledge claims one must provide total, absolutely exhaustive assurance for them.

∴ Experience can never validate knowledge claims that are genuinely universal.

It thus seems to emerge that experience and observation – always confined to particular episodes and occasions – can never establish universalized knowledge claims with that total assurance necessary to substantiate such claims as amounting to actual knowledge. If a general claim must be validated *in toto* to attain the status of genuine knowledge, it follows that – since experience is always of the particular – our general beliefs can never qualify as knowledge. We are back to the medieval precept: *latet dolus in generalibus*. General truths – and with them the whole fabric of laws on which our inductive knowledge of empirical relationships is built – defy our aspirations to knowledge.

Hume gave his own characteristic twist to this historic argument in the following terms:

The sceptic ... justly insists, that all our evidence for any matter of fact, which lies beyond the testimony of sense or memory, is derived entirely from the relation of cause and effect; that we have no other idea of this relation than that of two objects, which have been frequently *conjoined* together; that we have no argument to convince us, that objects, which have, in our experience, been frequently conjoined, will likewise, in other instances, be conjoined in the same manner; and that nothing leads us to this inference but custom or a certain instinct of our nature; which it is indeed difficult to resist, but which, like other instincts, may be fallacious and deceitful.[1]

H. A. Prichard was a more recent exponent of a closely cognate position, denying any possibility of there being any such thing as *inductive* knowledge,[2] seeing that *induction* is always data-transcendent (or *ampliative*, as Peirce puts it), while *knowledge* demands the total security of unqualified assurance. Such a stance is eminently useful for the sceptic's purposes. For one thing, it is quite clear that all our scientific claims go beyond the evidence – no significant generalization could fail to do so. Moreover, a good case can be made for holding that an element of universality is present in all matters of objective fact as to how things actually stand in the world, given the admixture of nomic generality implicit in all such claims because all of our descriptive and classificatory machinery in the empirical domain is law-laden.

The "No Generalizing" argument thus yields a decisively sceptical result. For if *experience* can never validate any generality-involving claims of objective fact, then it is clear that such claims cannot be validated at all. (Given the epistemic realities of the human condition, experience of the world – i.e., *interaction* with it – is the only basis on which information about matters of fact can be obtained.)

2. MEETING THE "NO GENERALIZING" ARGUMENT

The first premiss of the "No Generalizing" Argument seems secure enough: our experience, being inescapably finite, can never exhaust a potentially infinite range. To defeat the argument, one must thus tackle its second premiss and deny this contention that universal knowledge claims can only be validated by providing a *total,* exhaustive and logically airtight assurance for them. Let us accordingly begin by focus-

---

[1] *An Enquiry Concerning Human Understanding,* Sect. XII, Part II.

[2] H. A. Prichard, *Knowledge and Perception* (Oxford, 1950); see p. 97. To admit a view which, though prepared to allow some small smattering of items to qualify, puts nearly everything that we ordinarily think of as constituting "our knowledge" outside the admissible range, does not seem much more palatable than to join the sceptics in dismissing our claims to factual knowledge altogether.

ing on the thesis that to justify a universalized knowledge claim it is necessary to offer a detailed verification of each and every one of its endless instances. Such an insistence on verificational exhaustiveness is surely incorrect. What is needed to support a knowledge claim is not a total or exhaustive assurance, but an *adequate* assurance – a warrant that is "*realistically* sufficient" to validate the contention at issue.

The dialectic of "real" *vs.* "theoretical" thus once more removes a difficulty from our path. As we have seen time and time again, the governing consideration here lies in the *ultra posse* principle. What is needed is not an assurance that is exhaustive or *total* in some exaggerated logico-theoretical sense of this term, but *adequate* assurance in a sense which looks to the realistic possibilities of the situation.

This line of thought leads to the issue of just exactly what adequacy in the context of the cognitive validation of generalizations actually involves. The following objection will at once rear up in this connection:

> Surely, even after you have built up what you call a case that is "adequate" (or "circumstantially cogent" or whatever) for the claim "All X is Y," it is still not excluded that an X might turn up that is not a Y. This remains perfectly conceivable or possible. How, then, can you view the claim to *know* "All X is Y" as justified?

The core of this objection must be granted. Of course a counterinstance remains *conceivable*, and if (alas!) it arises we have no choice but to retract. But this unhappy eventuation would merely show that our claim was *false*, not that it was *unjustified*. Such falsification is indeed conceivable – it remains a possibility even in the face of an optimal justification. However, this (as we have seen in Chapter III) is exactly the point that the possibility in question is a "theoretical" and not a "real" one – it is one that we justifiedly regarded as "out of the question," a circumstance that certainly does not mean that it cannot conceivably occur – that its occurrence can be excluded as a *logical* possibility.

The very fact that – as a matter of theoretical principle –

one cannot possibly develop an experiential basis sufficient
to verify *seriatim* each and every one of the endless instances
of a universal claim means that it is inappropriate and improper to set this up as a requirement or preconditional requisite for knowledge. Carl G. Hempel has put the key point
incisively in the specific context of scientific generalizations:

> Precisely because science seeks knowledge that reaches
> far beyond the supporting evidence, its empirical claims
> cannot consistently be required or expected to be [de-
> monstratively] certain relative to that evidence; the ideal
> of empirical knowledge with [demonstrative] certainty is
> logically self-contradictory. And surely, science cannot
> be held to be limited because of its failure to meet a
> standard of perfection which is logically inconsistent.[3]

It is thus clear that the "No Generalizing" Argument fails to
achieve its sceptical objective. Its first premiss is indeed correct; experience cannot provide *logically* airtight guarantees
for claims to objective factual knowledge. But the second
premiss fails. It simply is not rationally appropriate to
demand that such guarantees should be forthcoming, setting
up a requirement that cannot in the very nature of things be
satisfied. The prospect of general or objective knowledge –
be it of the scientific or common-life variety – cannot validly
be undone by the imposition of a standard which embodies
conditions that cannot be met given the very nature of the
case.

3. THE PROSPECTS OF EMPIRICAL KNOWLEDGE: A THIS-OR-NOTHING ARGUMENT

If knowledge of matters of objective fact is to be potentially
obtainable (at least in principle) – if such cognitive claims are
to be validatable at all – then this *must* be so on the basis of
experience (supplemented by whatever principles and procedures of inductive systematization are needed to make its

---

[3] "Science Unlimited," *Annals of the Japan Association for the Philosophy of Science,* vol. 4 (1973), pp. 187–202 (see p. 190).

rational exploitation possible). Observation or, more generally, interaction with environing nature is our only avenue of contact with what happens in the world. We have no telephone line to the all-knowing recording angel.[4] If *anything* can validate claims to factual knowledge, then experience – *limited* experience, the only sort we can get hold of – can validate such claims. Here one encounters a characteristic instance of *this-or-nothing argumentation* in philosophical inquiry.[5] If we do not allow experience to validate, or at any rate be in a position to validate, our cognitive claims in the factual sphere, then *nothing* can do so: if *anything* can, then *experience* can. It is the only route to the destination: the only game in town. Accordingly, the sceptical imposition of a standard which, on the basis of theoretical general principles, would preclude all prospects of an experiential validation of factual knowledge is *eo ipso* improper and illegitimate. Being the *only* route, experience must be allowed to serve as a *possible* route.

These considerations do no more than to indicate that experience is the only available avenue to factual knowledge – the only *possible* route. But this leaves open the question: What justifies the stance that it is an *actual* route – i.e., what qualifies the "appropriate conclusions" to which experience leads us as actually representing valid claims to *knowledge*? How can one move from the hypothetical and possibilistic thesis "If *anything* can validate factual knowledge, then *experience* can validate factual knowledge" to the categorical and actualistic thesis that experience actually does so? After all, the history of man's cognitive endeavors makes clear that we may well be wrong in accepting experience-indicated generalities as affording genuine knowledge of the world.

In dealing with this issue, it is well to invoke once again

[4] The fact that we have no *direct* access to the truth in matters of objective fact – that our only avenue to it lies through the epistemological domain of inquiry, evidence, verification, or the like – is, as it were, the cognitive equivalent of the fall of man consequent upon original sin.

[5] This line of argumentation, much favored by the English idealists, was introduced by Bernard Bosanquet, who maintained that the ultimate basis both of deductive and of inductive inference is a matter of *this or nothing*. See his *Implication and Linear Inference* (London, 1920), pp. 3–4, 19, and *passim*. See also A. C. Ewing, *Idealism: A Critical Survey* (London, 1934), pp. 244ff., and Chaps. IV–V of the author's *Induction* (Oxford, 1980).

William James' cardinal principle that the adoption of a rule which would automatically prevent one's finding out something that is actually the case is simply irrational. It is thus irrational – in being self-defeating from the standpoint of the cognitive enterprise – to reject *a priori* the idea that claims to factual knowledge can be validated experientially. If we want to acquire information about the world and to be in a position to make correct cognitive claims about it, then we must not only use experience as a basis in actually making such claims, but must be prepared to treat these experientially validated claims (at any rate provisionally) as affording genuine knowledge. To be sure, this line of reasoning does not afford a *demonstration* that the rationally developed exploitation of experience does indeed yield authentic knowledge. It is a probatively weaker argument to the effect that it is rationally warranted and appropriate to take the stance that experience does so.

Such a line of reasoning is ultimately pragmatic in the broad sense of being purpose-oriented. It does not *demonstrate* correctness and somehow prove that the contention at issue is true. Rather, it only shows that in the purpose-relative context of our cognitive aims and objectives it is rational to maintain that it is true. Accordingly, it is not a conclusive *demonstration* of the claim, but a *pragmatic,* that is, teleologically geared vindication of it. However, there is no warrant for any feelings of dissatisfaction here. For we must face the fact that, in the circumstances, this sort of argumentation is the strongest that can reasonably be asked for because it is the strongest that can possibly be had. There is – there can be – no actual *proof* of the correctness of our experientially based knowledge claims: no demonstration to this effect can have *deductive* conclusiveness. All that we have – and can have – is the provision of appropriate rational warrant for accepting them as such. This should, nay *must*, suffice us.

XII

Skepsis and Reason

SYNOPSIS

(1) A sceptical abstention from the acceptance of objective factual claims about the world would be *irrational* because it frustrates any prospect of realizing our cognitive aims. (2) And this case against radical scepticism is not "merely pragmatic" in the sense of one oriented solely to the impeding of praxis; it shows that the sceptic's position infringes the demands of rationality itself. The sceptic cannot validly portray himself as "a partisan of rigid rationality," seeing that his posture violates the only *reasonable* methodological principles we have. (3) The radical sceptic is committed to the unpalatable view that, as far as any *reasons* go, there simply is "nothing to choose" between one assertion and another. (4) A radical, rigoristic scepticism which denies any and all basis for rational acceptance thereby precludes any prospect of viable communication and *rational* controversy. It is incompatible with the commitments and presuppositions of the mechanisms that are indispensably necessary for the conduct of our intellectual affairs.

1. THE IRRATIONALITY OF ACCEPTANCE-PROSCRIPTION: THE NO REASON, NO RATIONALITY ENTAILMENT

The preceding chapters have built up a positive theory of knowledge that rebuts the unattainability of *knowledge* as maintained by sceptics of every ilk. It remains to develop a more detailed critique of the radical scepticism that denies not just knowledge but even anything meriting the weaker designation of "reasonable belief." Let us for the present focus upon *radical* (rather than *qualified*) scepticism, the far-reaching scepticism that denies not just the attainability of *knowledge* but that of *reasonable belief* as well – in all the various forms of that venerable idea. To be sure, someone might argue that there is a distinction without a difference here because the only *good* reason is a *known* reason. But this seems unduly demanding.[1] Admittedly, there is a certain misleading plausibility to the idea that if someone accepts something "on good grounds" or "for good reasons" then these grounds or reasons must be something he takes himself to know. However shakily a contention is based on its grounds, so it might be argued, these grounds themselves must be solid. The idea is abroad that if anything is to count as plausible (probable, reasonable) then something – namely its ground or basis – must be altogether certain. But here appearances are misleading. A whole tissue of mutually re-inforcing appearances or plausibilities – none themselves amounting to knowledge of the items at issue – can provide a convincing case for a contention. If "it seems to me" that he looks familiar; if I "have a vague recollection" of having talked with him in a similar vein before; if I "am under the impression" that someone told me he would be here; and if in a similar way a vast gamut of such seemings reinforce the idea that an old acquaintance of mine stands before me once more; then I surely "have good reason" for holding this view, even though no single one of the couple of items constituting the 'good reason" at issue amounts to knowledge. To be sure, one would then have to characterize this contention as a matter of reasonable belief rather than actual knowledge, but that's just part of the point at issue – viz., that there can be reasonable belief in the absence of knowledge. Such consider-

---

[1] Peter Unger in *Ignorance* (Oxford, 1975) maintains that "*S*'s *reason* [for accepting *q*] was that *p*, but *S* wasn't absolutely certain that *p*" is substantively inconsistent (see p. 209). But this contention is incorrect. For one thing, there is no anomaly in saying "*S* saw *p* as virtually certain (or: as a most likely prospect), and this was his reason for accepting *q*." Moreover, a sufficiently intricate concatenation (*syndromē*) of individually feeble and weakly evidenced considerations can also provide grounds for knowledge. One must reject the idea that knowledge can be based only on knowledge (See p. 166.)

ations indicate that it is a viable theoretical option to espouse a merely qualified or mitigated scepticism, one that accepts the prospect of warranted belief despite rejecting the availability of authentic knowledge. But our present deliberations will put this prospect aside to focus upon the radical scepticism that rejects any sort of warranted assertability.

If our claims about factual matters are all in theory defeasible – if, as the evidential gap indicates, they are in principle always *potentially* flawed – then caution might well be the best policy and we would do well to assume a totally sceptical posture. For in this circumstance, why not adopt the radical sceptic's traditional policy of universal nonassertion (*aphasia*) and suspension of judgment (*epochē*). Why not simply let discretion be the better part of epistemic valor and systematically avoid accepting anything whatsoever?

The answer is that this sceptical policy of systematic avoidance of acceptance is fundamentally *irrational*, because it blocks from the very outset any prospect of realizing the inherent goals of the enterprise of factual inquiry. The obtaining of *information about the world* is, after all, the aim and purpose that governs the entire cognitive venture. To be sure, when we set out to reach this goal we may well discover in the end that, try as we will, success in reaching it is beyond our inadequate means. But we shall *certainly* not reach the goal if we do not set out on the journey at all – which is exactly what the blanket proscription of acceptance amounts to. The rigorous sceptic writes off at the very outset a prospect whose rejection would only be rationally defensible at the very end.

In "playing the game" of assertion and claims to credence, we may well lose: our contentions may well turn out to be mistaken. But in a refusal to play this game at all we face not just the possibility but the certainty of losing the prize.

The sceptic too readily loses sight of a crucial fact regarding the teleological *raison d'être* of our cognitive endeavors. Their aim – as we have seen – is not just to avoid error but to engross truth. The object of rational inquiry is to secure *information* about the world. And here, as elsewhere, "Nothing ventured, nothing gained" is the operative principle. Granted, a systematic abstention from cognitive involvement is a sure-fire safeguard against error. But it affords this security at too steep a price, seeing that it calls for abandoning the whole cognitive enterprise. Given the very nature of the enterprise of inquiry, there is no alternative to a rejection of scepticism. (We once again encounter a course of this-or-nothing argumentation analogous to that considered on p. 195 above.)

The appropriate stance here was indicated with trenchant cogency by Charles Sanders Peirce:

> The first question, then, which I have to ask is: Supposing such a thing to be true, what is the kind of proof which I ought to demand to satisfy me of its truth.[2]

A general epistemic policy which would make it impossible, as a matter of principle, for us to discover *something which is ex hypothesi the case* is clearly irrational. And the proscription of accepting is obviously such a policy – one which aborts the whole project of inquiry at the very outset, without according it the benefit of a fair trial.

Nor can a workable alternative to a policy of acceptance be found in a probabilism that in effect says: "You must never accept categorically and outright a thesis regarding matters of objective fact: given the "evidential gap," an explicit qualification of tentativity must characterize all of your factual claims, and so you should only endorse such a thesis as being probable in this or that degree."[3] Such a policy again does not meet the requirements of the case. It runs afoul of the teleology of inquiry because *it affords no descriptive information about the world.* All determination is negation (*omnis determinatio est negatio*), as Spinoza's dictum wisely has it, and a (zero-free) probability distribution across *all* of the possibilities rules none of them out. To be told that an

---

[2] *Collected Papers*, vol. II, §2.112.

[3] See R. Carnap, *Logical Foundations of Probability* (Chicago, Ill., 1950; 2nd edn., 1960), sect. 50, and P. A. Schilpp (ed.), *The Philosophy of Rudolf Carnap* (La Salle, Ill., 1963), pp. 972–973. Carnap's position is followed by R. Jeffrey. See his "Valuation and Acceptance of Scientific Hypotheses," *Philosophy of Science*, vol. 23 (1956), pp. 237–246.

object is black with probability 0.7 and white with probability 0.1 and neither with probability 0.2 is not to be given any *descriptive* information about its color at all. Accordingly, such an omnivorous probabilism also has the effect of aborting the enterprise of inquiry at the very outset. Insofar as the aim of factual inquiry is to provide a descriptively informative picture of the world, a *probabilistically* conditioned strategy of acceptance does not provide a viable alternative to a *categorical* approach (Cp. pp. 79–80.)

There remains also the no less serious fact that in insisting that we abandon acceptance in all its modes, the sceptic blocks any prospect of our achieving (cognitive) rationality. Rationality requires that we have (or at any rate purport to have) good *reasons* for the things we maintain. But if I adduce Q as constituting a reason for maintaining P, then I must commit myself to accepting Q – that is, accepting it as actual – and not merely as possible or probable. One must acknowledge the cogency of the "No reason, no rationality" argument that the only *good* reason is an *acceptable* reason.[4] The ancient sceptics, as we know from Sextus Empiricus, saw reason, acceptance, and truth as interdependent and co-ordinate resources which stand or fall together. They preached *isosthenia*, the balancing between pro- and con-consider-ations, so that *yes* and *no* alike are always *equally* proper (or, rather, equally *improper*) answers to our questions. But in the face of such equipoise, any sort of rational validation clearly becomes impossible. The whole project of giving and seeking for reasons collapses if one adopts the idea that as a matter of general principle there is nothing one is entitled to maintain as true. To repeat, rationality requires reasons, and the only [plausibly-held-to-be] *cogent* reasons are [plausibly-held-to-be] *acceptable* reasons.

As the sceptic sees it, the appeal to reason in all forms must be replaced with the appeal to *extra-cognitive* mech-anisms on the order of instinct, revelation, taste, or the like – all equally devoid of any claims to *justification*. In refusing to undertake cognitive commitments the sceptic would have us

---

[4] Note, however, that to say this is not to say that the only *good* reason is a *known* reason. For a critique of this altogether too demanding thesis see pp. 165–166.

withdraw from the enterprise of rationality as well.[5] Posing
as a partisan of rigid rationality he comes not to fulfil but to
destroy the commandments of reason.

2. THE SCEPTIC AS ENEMY OF RATIONALITY

This sacrifice of rationality – at any rate within factual
inquiry – is a step a committed sceptic may well be prepared
to take: he sees it as something that may be a loss from the
angle of *our* parochial precommitments, but that *he* in his
"superior wisdom" is not prepared to regard as such. How,
then, can the reality of the loss engendered by this position
be brought home?

One major traditional pragmatic argument against scepticism goes roughly as follows: /

> Scepticism founders on the structure of the human con-
> dition, since man is a creature that finds itself emplaced
> *in medias res* in a world where his very survival demands
> action. And the action of a rational being requires the
> guidance of belief. Not the requirements of theory and
> cognition but the exigencies of practice and action make
> manifest the untenability of the sceptic's position.

And so, since the days of the Academic Sceptics of Greek
antiquity, philosophers have often answered our present
question "Why accept anything at all?" by taking the following line: "Man is a rational animal. *Qua* animal he must act,
since his very survival depends upon action. But *qua* rational
being he cannot act availingly save insofar as his actions are
guided by what he accepts. The *practical* circumstances of
the human condition preclude the systematic suspension of
belief as a viable policy." This same line of argumentation
was revived by thinkers ranging from David Hume to William James.[6]

[5] This consequence is persuasively argued by Peter Unger in Chap. V, "From
Ignorance to Irrationality" of his book *Ignorance* (Oxford, 1975), pp. 197–249.
[6] William James said:
[Someone] who says "Better to go without belief forever than believe a lie!"
merely shows his own preponderant private horror of becoming a dupe . . . but

But this praxis-oriented appeal has not been operative in our present argumentation, which has addressed itself wholly to the issue of *cognitive* rationality – of "theoretical" rather than "merely practical" reason. To this point, our line of reasoning has not run "If you want to act effectively then you must accept something," but rather: "If you want to enter into 'the cognitive enterprise' – that is, if you wish to be in the position to obtain information about the world – then you must accept something." Both approaches take a line that is not categorical and unconditional, but rather hypothetical and conditional – by hinging the matter on the espousal of a predesignated goal. But in the strictly pragmatic case, the condition relates to the requisites for effective action, while in the cognitive case, to the requisites for rational inquiry. And this second domain is where the present deliberations place their weight. They have urged that the price the sceptic pays for refusing to subscribe to the accepted probative standards of rational deliberation in inquiry is paid in terms of compromising the very aim of the cognitive enterprise – the objective of securing, as best we can, information about the world and its ways. This prudential loss inherent in the frustration of our basic cognitive aims (no matter how much the sceptic himself may be willing to turn his back upon them) is the key theoretical reason for the rejection of scepticism.

Any strictly practical, pragmatic and praxis-oriented critique leaves it open for the sceptic to take to the high ground of a partisan of rigorous rationality, by adopting the following stance:

This charge of stultifying practice is really beneath my notice. Theoretical reason and abstract rationality are what concerns the true philosopher. The issue of what is *merely practical* does not concern me. As far as "mere practice" goes, I am perfectly prepared to conform my actions to the pattern that men in general see fit to follow. In matters of *practice* let us by all means go

---

I can believe that worse things than being duped may happen to a man in this world. . . . . (*The Will to Believe and Other Essays in Popular Philosophy* [New York, 1899], pp. 18–19.)

along at the common level. But one should recognize that the clarity of the theoretical intellect points in another – and altogether sceptical – direction.

The present line of argumentation does not afford the sceptic this comfortable option. Its fulcrum is not the issue of *practice* as such, but the issue of cognitive praxis – of *rationality* as it relates to inquiry, communication, and rational controversy. In affecting to disdain *this* line of approach, it is not simply the practice or ordinary life, but the cognitive enterprise itself on which the sceptic must now turn his back.

The sceptic is not embarked on a *defense* of reason, but on a self-imposed *exile* from the enterprise of rational deliberation and the community of rational inquirers. And at this juncture he is no longer left in possession of the high ground. In refusing to give to the standard evidential considerations the presumptive and *prima facie* weight that is their established value on the market of rational interchange, the sceptic, rather than being the defender of rigid reason, is in fact profoundly irrational.

Historically, sceptics have sometimes not hesitated to accept the charge that they are destroyers of reason, insisting that their use of reason is simply as an instrument for its own destruction. Acute sceptics have generally been alive to this issue, and some of them have been prepared to grasp the nettle and admit (and even exult in) the consequence that their position does not only gainsay knowledge, but actually rejects the whole project of cognitive rationality – at any rate at the level of our factual beliefs. But whatever satisfaction this posture may afford the sceptic, it is hardly likely to appeal to those who do not already share his position. After all, to *refute* the sceptic it is not necessary to dislodge him from his position – to *convert* him, as it were; it suffices to render his position unavailable to "the rational man."

The sceptic *seemingly* moves within the orbit of rationality, but only seemingly so, for in fact scepticism violates the only reasonable epistemological principles we have. To be sure, there will always be a rationale of justification for such methodological ground-rules. And if it were simply this rationalization that the sceptic was asking for, his demands would *not* be unreasonable, and could always in principle be met. But this defense itself would, of course, have to be conducted subject to the standard *modus operandi* of rational argumentation. There is and can be no rational justification outside the domain of rationality itself.

One could – to be sure – press the issue still one step further. For a committed sceptic might take the following line:

Very well – let it be granted that cognitive acceptance by way of knowledge or reasonable belief is necessary to the project of rational inquiry or what you have called the "cognitive enterprise." So what? Why should one seek to play this "rationality game" at all? After all, to call someone "a rational person" is just giving him an honorific pat on the back for comporting himself in intellectual affairs in an approved manner. It begs – or leaves open – the questions: Why is this "rationality" really a good thing? What *point* is there to being rational?

This line of objection raises the spectre that our standards of rationality might be altogether arbitrary, lacking any and all appropriate legitimation.[7]

We come here to the sceptic's case against the utility of reason. In war, victory does not always lie on the side of the big battalions. In inquiry, truth does not always lie on the side of the stronger reasons. And here we face the sceptic's ultimate challenge: What basis is there for the belief that the real is rational (to put it in Hegelian terms)? What assurance do we have that aligning our beliefs with the canons of the

---

[7] Max Black has formulated this key issue with characteristic clarity:

The ... [cognitive] philosopher necessarily uses such key words as "reasonable" against the traditional [sceptical] approaches to the problem [of inductive knowledge]. But to use these crucial terms in a discussion of the inductive problem, it might be argued, is to beg the very question at issue. A lunatic or an eccentric philosopher might well use the expression "good reason" in a way that would be blatantly improper [by established standards], yet he might be able to prove, by appeal to his own criteria, that he had "good reasons" to use the phrase in the way he did. But are we ourselves in any better position? Are we not obligated to break through the linguistic barrier and at least to show why the alleged criteria for good reasons to which appeal is made should continue to receive our allegiance? (Art. "Induction" in *The Encyclopedia of Philosophy*, ed. by P. Edwards, vol. 4 (New York, 1967), p. 178.)

logical and the reasonable leads us any closer to *the truth?*

We must begin by acknowledging that there is no way of producing a demonstrative proof here on the basis of theoretical principles alone. The only strictly theoretical – i.e., non-pragmatic – defense available here proceeds via the cycle of selfsubstantiation, by holding that *it is rational to believe that the best we can do is to govern our acceptances by the canons of rationality.* This theoretical line is correct as far as it goes, but it is not altogether satisfactory. It clearly stands in need of extratheoretical supplementation. But such supplementation is in fact available through experiential *retrovalidation* (retrospective revalidation). For the clear indications of experience are (1) that we do well in adhering to the processes of scientific rationality, and (2) that no alternative that has come to hand through trial and error has manifested a capacity to do comparably well.[8]

3. THE "NOTHING TO CHOOSE" OBJECTION TO RADICAL SCEPTICISM

Perhaps no other objection to radical scepticism in the factual domain is as impressive as the fact that, for the all-out sceptic, all assertions about the objective facts must lie on the same cognitive plane. No contention about the world – no matter how bizarre – is any better off than any other in point of credentials. As far as the cognitive venture goes, such scepticism is a doomsday bomb that levels everything in sight. For the radical sceptic there just is no rationality-relevant difference between "More than three people are currently living in China" and "There are fewer than three automobiles in North America." He is committed to the view that there is "nothing to choose" in point of warrant between one factual claim and another, and puts "There are unicorns" and "There are elephants" into the same epistemological box. And so we are led to the complaint which C. I. Lewis has put so cogently:

---

[8] See the author's *Methodological Pragmatism* (Oxford, 1976) for a full-scale development of this line of thought.

I consider skepticism something worse than unsatisfactory; I consider it nonsense to hold or to imply that just any empirical judgment is as good as any other – because none is warranted. A theory which implies or allows that consequence is not an explanation of anything but merely an intellectual disaster.[9]

The radical sceptic stands committed to the view that what we would ordinarily call wild fancy, idle speculation, and lunatic ravings are nowise rationally inferior as a basis for belief to the most carefully derived and thoroughly tested assertion of the historian or scientist. This view of the cognitive enterprise is clearly untenable. Only at the price of turning his back on the "lessons of common experience" and the "precepts of common sense" can the sceptic's position attain even a semblance of cogency.

Still, the sceptic might well reply as follows, adopting the stance of his Pyrrhonian forefathers:

You do me an injustice. I do not put all assertions on the same plane. I follow this or that *noncognitive* guide: "appearances," "custom," "the general consensus," or the like.

But this reply misses the point. The burden of the objection is not simply that the sceptic fails to favor some assertions over others. It is, rather, that he insists that there just are no REASONS for doing so. And just this is so objectionable: that the sceptic turns his back on reason and finds no alternative but to insist on rejecting the operation of our (indeed of any and all) principles of probative cogency. This is a line the sceptic himself may willingly take, but there is no earthly reason why those of us who are not *already* precommitted to his views should join him in doing so.

---

[9] C. I. Lewis, "The Given Element in Empirical Knowledge," *The Philosophical Review*, vol. 61 (1952), pp. 168–175; reprinted in R. M. Chisholm and R. J. Swartz, *Empirical Knowledge* (*op. cit.*), pp. 368–375 (see p. 375). See also John Kekes, *A Justification of Rationality* (Albany, 1976).

4. PERVASIVE SCEPTICISM PRECLUDES RATIONAL COMMUNICATION

It is thus our contention that the radical sceptic is being unreasonable in that – by rejecting the established probative ground-rules – he forsakes cognitive rationality in the factual area. But in striving against this conclusion, the following reply remains open to him: "If I am departing from what on *your* view is 'rationality,' that doesn't show anything that *I* need be prepared to regard as a genuine flaw. Indeed my very thesis is that your 'rationality' is, in a basic regard, deficient." To meet this desperate but profound objection we must shift the ground. It now becomes advantageous to approach the whole issue from a new point of departure, namely that of the very prospects of communication. For not only does his refusal to accept claims preclude the radical sceptic from participation in the enterprise of *inquiry*, he is blocked from the enterprise of communication as well.

As was observed in the opening chapter, the inventory of untenable knowledge-locutions also includes: "*p*, but I don't accept that *p*" and "*p*, but there's no good reason for holding that *p*." [10] Simple assertion as such not only evinces commitment to a thesis, but also lays claims (albeit tacit claims) to *cognitive entitlement*. This fact does (or should) cause discomfiture for the radical sceptic. [11] A rigorous scepticism ruthlessly severs the links which alone make rational discussion possible. All communication is predicated on the fundamental convention that normally and standardly what one declares to be so is something that (1) one accepts as true, and (2) one claims to be rationally warranted in thus accepting. [12]

[10] In fact, even "*p*, but I don't know that *p*" is pragmatically inconsistent. The conscientious user of language would have to say something like "*p* seems a virtually sure thing to me, but I don't actually know it to be true."

[11] Note that since simply declaring or asserting something is tantamount to maintaining that one accepts it, and does so in a responsible way, then the sceptic cannot – i.e., cannot *self-consistently* – at once *propound* a thesis and concurrently insist that he does not (since one cannot) warrantedly accept anything. The closest the sceptic could come to the maintenance of a philosophical position is studied adherence to the silence of the ancient Cynic philosophers.

[12] Peter Unger suggests a "reformation" of language in the interests of scepticism: "We want linguistic institutions and practices where our [universal] ignorance will not enjoin silence." (*Ignorance* [Oxford, 1975], p. 271). But he offers no concrete proposals along these lines, and this is very understandable. It is difficult to see how

In rejecting the ground-rules of our reasoning as inappropriate the sceptic also abandons the ground-rules of communication. In denying the prospect of any sort of rational warrant – however tentative – the rigorous sceptic enters a self-imposed exile from the community of communicators.

Most sceptical writers are ultimately led, however reluctantly, to a recognition that a rigoristic scepticism leads to radical departures from the use of language and the established procedures of social communication and rational interchange. Thus Peter Unger is driven in the course of his enthusiastic defense of scepticism to the confession that "there is no appropriately accepted way for a sceptic about knowledge to express his view without falsely representing himself in the process." [13] And Arne Naess writes:

> If he makes the sources and frequences of error a subject of special study, the epistemologist *continues* [sceptical] dialogues (of a kind rarely observed in the community) with such tenacity . . . that he must be considered a more or less neutral bystander [i.e., an *outsider*], rather than a member of the community in these matters. [14]

Such passages indicate that acute sceptics are aware that their insistence on the inappropriateness of knowledge claims commits them to a conception of "knowledge" substantially at variance with that actually operative in knowledge-discourse as actually practised in the linguistic community. In his refusal to put his views in writing Pyrrho saw aright that there is an ultimate inconsistency in any endeavor to codify or promulgate the sceptical position. And his followers have generally anticipated the ruling idea of Wittgenstein's *On*

---

a language could be formed, taught, and (above all) *used* in which assertion played no role and declaration carried with it no claims to veracity. Even if (per impossible) one had such a "language" what would be the *point* of using it in communicative contexts?

[13] Peter Unger, *Ignorance: A Case for Scepticism* (Oxford, 1975), p. 268.

[14] *Scepticism* (London, 1968), p. 155.

Certainty that our everyday talk is a praxis rendered unworkable by scepticism.[15]

Confronted with this sort of charge, the sceptic turns tough, arguing that our ordinary use of language is simply sloppy – that in common-life affairs we generally speak loosely and casually, tending to construe charitably and let what is said pass as being true. The party line is simply that if scepticism is at variance with the *modus operandi* of everyday discourse, then so much the worse for everyday discourse. The sceptic falls back on the high line of the contention "Our concern is not with the careless doings of common life, but with issues of philosophical rigor."

But this tactic will not serve. The philosopher cannot be permitted to rewrite the established norms for our talk of "knowledge." They are given by the ground-rules of our language – the preestablished framework for our knowledge-pertinent discourse. The philosopher is bound to honor them – exactly like other members of the community. If he changes these standards in the context of his analysis of knowledge, then he *changes the subject* as well.

The sceptic lays himself open to the line of argumentation used by Aristotle against those who (like Protagoras and Cratylus and certain Heracleiteans) sought to question the Law of Contradiction – the *apodeiksis elektikōs* or so-called "proof by refutation." For any attack on this law in the context of rational discussion would require of its proponent "that he should say something that is meaningful both to himself and to another – this is necessary if there is to be any discussion at all, for otherwise there will be no reasoning (*logos*), either with himself or with another" (*Metaph.*, 1006a23). The point is that to enter into a discussion at all, one must acquiesce in the ground-rules which alone make discussion-in-general possible. To *reason* to any conclusion – even a conclusion that gainsays a principle of reasoning – calls for subscribing to the principles of reasoning. In entering the lists of reasoned deliberation and controversy one has

---

[15] Nowadays this point is often put in the more sophisticated guise of a "transcendental argument" from a praxis, viz., discourse, to its presuppositions – a line of argumentation which renders scepticism untenable relative to this praxis in being logically incompatible with its presuppositions.

already subscribed to the norms of rational discourse – it is already too late, so to speak, to take a questioning stance towards them.

A sceptic can, to be sure, deny that he is involved in any form of "advocacy" or that he has any "position" to offer. He can motivate his whole undertaking as being negative and therapeutic – a matter of getting us to refrain from undertaking any cognitive commitments and adopting a certain intellectual (anticognitive) point of view. He can portray his own discourse as simply a dispensable device to be thrown away once he has securely motivated us in the *via negativa* of suspension of judgment (*epochē*) and nonassertion (*aphasia*). He will insist that he offers no positive claims and contentions about the world. The sceptic must view all his sceptical *contentions* and *arguments* as vehicles that ultimately self-destruct enroute to silence, akin to the Wittgensteinean ladder that must be kicked down after its work is done.[16] But if we do not favor him from the outset in rejecting the utility of reasons, then the admission that he can provide us no *reasons* for joining him (for he cannot candidly purport to offer us by way of a *reason* such a consideration as the attainment of peace of mind or *ataraxia*) precludes from the very start any likely prospect of his converting the not already converted (let alone of his *persuading* them).

A radical scepticism regarding matters of fact in the final analysis engenders the collapse of communication and – since man is the *rational* animal – leads thereby to a withdrawal from the human community. Perceptive sceptics have not been blind to this fact; it was already perceived – and regretted – by Pyrrho himself, as witness his famous reply to a critic that it is not easy to divest oneself entirely of one's humanity.[17]

The collapse of the prospect of rational inquiry and communication is the ultimate sanction barring the way to any rational espousal of radical scepticism. It is a price that a fanatically dedicated devotee of the sceptical position may be

---

[16] See M. F. Burnyeat, "Protagoras and Self-Refutation in Later Greek Philosophy," *The Philosophical Review*, vol. 85 (1976), pp. 44–69 (especially p. 63).

[17] Diogenes Laertius, IX, 66.

willing to meet, but it is clearly one that *we*, who are not so precommitted, cannot possibly pay.[18]

[18] To be sure, as we remarked at the outset, the present argumentation addresses itself only to the radical sceptic who rejects not merely knowledge, but warranted acceptability (reasonable belief) as well. The qualified sceptic, who, while proscribing *knowledge*, yet allows warranted acceptability, must be dealt with by other, somewhat less drastic means.

XIII

Skepsis and Action

SYNOPSIS

(1) Some of the ancient Academic Sceptics argued (quite correctly) that rational action need not be based on *knowledge* because noncognitive decision-guides are available to provide a suitable warranting basis for action. (2) But it will *not* do to join the radical sceptics in holding that action can be based on such wholly noncognitive considerations. For the demands of rationality are sacrificed thereby: rigorous scepticism does not block *praxis* as such, but it precludes any prospect of *rationality* in praxis. A this-or-nothing argument is at issue here: the maintenance of rationality in action presupposes a cognitivist stance. (3) And we should be rational in action because this affords the best basis for expecting the realization of our goals. (4) Yet another form of sceptical argumentation maintains that our claims to knowledge always involve the prospect of unacceptable risks. But this distorts the issue, because acceptance as known certainly need not engender such unacceptable risks. (5) Why be rational in action? Because this – as best we can tell – holds the optimal promise for achieving the goals at which action is directed. The basic justification of cognitive rationality runs thus: rationality in belief is a prerequisite of rationality in action, and rationality in action is a matter of *prudence*, of self-interest oriented in achieving an optimal expectation of realizing one's own objectives.

1. SCEPTICISM AND THE GUIDANCE OF ACTION

Even the most dedicatedly rigorous of sceptics has generally recognized that man must *act* to survive and thrive in the world. Like everyone else, sceptics have realized that we humans find ourselves emplaced *in medias res* in an environment which will not satisfy our needs, wants, and desires automatically, without the intervention of activity on our part. But how are we to choose among alternatives here? If we wish to relieve those hunger pangs – for example – should we eat or hold our breath or stamp our feet or close our eyes and wish very hard? The sceptic too must act. And historically sceptics have been little more prone than other men to stand at the brink of a perceived precipice and take an unhesitating step forward, banking on the deceitfulness of the senses.[1] How, then, can they tackle the problem of the appropriate choice? What sorts of considerations should guide our actions?

Sceptics throughout the ages have denied the prospect of man's attainment of knowledge (*epistēmē*). Now one clearly cannot make use of what one does not have. And so sceptics have always taken the stance that men cannot guide their activities by knowledge – that we *cannot* base our actions on the recognition that fire burns or that eating assuages hunger. This position has laid scepticism open to the charge of immobilizing action. It has invited a Dr. Johnsonesque "refutation" of scepticism on the grounds of making the very conduct of life itself impossible. David Hume put this point as follows:

> But a Pyrrhonian ... must acknowledge, if he will acknowledge anything, that all human life must perish, were his principles universally and steadily to prevail. All discourse, all action would immediately cease; and men remain in a total lethargy, till the necessities of

---

[1] In antiquity, stories circulated as to how Pyrrho comported himself so recklessly that friends had to guard him from being run over by carts or walking over precipices. (See Diogenes Laertius, IX, 62.) Given that he lived to nearly 90, one suspects them as an apocryphal product of opponents' endeavors to give scepticism a bad press by impugning with ridicule what they could not defeat with argument.

nature, unsatisfied, put an end to their miserable existence.[2]

To this sort of charge, the ancient sceptics always replied that action need not be based on *knowledge* at all. They insisted on the sufficiency of *noncognitive* guides for action. The main alternatives proposed here have included the following four:[3]

1. *intuitionism:* action is to be based on instinct, bodily drives, and natural inclination.
2. *indifferentism:* action is to be based on whim, spur-of-the-moment impulse, or haphazard ("just toss a coin").
3. *conformism:* action is to be based on custom, "the done thing," the customary practice of the community.[4]
4. *praxism:* action is to be based on "know-how" (i.e., on "how-to-do" precepts) alone, where this does not involve any sort of "knowledge-that," but simply adhering to the established rules of *praxis* in the various practical arts and enterprises.

All these, however, are to be thought of as matters of *practical motives* for choosing to act one way rather than another and not as affording a *theoretical good reason* for such choices. The sceptic simply refuses, *ex officio,* to endorse any reasons for acting. Above all, the ancient Pyrrhonians held that the conduct of life can be governed not by knowledge but by *appearances*: "we neither affirm nor deny . . . but we

---

[2] David Hume, *An Enquiry Concerning Human Understanding,* Sect XII, Pt ii. Compare John Locke:

> He that will not eat till he has a demonstration that it will nourish him; he that will not stir till he infallibly knows the business he goes about will succeed, will have little else to do but to sit still and perish. (*Essay Concerning Human Understanding,* Bk. IV, Chap XIV, §1.)

[3] "It would appear that this regulation of life is fourfold and that one part of it lies in the guidance of nature, another in the constraint of the passions, another in the tradition of laws and customs, and another in the instruction of the arts." (Sextus Empiricus, *Outlines of Pyrrhonism,* Bk. I, Chap. 11, Sect. 23.)

[4] Compare Descartes' *Discourse on Method.*

yield to those things which move us emotionally and drive us compulsorily to assent."[5]

As Sextus Empiricus insists time and again, the springs of action are desire and aversion – seeking and avoiding – and these can operate without the intervention of any sort of credence, without our subscribing to a doctrine of any kind, or endorsing any actual thesis to the effect that this or that *is really the case.* Life without knowledge, reason, or belief is certainly not in principle impossible: animals, for example, manage very well. Or again, a somewhat less radical strategy is available – one that countenances acceptance (and belief), but only on a wholly unreasoned basis (e.g., instinct, constraint by the appearances, etc.). The sceptic can accordingly hold – and act on – all those beliefs which people ordinarily adopt, with only this difference, that he regards them as reflecting mere appearances, and denies that the holding of these beliefs is rationally justified. Hume's objection hits wide of the mark: scepticism need not immobilize action.

2. DIFFICULTIES IN THE *EPOCHĒ* OF SCEPTICISM

Although the sceptic may indeed have guides to action–namely, noncognitive guides – scepticism remains gravely deficient in a closely cognate respect. For while the sceptic can indeed act on appearances (or custom, etc.), he cannot *defend* his actions. He cannot *justify* doing *A* rather than *B*. He can tell us that he eats food to assuage hunger (rather than merely rubbing his stomach) because that's the done thing, but this mere *explanation* of what he does does not constitute a *ground* for it. Scepticism thus destroys the prospect of any *rational* recourse of the techniques of praxis. Given all-out *epochē*, our behavior becomes not irrational but irrationalizable. All linkage between action and rationality is severed. Accordingly, it is not difficult to discern the unsatisfactory nature of all noncognitive strategies for the guidance of action. For in being *noncognitive,* these approaches are also *nonrational* (which is, to be sure, something quite different

[5] Sextus Empiricus, *Outlines of Pyrrhonism,* Bk. I, Chap. 20, Sect. 193; and compare 121–124.

from the irrational). While they indeed tell us *what* to do, they are stonily silent on the crucial issue of *why* it is to be done.

Man, however, is an ineradicably *rational* animal. In every circumstance and situation he seeks "to know the reason why." Such a creature is geared to satisfy not only its *physical,* but its intellectual hunger as well: to insist upon having some *reason to suppose* the adequacy of its doings and unable to rest content to proceed in blind faith or in a purely experimental spirit.[6]

Where the guidance of action is concerned, we aspire to the rationalizing reassurance that we are doing the best that is possible for us in the circumstances – the most that can *realistically* be asked of us. And this quest establishes the need for *information*: for the recognition – and thus *cognition* – that our actions bear an appropriate sort of relationship to the situations in which we find ourselves. Scepticism can offer nothing by way of satisfactory response to such a demand. (To be sure, if the sceptic's argumentation were definitive – if a cogent demonstration of the impossibility of factual knowledge were indeed at hand – then one would have no alternative but to fall back on the non-cognitive guides; but this perspective clearly begs the conclusion at issue.) The upshot of this line of consideration is that while the sceptic is quite correct in holding that scepticism need not stultify action *per se*, it does nevertheless abolish all prospects of *rational* action, thereby flying in the face of what is – in fact and in appearance as well – a fundamental requisite of the human condition.

In antiquity, this objection was met by certain thinkers within the Academic school of scepticism by a counter-proposal which, though maintaining unattainability of *knowledge* (*epistēmē*) – and thus still sceptical in tendency – held that there is a cognitive resource short of *knowledge*, namely "reasonable belief" (*to eulogon* = the plausible). Continuing to espouse the usual sceptical proscription of knowledge, these "mitigated" sceptics espoused an attenuated form of "knowledge" that is adequate for the rational guidance of

[6] See Arne Naess, *Scepticism* (London, 1968), pp. 41–42, for advocacy of this "experimental" approach.

action (*praxis*) despite its inability to meet the demands of theoretically valid cognition. And it was argued that man *can* – and that the rational (or "wise" = *sophos*) man actually *does* – base his action upon such reasonable belief. In the view of these semi-sceptics (Carneades in particular), not *knowledge* but *plausibility* is the guide to life.

The tenor of this approach has much in common with the present position as set out in Chapter VII on "Mundane Knowledge." Nevertheless, from our point of view, the decisive shortcoming of this mitigated scepticism is its studied refusal to stake claims to *knowledge* and its continued acceptance of the sceptic's conception of what "knowledge" in fact involves. For – as we have argued throughout – there simply is no valid reason for refraining from talk of *knowledge* in the sort of cases where the mitigated sceptics insist upon speaking of "plausibility" (or the Deweyite pragmatists of "warranted assertability").

The recourse to plausibility among the later Academic sceptics was, however, denied by the more orthodox and rigorous Pyrrhonian sceptics. As we know from Sextus Empiricus, these all-out sceptics not merely argued that man is unable to achieve *knowledge*, but also denied that he can attain any such thing as *reasonable* belief. And this more extreme position is straightforwardly incompatible with any prospect of rational action, that is, action based on justifiedly held reasons.

The radical sceptics of antiquity accordingly maintained that the "wise" (reasonable) man can get by in all the practical affairs of life on the basis of how-to knowledge alone. He can dispense altogether with claims to knowledge-that; he need merely know how to quench his thirst – viz., by drinking the water – and need not claim to know *that* drinking water will do so. Practical "knowledge" is enough; all credence, all acceptance with regard to factual matters, can be dispensed with. Appropriate *praxis* – so it was held – is altogether compatible with the suspension of judgment of sceptical *epochē*.

This seems quite wrong, at any rate as long as the quest for rationality is not wholly abandoned. Consider the exchange:

A. Why did you do that – that is, drink that glass of water?

B. To quench my thirst.

A. But what led you to think that this particular action (drinking the water) would produce this effect?

B. Because that's the generally done thing in such cases.

A. But what sorts of grounds are there to think that "the done thing" is the *correct* thing to do in this case?

B. No such idea ever entered my mind; I make no claim that it (custom) can serve as a *reason*.

Clearly in these circumstances we can hardly characterize *B* as acting rationally in the case at hand. To be considered *rational*, a person must be willing and able to adduce some *reasons* to back up his claim to how-to knowledge. And these reasons must be of a knowledge-that form.

To be sure, it is not the *use* of a technique, procedure, process, instrument, *modus operandi* (etc.) as such, but its *rational* use that requires a recourse to knowledge-that. Specifically, the *rational* use of ANY technique requires a great deal of factual knowledge, since we must establish such things as:

1. that "it works" with respect to a realization of the end-in-view (or that there is a reasonable prospect of its working)
2. that it works better than "plausible" alternatives (those to be had – *inter alia* – for roughly the same time, money, effort, etc.)
3. that it produces no untoward side-effects (or none so large as to offset the benefit we would attain by realizing the end-in-view).

It is obvious that the warranting of all such judgments presupposes a great deal of factual information of the standard knowledge-that type.

Action in a purpose-realizing way is not enough for rationality – the successes at issue may be wholly fortuitous and accidental. To meet the conditions of rationality, we must not only *do* what realizes our aims, but do it in an adequately grounded expectation that it will (or well may) realize them. And this calls for the factual knowledge that this amalgam of technology-cum-technique is *appropriate* to the tasks at hand.

Ludwig Wittgenstein wrote:

> The squirrel does not infer by induction that it is going to need stores next winter as well. And no more do we need a law of induction to *justify* [*rechtfertigen*] our actions or our predictions.[7]

This gets the matter exactly wrong. Had Wittgenstein written *perform* (or "carry out") in place of *justify*, all would have been well. But once *justification* (*Rechfertigung*) is brought upon the stage, induction or some functional equivalent for establishing the need is just exactly what does become necessary. Saying that someone is being rational commits us to holding that this person is in a position to *rationalize* what he says and what he does – to justify it and exhibit it as the sensible thing to do. The rational use of a technique inevitably requires a great deal of *factual* backing from our knowledge – our purported knowledge – regarding how things work in the world.

To be sure, the determined sceptic may still argue as follows:

> You move too glibly when you say that I propose to abandon all belief. For one must distinguish between
> 1. C-beliefs (cognitive beliefs), as held by one who accepts (by way of intellectual subscription) the truth of a certain claim.
> 2. P-beliefs (pragmatic beliefs) as held by one who "accepts" a certain thesis simply as a basis for action, but as a "working hypothesis," without granting it actual *credence* in the sense of intellectual subscription or actual acceptance.
>
> Now my absention from the former mode of "belief" does not imply any rejection of the latter.[8]

[7] *On Certainty* (Oxford, 1969), Sect. 287; italics supplied.
[8] Cf. Naess, *Scepticism* (London, 1968), pp. 47 ff.

But this will not do. For the issue of *rationality* ultimately blocks the opening of such a gap between these two modes of belief. If we insist on knowing *why* we should act on the basis of a certain claim, we generally are not – or at any rate *should* not be – rationally satisfied until the truth of this thesis is established, or at any rate its acceptability somehow made manifest.

These considerations render the radical sceptics' insistence on a noncognitive basis for action unacceptable from the rational point of view. Only a position which – like that of the mitigated sceptics – is prepared to countenance the prospect of "reasonable belief" or some comparable cognitive resource is capable of satisfying the rational man. For the rational man requires a cogent reason for action, and only with the abandonment of a rigoristic all-out scepticism can such reasons be obtained.

3. WHY BE RATIONAL IN ACTION?

The preceding argumentation has it that reasonable beliefs are needed to underwrite rational action, so that rationality in action *requires* cognitive rationality. But this leaves open the residual question: *Why be rational in action?* What is to be gained thereby? And at this stage we confront once more the sceptical extremist who asks: "Why should I subscribe to your 'rationality'? So call me irrational! Sticks and stones may break my bones, but names will never hurt me."

One possible response here is represented by the position of *analytical* rationalism, which holds that rationality cannot be rationally justified at all because here, with rationality, we have come to "the end of the line." An instance of this position is A. J. Ayer's observation that any justification of induction will

assume that the future can . . . be relied on to resemble the past. No doubt this assumption is correct, but there can be no way of proving it without its being presupposed. So, if circular proofs are not to count, there can be no proof. . . . This does not mean that the scientific method is irrational. It could be irrational only if there were a standard of rationality which it failed to meet; whereas in fact it goes to set the standard: arguments are judged to be rational or irrational by reference to it.[9]

And in a closely analogous way, a this-or-nothing argument might be deployed as well:

If ANY policy of acting can be rationally warranted (i.e., be cogently argued for as superior on the basis of available evidence), then the policy of basing action on "reasonable belief" (or some appropriate suchlike cognitive resource) can be so warranted.

If "reasonable belief" cannot provide a valid basis for rational action, then nothing can: by definition, as it were, a "reasonable belief" *establishes itself as such by being the one to do this job.*

This view that rationality represents a *ne plus ultra* that must be construed to set its own standard is not, however, altogether satisfying. Rationality itself makes it incumbent on us to give a reason for its adoption.[10] (Though, to be sure, this reason must be a rational one.)

Our own approach to this issue proceeds along relatively straightforward lines. A person should be rational in action simply because – as best one can judge the matter – it is to one's advantage to be so. The imperative at issue is at bottom a *prudential* one.[11] A pivotal facet of the justification of rationality and the rational enterprise lies in its efficient realiz-

---

[9] *The Problem of Knowledge* (Harmondsworth, 1956), pp. 74–75.

[10] As John Kekes trenchantly puts the problem: "Why believe because it is reasonable, why not believe with the beatific Tertullian because it is absurd?" (*A Justification of Rationality* [Albany, 1976], p. 19.)

[11] William James made the point with characteristic cogency:

"The possession of truth, so far from being here [i.e., in human affairs] an end in itself, is only a preliminary means towards other vital satisfactions." And again: "Our obligation to seek truth is part of our general [prudential] obligation to do what pays." (*Pragmatism* [New York, 1907], pp. 203 and 230.)

ation of that key cognitive goal: the *expectedly* adequate guidance of life in a difficult environment.

To be sure, this line of deliberation calls for an immediate concession. There is not – and cannot be – any categorical *guarantee* that rationally guided action will be successful in the sense of assured and failproof goal-attainment. Even the most rationally laid plan can misfire. Reality is not always and inevitably on the side of the strongest arguments. But while one cannot *guarantee* success here, one can indeed extend a *reasonable assurance* of it – recognizing that that of which we are "reasonably assured" may on occasion fail us, and that we may find ourselves disappointed in even our most rational expectations. The assurance at issue here is not a failproof guarantee, but the reassurance of having made the best rational bet – of having done as well as one can in the circumstances of the case.

Still, just *why* is "implementing our *reasonable* beliefs" the best rational bet? The answer is straightforward: because that is exactly what "reasonable" beliefs are – i.e., what qualifies a belief as *reasonable*. The reasonable belief is precisely and by definition that whose acceptance – to the very best of our available knowledge and belief – affords the best promise for realizing our goals. And so, sceptical charges to the contrary notwithstanding, the pursuit of reasonable beliefs offers us the best available prospects of cognitive adequacy and successful praxis.

4. SCEPTICISM AND THE IMPLEMENTATION OF KNOWLEDGE: THE UNACCEPTABLE RISK ARGUMENT

However, there is also on the other side a sceptical line of argumentation which rests on practical considerations, maintaining that any espousal of cognitive claims involves the prospect of unacceptable risks. This argumentation is conveniently formulated in the following passage:

A statement enjoys the highest degree of certainty only if it is supported by evidence which justifies a willingness to risk the greatest possible penalty on the truth of the statement. For a person to regard a statement as being certain in the highest degree, he must be willing to risk *anything* on its truth. . . . I propose to use the term "philo-sophical certainty" to refer to the highest degree of certainty. In offering . . . [this criterion] I believe I have preserved the standard for measuring degrees of cer-tainty that is implicit in the ordinary usage of terms like "certain." In my opinion, when . . . [sceptics] maintain that no empirical statement can be certain, they mean that none can be philosophically certain. . . .[12]

It is now easy to see how a thoroughly sceptical position dovetails with such a conception of philosophical certainty. For a sceptic would argue thus:

In claiming knowledge you claim absolute certainty – certainty in the highest degree, beyond any possibility of error. But consider now the issue of "acting on know-ledge" – of *implementing* in action what is *accepted* as known. Clearly our actions should reflect the certainty and incorrigibility of our claims to knowledge. We should act on what we claim to know in all conditions and circumstances, and accept *any* sort of bet or gamble on it. But surely there will be some risks we would not run. There are some consequences of erring that are just too awful to be acceptable when there is *any* prospect of error – the "end of the world" say, or extinction of life on earth, or the suffering of eternal hellfire. These risks would give any rational person pause before acting on his knowledge. Accordingly we would never really claim to know.

We thus arrive at the sceptic's "Unacceptable Risk" Argu-ment:

[12] Harry G. Frankfurt, "Philosophical Certainty," *The Philosophical Review*, vol. 71 (1962), pp. 303–327 (see p. 323). Compare also Norman Malcom, "The Verifica-tion Argument" in R. Chisholm and R. Swartz (eds.), *The Theory of Knowledge* (Englewood Cliffs, 1973), p. 202.

1. Acceptance as known demands maximal (philosophical) certainty.
2. Maximal (philosophical) certainty calls for implementation in all cases and the acceptance of all risks.

∴ 3. Acceptance as known calls for implementation in all circumstances and the acceptance of all risks.
4. In all or virtually all cases, there are some risks which a rational man would not run in implementing his beliefs.

∴ 5. In all or virtually all cases, the rational man could not claim that his beliefs deserve to be classified as knowledge.

The sceptic bolsters this line of argumentation by parading before us all sorts of horrendous risks we would naturally refrain from running in any circumstances: the extinction of all thought in the world or other awesome disasters.

Notwithstanding such emotive appeals, the reasoning at issue is invalid. The flaw lies with Premiss 2. Frankfurt's *obiter dictum* to the contrary notwithstanding, "philosophical certainty" in his risk-anything sense is emphatically *not* "implicit in the ordinary usage" that governs our claims to certainty and incorrigibility. The certainties of the philosophers are one thing and those of the plain man another – and it is clearly with a view to the latter that ordinary usage operates. (For better or for worse, ordinary usage just does not defer to philosophical strictures.)

As the argumentation of Chapter III indicated, the certainty of knowledge is *mundane* certainty, the certainty of life. The validation of our knowledge claims requires the preclusion of every *realistic* possibility of error, but not every *conceivable* possibility whatsoever. The cognitivist need not deny that our claims to factual knowledge are defeasible. He need not shut his eye on the fact that there is always some risk, some chance of error, however remote, some possibility (often far-fetched, or even fantastic and "unthinkable") that we are wrong.

What is at issue with knowledge is not the "highest conceivable certainty" (in some theoretical sense), but *adequate* certainty given the general nature of the case. It is a matter of rendering the thing in question as certain as it can be made on the basis of those steps it is reasonable to take. And the risks at issue with the certainty-component of our everyday knowledge claims are the prosaic and causal risks of everyday life (preeminently including the usually minor embarassment of being proven wrong), and not the horrendous and fanciful risks by which the sceptic seeks to intimidate us.

The first syllogism of the "Unacceptable Risks" Argument accordingly collapses. To profess warrant for a claim to knowledge is perfectly compatible with refusing to run absurd risks in its wake. It is simply false that the conception of knowledge we actually work with is so hyperbolically absolutistic that someone who stakes a claim to knowledge would be called on (in mere selfconsistency) to act on it in all conditions and circumstances and to be willing to accept any and all risk whatsoever. The certainty of knowledge is not the certainty of "having probability 1" in decision-making contexts.

The effect of the "Unacceptable Risk" Argument is thus not to show that we have no knowledge, but rather to show – once again – that the sceptic's conception of knowledge is inappropriate in its hyperbolic exaggerations. The conception of knowledge that we actually operate with is inherently defeasibilist and emphatically does *not* establish it as a precondition of a warranted claim to knowledge that there be implementation in all cases and a preparedness to run all risks.

5. A DEFENSE OF COGNITIVE RATIONALITY CANNOT PROCEED ON THEORETICAL GROUNDS ALONE: PRAGMATIC CONSIDERATIONS MUST PLAY A ROLE

An ongoing succession of philosophers of pragmatic inclination has always stressed the ultimate inadequacy of any strictly theoretical defense of rationality. And their instincts in this regard are basically correct. To rely wholly upon considerations of cognitive or theoretical rationality in the defense of rationality is to move in a circle in justifying rationality by its own standard. The time must come for stepping outside the whole cognitive/theoretical sphere: one clearly cannot marshall an ultimately satisfactory defense of rational cognition by an appeal that proceeds *wholly* on its own ground. It becomes necessary to seek some cognition-external support for cognitive justification. And at just this stage, the aforementioned pragmatic appeal to the condition of effective action properly comes into operation.[13]

As we have argued time and again, the "ought" in "Men ought to be rational" is in the final analysis a *prudential* ought and not a *moral* ought. That is, one should be rational *if one is to be efficient in the realization of one's chosen objectives* (whatever they may happen to be), so that the constraints at issue are not those of *morality*, but those of *prudence* and intelligent self-interest. The guidance of action by rational belief is the policy which – as best we can tell – holds the optimal promise for achieving the goals at which action is directed.

It might seem on casual inspection that this line of argumentation leaves the matter in a somewhat unsatisfactory state. It says (roughly): "You should be rational in action – i.e., conform your actions to those strictures which it is rational to accept (roughly, which are true as best one can determine) – because *it is rational to believe that* success in goal attainment is most effectively realized in this way." And one might prefer it if the italicized clause were wholly suppressed – at any rate in this epistemic dispensation, where we have no way of getting at the facts directly, without the epistemic detour of securing grounds and reasons for them. But (and this is the key point) it is absurd to ask for what cannot be (*ultra posse* . . .). In the inescapable circumstances of the case there is no basis for any rational discontent, no room for any dissatisfaction or complaint.

Admittedly, the reasoning at issue has an appearance of a vitiating circularity here because the force of the argument

---

[13] The line of thought now being broached is worked out in considerable detail in the author's *Methodological Pragmatism* (Oxford, 1976).

itself rests on a stipulation (or hypothesizing) of rationality: "If you are going to be rational in your beliefs then you must also act rationally because it is rational to believe that rational action is optimal in point of goal attainment." But this sort of question-begging is *inevitable* in the circumstances. The presupposition of rationality is not vitiating but essential. If we bother to want an answer to the question "Why be rational?" at all, it is a *rational* answer that we want. Already embarked on the sea of rationality, we want such assurance as can now be made available that we have done the right thing. And such reassurance can indeed be given – exactly along the lines just indicated. Given the very nature of the justificatory enterprise at issue, one just cannot avoid letting rationality sit in judgment on itself. (What is being asked for – after all – is a rational argument for rational action, a basis for rational conviction and not persuasion by something probatively irrelevant like threats or *force majeure*.) One would expect – nay demand – that rationality is self-substantiation in this way – that it *must* emerge as the best policy on its own telling.

This rejection of scepticism – this rationalization of the usual methods and standards of rationality – thus turns on a cycle of justificatory reasoning whose overall structure is as follows: Q. – Why be rational? A. – (1) In cognition (i.e., on the side of strictly intellectual considerations) because rational belief is a precondition of *rational action,* and (2) In action (i.e., on the side of praxis) so that we can achieve a *reasonable expectation* of success. The two components of this justificatory argumentation interlock in a smooth dovetailing of mutual supportiveness. Rationality of belief is a prerequisite of rationality in action, and rationality in action is a matter of *prudence*, of self-interest oriented at the rationally optimal expectation of realizing one's own objectives. It is the fact that they are geared to efficient praxis that prevents our standards of rationality from being arbitrary, yet the element of reasonable expectation in this gearing introduces an inevitable rational component into the concept of "efficient praxis" itself. The two dimensions are interlocked in symbolic union: theoria without praxis is futile, praxis without theoria ineffectual.

In a cognate context one acute commentator has written:

> If rationality is what we as self-interested agents do . . .
> [one] probably need not worry about the survival of
> rationality. If rationality rides on self-interest, I'd say
> it's on to a very good thing.[14]

But the matter is not quite so simple. Rationality rides not
on self-interest as such, but on *intelligent* self-interest. This
circumstance renders its position a bit more precarious.

A further sceptical objection yet remains:

> Your validation of rationality has proceeded in teleo-
> logical, purpose-relative terms with reference to our *cog-
> nitive* aims (information, communication) and our *prag-
> matic* aims (effective action, successful intervention in
> the course of events). But our own intellectual tradition
> – with its heavily cognitive and practical orientation – is
> surely not the only one. Consider such alternatives as
> the mysticism of the Zen Buddhist, the otherworldly re-
> ligiosity of monasticism, the aestheticism of the Bo-
> hemian, the utopianism of the political visionary, etc.
> Pragmatic success and factual truth will not occupy a
> high place in such alternative value-hierarchies, since
> variousothervalues(desirelessness,self-control,godliness,
> attunement to the march of history, etc.) would take a
> superior place. How then – the sceptic asks – can you
> ultimately justify a determinative role for the value com-
> mitments of *your* own particular tradition (with its empha-
> sis on cognitive truth and pragmatic success), in contrast
> to the values of these alternative traditions?

Two points must be made. (1) If it is *rational* justification
that the objector demands of us, then *we* have no alternative
but to construe this as being "rational justification" on the
standard interpretation of this conception. (If it were something else that the objector wanted, this would doubtless
emerge in the discussion, at which point we would tend to

[14] S. E. Hughes, review of John Kekes, *A Justification of Rationality* in *Australasian Journal of Philosophy*, vol. 55 (1977), pp. 221–225 (see p. 225).

lose interest in it.) Accordingly, the justification at issue will (*ex hypothesi*) have to fall subject to the usual standards of rationality given what we have spoken of as "the conditions of the problem." And this consideration gives these standards a special standing of (context-relative) preeminence from the very outset. Moreover, (2) insofar as *efficient* goal attainment is the issue (never mind for the moment what the operative goals are), this very fact suffices to underwrite a basis for speaking of "success in the pragmatics of goal-attainment," and thus provides a place at which some purchase can be had for the Archimedean lever of the orthodox cognitive values, geared as they are to providing an appropriate basis for an expectantly efficient praxis.

$$* \quad * \quad *$$

These deliberations conclude the unfolding of our argument against a radical scepticism that rejects a policy of thesis-acceptance based on the standard probative ground-rules. The preceding chapter considered the *cognitive* sanctions to such scepticism – its impeding the realization of our cognitive purposes in blocking the acquisition of information about the world and impeding the prospects of communication. The present chapter has indicated its *pragmatic* sanctions[15] – its impedence of any reasonable prospect of achieving our practical purposes. The untenability of radical scepticism inheres in the fact that it is demonstrably rational to take the stance that its adoption produces unfortunate results both on the side of *theoria* (intellectual understanding) and on that of *praxis* (effective action). We arrive at the stance that scepticism thwarts those cognitive commitments which *as best we can tell* (on the established canons of reason) offer the most promising and conducive bases for the realization of our cognitive and practical goals. Such a line of justificatory reasoning admittedly does not refute the radical sceptic on his own ground, but it does render it impossible for us to join him there.

[15] No pun intended.

XIV

Elements of Truth in Scepticism

SYNOPSIS

(1) There is substantial justice to the sceptics' critique of the *completeness, correctness,* and even the *consistency* of "our knowledge," (2) For one thing, there is no prospect of rendering our knowledge of the world complete. (3) Moreover, the dynamical aspect of our knowledge indicates its inherent weakness of completeness claims at any one, particular historical juncture. (4) Also, there are good grounds for regarding it as not only incomplete but also presumptively incorrect and corrigible. (5) Matters could even so eventuate that the ideal of the consistency of knowledge may have to be abandoned. (6) In consequence, there is a large kernel of truth to sceptical complaints about the deficiences of the body of "our knowledge." Nevertheless, the sceptic's argumentation fails to achieve its main object of demonstrating the impropriety or illegitimacy of our specific claims to knowledge.

1. ELEMENTS OF TRUTH IN SCEPTICISM

The preceding discussion has argued the untenability of scepticism, maintaining that the sceptic is wrong in renouncing the cognitivist policy of propositional acceptance under the aegis of the standard probative ground-rules. However, the aim of this concluding chapter is to maintain that the sceptic does not leave the arena of controversy empty-handed. In fact, many of his key contentions are not only correct, but highly useful for gaining a proper understanding of the nature of knowledge. When the sceptic insists upon the inadequacy of "our knowledge," there is much that can be said for his case. The best explanation for the longevity of scepticism and its tenacious hold upon an ongoing sector of philosophical tradition lies in recognizing that scepticism gives a correct account of various important facets of the cognitive situation. For what we vaunt as our knowledge is no doubt deficient as regards completeness, correctness, and even consistency. This situation requires closer examination.

2. PROBLEMS OF COMPLETENESS

It must be recognized that the totality of facts about a thing – any thing – is inexhaustible, that the number of facts about any given thing is infinite. To become clear about this, it is helpful to heed a useful distinction – that between *truths* and *facts*. A "truth" is a *linguistic* entity – the formulation of a fact in some language or other. Any correct statement in some (actual) language formulates a truth. And the converse obtains as well: a truth must be embodied in a statement, and cannot exist as a disembodied ghost. A *fact*, on the other hand, is *not* a linguistic entity at all – it is an actual circumstance or state of affairs obtaining in "the real world." Any objective circumstance that is correctly statable in some *possible* language is a fact. It is thus to be expected that there are more facts than truths: Every truth must state a fact, but it is undoubtedly possible that there will be facts that are never statable in any actually available language. Facts stand in correlation with *potential* truths whose actualization as such hinges on the availability of appropriate linguistic apparatus for their formulation. Truths involve a one-parameter possibilization – they embrace whatever *can* be stated truly in some *actual* language. Facts, on the other hand, involve a two-parameter possibilization – they embrace whatever *can* be stated truly in some *possible* language. Two very different equations are operative:

truth = something *truly stated* in some (actual) language
fact = something *truly statable* in some (possible) language

Truths are *actualistically* language-correlative, while facts are only *possibilistically* language-correlative. It must accordingly be presumed that there are facts which will never be captured as truths – though it is obviously impossible to adduce any concrete illustrations of this phenomenon.

The number of truths (or purported truths) that is articulated about a thing is always (at any historical juncture) *finite*. But our concept of "the real world" is such that there will always be infinitely many facts about a thing. Accordingly, we cannot begin to exhaust – and thus to know explicitly – "the whole truth" about a thing. For knowledge, or at any rate, knowledge of the sort that concerns us here – linguistically formulated knowledge-that – is always a recognition of *truths* as such. Accordingly, it transpires that the range of facts regarding something is inevitably larger than that of the body of knowledge about it we can ever possibly possess. The domain of fact transcends the limits of our capacity to *express* it, and, *a fortiori*, those of our capacity to *know* it.

But surely – it might be said – one can have potential or implicit knowledge of an infinite domain. For a general truth will always encompass many particular ones by way of deductive consequencehood – even infinitely many of them. The finite set of axioms of a system will yield infinitely many theorems. And so when we shift from overt or explicit to implicit or tacit knowledge, we have the prospect of capturing an infinite knowledge-content within a finite propositional basis by recourse to deductive systematization.

While this is so, however, it does not fully remove the relative limitedness of the resulting "body of knowledge." For the totality of the deductive consequences that can be obtained from any finite set of axioms is itself always enumerable. The most we can ever hope to encompass by any sort of *deductively* implicit containment within a finite basis of truths is a *denumerably infinite* manifold of truths. And so, as long as the mechanism of implicit containment remains a recursive process, it too can never hope to transcend the range of the denumerable, and thus cannot hope to encompass the whole of the transdenumerable range of descriptive facts about a thing – seeing that there is no reason to suppose that the number of *possible* languages will itself be denumerable.[1] (Moreover, even within the denumerable realm, our attempt at deductive systematization can run into difficulties: as we know from Gödel's work, one cannot even hope to systematize – by any recursive, axiomatic process – all the truths of arithmetic.)

Considerations along these lines indicate one aspect of the inherent incompleteness of our factual knowledge. There are others as well.

3. A FURTHER SOURCE OF INCOMPLETENESS: THE DYNAMICAL DIMENSION OF KNOWLEDGE DEVELOPMENT

The preceding deliberations relate to the limits of the knowledge that can be rationalized on a *fixed and given* conceptual basis (i.e., relative to a *determinate* body of linguistic and conceptual machinery). But in real life a linguistic/conceptual basis is never "fixed and given." Our conceptions of things do not present a stable object of scrutiny – they are a *moving* rather than a *fixed* target for analysis. We form our conception of the sun in terms of reference very different from those of Aristotle, and that of a heart in terms of reference very different from those of Galen.

Consider how many facts about his own sword were unknown to Caesar. He did not know that it contained carbon or that it conducted electricity. The very concepts at issue ("carbon," "electricity-conduction") were outside Caesar's cognitive range. There are key facts (or presumptive facts) even about the most familiar things – trees and animals, bricks and mortar – that were unknown 100 years ago. And this is so not just because of an ignorance of items of detail (as with a missing word in a crossword puzzle). Rather, the ignorance in question arises because the very *concepts* at

---

[1] Indeed one can readily visualize a diagonalization argument to show that it is not.

issue had not been formulated. It is not just that Caesar did not *know* what the half-life of californium is, but that he couldn't have *understood* this fact if someone had told it to him.

Any adequate view of metaphysico-epistemological realities of inquiry must recognize that this is always so. It must realize that the ongoing process of science is a process of conceptual innovation that always leaves certain theses wholly outside the cognitive range of the inquirers of any particular period. And this means that there will always be facts (or plausible candidate-facts) about a thing that we do not *know* because we cannot even *conceive* of them. To grasp such a fact calls for taking a perspective of consideration that we simply do not have, since the state of knowledge (or purported knowledge) is not yet advanced to a point at which its formulation is possible.

The language of emergence can perhaps be deployed profitably to make the point. But what is at issue is not an *emergence of the features of things*, but an emergence in our *knowledge* about them. The heart pumped so as to circulate blood in the human body well before Harvey; uranium containing substances were radioactive before Becquerel. The emergence at issue relates to our cognitive mechanisms of conceptualization, not to the objects of our conceptualization in and of themselves. We can continue to talk about the same things even when making altogether novel observations about them.

The properties of a thing are literally open-ended: We can always discover more of them. Even if we view nature as inherently finitistic, and espouse a Principle of Limited Variety to the effect that the world can be portrayed descriptively with the materials of a finite taxonomic scheme, there can be no *a priori* guarantee that with the progress of science we will not go on *ad indefinitum* to change our mind about the membership of this finite register of descriptive materials.

In view of this "cognitive inexhaustibility" of things we must never lay claim to cognitive monopoly or to cognitive finality. Indeed, a recognition of the "inexhaustibility" of the potential knowledge of things is implicit in the very conception of a "real thing" as it figures in our conceptual scheme. Our very notion of a real thing is such that the possibility of learning to think differently about any thing will always have to be kept in mind as an open prospect. It is a crucial fact about our epistemic stance towards the real world to recognize that every part and parcel of it contains compartments that lie beyond our *present* cognitive reach – at *any* "present" whatever.

Moreover, we do – and must – recognize that we may well be wrong about the nature of a thing, not only in regard to its descriptive make-up, but in more fundamental regards as well. Things may be misconceived in very basic ways (for example, a pre-Copernican "sunrise," or again past ideas about a "case of cancer," should it turn out that the medicine of the future takes a very different view of what goes on where one previously saw the occurrence of a particular "disease entity").

It is of course conceivable that natural science will come to a stop, and do so not in the trivial sense of a cessation of intelligent life, but in C. S. Peirce's more interesting sense of eventually reaching a condition after which even indefinitely ongoing inquiry will not – and indeed in the nature of things *cannot* (perhaps only because of the inherent limitations in our ability to enhance man-nature interactions) – produce any significant change. Such a position is in theory possible. But we can never *know* – be it in practice or in principle – that it is actual. We can never ascertain that science has attained such an ω-condition of final completion – from our point of view, the possibility of further change lying "just around the corner" can never be ruled out finally and decisively. The situation in natural science is such that our knowledge of nature must ever be presumed to be incomplete. One is thus brought back to the stance of the great Idealist philosophers (Plato, Spinoza, Hegel, Bradley, Royce) that human knowledge inevitably falls short of "perfect science" (the Idea, the Absolute), and must accordingly be looked upon as incomplete.

A further line of consideration is important here. Man's material resources are limited. And these limits inexorably circumscribe our cognitive access to the real world. There will always be interactions with nature of such a scale (as measured in such parameters as energy, pressure, temperature, particle-velocities, etc.) that their realization would require the deployment of resources of so vast a scope that we can never realize them. And if there are interactions to which we have no access, then there are (presumably) phenomena which we cannot discern. It would be unreasonable to expect nature to confine the distribution of phenomena of potential cognitive significance to those ranges that lie within the horizons of our vision.

Where there are inaccessible phenomena, there must be cognitive incompleteness. To this extent, at any rate, the empiricists were surely right. Only the most fanatical rationalist could uphold the capacity of sheer intellect to compensate for the lack of data. Where there are unobserved phenomena we must reckon with the prospect that our theoretical systematizations may well be (nay, presumably are) incomplete. Moreover, if certain phenomena are not just undetected but in the very nature of the case inaccessible (even if only for the merely economic reasons mooted above), then our theoretical knowledge of nature is (presumably) incompletable. Certain fundamental features inherent in the very structure of man's inquiry into the ways of the world thus conspire to indicate the incompleteness of the knowledge we can attain in this sphere.[2]

4. PROBLEMS OF CORRECTNESS

Not only is "our knowledge" *incomplete*, but we have little alternative to regarding it as presumptively *incorrect and corrigible*. Evidence-in-hand is necessarily limited and finitistic. But our claims to objective factual knowledge always incorporate elements of nomic universality. And this brings us back to the circumstance of the "evidential gap," which means that there will always be a discrepancy between claim-evidence and claim-content where factual issues are concerned. And now the Humean pitfall looms: we can never

---

[2] This somewhat telegraphic discussion is developed more fully in the author's book on *Scientific Progress* (Oxford, 1977).

secure categorical guarantees that the future will not upset generalizations based on the data of the past. Thus all claims to objective knowledge about the real world are "in principle" and "in theory" defeasible.

This defeasibility of our factual knowledge of the world is rather exhibited than *refuted* by a consideration of scientific knowledge. For the status of our knowledge as merely *purported* knowledge is nowhere clearer than with science. Our scientific "knowledge" is by no means as secure and absolute as is sometimes pretended. There is every reason to think that where scientific knowledge is concerned further knowledge does not just supplement but generally corrects our knowledge-in-hand, so that the incompleteness of our information implies its presumptive incorrectness as well. We must come to terms with the fact that, at any rate at the scientific level of generality and precision, *each* of our accepted beliefs *may* eventuate as false and *many* of our accepted beliefs *will* eventuate as false.

If there is any one thing we can learn from the history of science, it is that the science of one day is looked upon on the next as naive, deficient, and basically wrong from the vantage point of the wisdom of hindsight. The clearest induction from the history of science is that science is always mistaken – that at *every* stage of its development its practitioners, looking backwards with the vision of hindsight, view the work of their predecessors as seriously misinformed and mistaken in very fundamental respects. And if we adopt (as in candor and realism we must) the realistic view that we ourselves and our contemporaries do not occupy a privileged position in this respect, then we have no realistic alternative but to suppose that much or all of what we ourselves vaunt as "scientific knowledge" is itself presumably wrong.

We must confront the thrust of the simple syllogism:

1. The vaunted scientific knowledge of our predecessors has always turned out to need correction, and so not to be real knowledge after all.
2. No human generation is in privileged epistemic position: what has always held in the past is possibly –

even probably – the case with the present as well.

∴. Our vaunted scientific knowledge does not qualify as authentic knowledge either.

In all due realism it is necessary to adopt the *epistemological Copernicanism* of the second premiss here – a view that rejects the egocentric claim that we ourselves occupy a pivotal position in the epistemic dispensation. We must recognize that there is nothing inherently sacrosanct about our own present cognitive posture *vis-à-vis* that of other, later historical junctures. A kind of intellectual humility is called for – a self-abnegatory diffidence that abstains from the hubris of pretentions to cognitive finality or centrality.

Our attempts at the scientific description and explanation of how things work in the world represents no more than "the very best we can do" at this level of generality and precision and rigor. And we realize in the abstract that it will in due course eventuate that our best is not quite good enough, that our "scientific knowledge" contains an admixture of error. The idea that science does – or sooner or later must – arrive at "the truth of the matter" is not easy to substantiate. There seems no realistic alternative to the supposition that science is wrong – in various ways – and that much of our supposed "knowledge" of the world is a tissue of plausible error. We are thus ill advised to view the science of our own day – or *any* day – as "the final truth of the matter." All we can do is the best we can, the most that can be asked of us in the epistemic circumstances in which we labor. (*Ultra posse. . . .*) There is thus every reason to regard our scientific knowledge as no more than an imperfect estimate, essentially corrigible, subject to revision, inherently uncertain, and liable to be modified or even wholly abandoned in the wake of further scientific innovation.

There is no reason to think that *our* view of things – be it of individual things (the moon, the great wall of China) or of types thereof (the domestic cat, the common cold) – is any more definitive and final than that taken by our own predecessors in the cognitive enterprise. Such an analysis calls for the humbling view that just as we think our predecessors of 100 years ago had a fundamentally inadequate grasp on the furniture of the world, so our successors of 100 years hence will take the same view of *our* knowledge (or purported knowledge) of things. The classical, pre-Kantian view of epistemology embodies a particular approach to things through the contrast between how they appear to us (in terms of our present knowledge or purported knowledge about them) and how they are absolutistically and *an sich* (in terms, say, of God's knowledge about them). The approach taken here exchanges this perspective for one based on the contrast between the *present* view of things and the prospect of an "improved" *future* view of them. It is prepared to dispense with the old-line epistemologists' myth of the God's eye view.

The original Copernican revolution made the point that there is nothing *ontologically* privileged about our own position in space. The doctrine now at issue effectively holds that there is nothing *cognitively* privileged about our own position in time. It urges that *there is nothing epistemically privileged about the present* –ANY present, our own prominently included. Such a perspective indicates not only the incompleteness of "our knowledge" but its presumptive incorrectness as well.

Realism requires us to recognize that, as concerns our scientific understanding of the world, our most secure knowledge is presumably no more than presently accepted error. But this recognition of the fallibilism of our cognitive endeavors must be construed rather as an incentive to do the best we can than an open invitation to scepticism. In human inquiry, the cognitive ideal is correlative with the striving for optimal systematization. And this is an ideal which, like other ideals, is worthy of pursuit, despite the fact that we must realistically recognize that its full attainment lies beyond our grasp.

5. PROBLEMS OF CONSISTENCY

So much for the completeness and correctness of our knowledge. The question of consistency yet remains. For any

but a convinced Marxist, the thesis of the consistency of
nature may seem to be a trivial truism. But the idea that
man's endeavors to systematize his knowledge of nature
might end in inconsistency is a real prospect that cannot be
dismissed out of hand.

Consider how the "natural" endeavor to achieve the best
possible systematization of our knowledge might realistically
come to issue in consistency. Take the example of a theoretical regimentation of limited data as in the curve-fitting situation of Figure 1. Projecting a "best-fit" curve basis of data

FIGURE 1
CURVE-FITTING IN RESTRICTED PURVIEW CASES

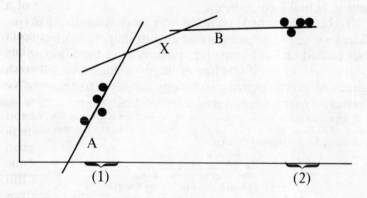

obtained in region (1) alone we might well arrive at the line
A. Again, on the basis of region (2) data we might well arrive
at the line B. Moreover – so let us assume – no practicable,
physically accessible way is open to us for securing data outside of regions (1) and (2). Now if our "science" were to
contain two separate branches, one of which deals with the
data of region (1) alone, and the other with those of (2), then
an inconsistency would at once result. The prospect of a
transitional phase X would not arise to yield a unified picture. The one branch of science would hold the overall situa-

tion to be A-like, while the other would hold it to be B-like.[3]

The examples also illustrate the important point that it is not the bare "facts" of the case in and by themselves, *but the very drive to achieve their smooth systematization* that produces the inconsistency at issue in such circumstances. In each case we have several *partial* perspectives on an over-all set of facts – incomplete and to all appearances mutually inconsequent. But the isolated and separate *systematization* of each context then leads to extrapolation-results which are mutually incompatible.[4] Accordingly, it is important (and perhaps shocking) to recognize that as long as our purported knowledge of the world remains – as it always must – both fragmented and incomplete, this may well exact its price not simply in *ignorance* – that is, in blanks in our knowledge – but in actual *inconsistency*.

To be sure, if our knowledge were more synoptic, then (perhaps) we would presumably be able to shape a more complex but unified and self-consistent picture, as in the Figure 1 diagram itself. (Thus if one line of inquiry addresses itself to the issues of physiological psychology, another to those of behavioral psychology, inconsistencies of perspective might

[3] An amusing but vividly clear picture of the problem is given in John G. Saxe's poem "The Blind Men and the Elephant" Which tells the story of the wise men of Indostan who investigated the elephant:

> . . . six men of Indostan,
> To learning much inclined,
> Who went to see the elephant,
> (Though all of them were blind).

One sage stumbled against the elephant's "broad and sturdy side" and declared the beast to be "very like a wall." Another, who had felt its tusk, pronounced the elephant to be very like a spear. The third, who took the elephant's squirming trunk in his hands, compared it to a snake; while the fourth, who put his arms around the elephant's knee, was sure that the animal resembled a tree. A flapping ear convinced another that the elephant had the form of a fan; while the sixth blind man was persuaded that it had the form of a rope, since he took hold of the tail.

> And so these men of Indostan,
> Disputed loud and long;
> Each in his own opinion
> Exceeding stiff and strong:
> Though each was partly in the right,
> And all were in the wrong.

[4] Just here lies the profound lesson of the story of the blind men and the elephant. The inconsistencies at issue do not result from "the data" available to the men – what they feel and experience. It is their systematizing extension of these data that produces the conflict.